Third World Politics

Third World Politics

A Comparative Introduction

Paul Cammack, David Pool, and William Tordoff

The Johns Hopkins University Press

Baltimore

Second printing, 1989

The Johns Hopkins University Press
701 West 40th Street
Baltimore, Maryland 21211

Library of Congress Cataloging-in-Publication Data

Cammack, Paul.
    Third World politics: a comparative introduction/Paul
Cammack, David Pool, and William Tordoff
p.   cm.
Bibliography: p.
Includes index.
ISBN 0-8018-3649-2.   ISBN 0-8018-3661-1 (pbk.)
1. Developing countries–Politics and government. I. Pool,
David.   II. Tordoff, William.   III. Title.
JF60.C36 1988
302.9172′4–dc19   87-31140
                                             CIP

In memory of Jack Cammack, Margaret Pool
and Dora Tordoff

Contents

List of Maps

Changes in Country Names

Throughout the text, the name by which the country was known at the date relevant to the discussion is used. Changes of name usually occurred at independence; post-independence changes are indicated in brackets.

Present	*Pre-independence*
Benin (1975)	Dahomey
Botswana	Bechuanaland
Burkina Faso (1984)	Upper Volta
Cameroon	{ French Cameroons British Southern Cameroons[1]
Central African Republic	Oubangui Chari
Djibouti	French Territory of the Afars and Issas[2]
Equatorial Guinea	Spanish Guinea
Gambia/Senegambia[3]	Gambia
Ghana	Gold Coast and British Togoland
Lesotho	Basutoland
Malawi	Nyasaland
Mali[4]	French Soudan
Namibia[5]	South West Africa
Saharan Arab Democratic Republic[6]	Spanish Sahara/ Western Sahara
Senegal/Senegambia[3]	Senegal
Somalia/Somali Democratic Republic	{ British Somaliland Italian Somaliland
Tanzania (1965)[7]	{ Tanganyika Zanzibar

Togo	French Togoland
Zaire (1971)	Belgian Congo[8]
Zambia	Northern Rhodesia
Zimbabwe	Southern Rhodesia/ Rhodesia

Notes:

1. The Southern Cameroons, a British-administered UN trust territory, joined the Republic of Cameroon following a plebiscite in 1961; the people of the Northern Cameroons opted for integration with Nigeria.
2. Often referred to as French Somaliland.
3. The names 'Gambia' and 'Senegal' are retained, but in 1981 the two states formed the confederation of Senegambia.
4. The Mali Federation was formed by Senegal and Soudan in 1959, but survived for less than three months after being granted political independence by France in June 1960. France then recognised the separate independence of Senegal and Soudan, and the Union Soudanaise changed the name of Soudan to the Republic of Mali.
5. Not yet independent.
6. Also known as the Sahrawi Arab Democratic Republic. Its international status is disputed by Morocco, which claims the territory.
7. The United Republic of Tanganyika and Zanzibar came into being on 26 April 1964, as a consequence of the union between Tanganyika and Zanzibar; the name 'United Republic of Tanzania' was officially adopted a year later.
8. Often referred to as Congo–Léopoldville and subsequently (from 1 July 1966) as Congo–Kinshasa.

Introduction

Third World Politics: A Comparative Introduction aims to provide an introduction to the Third World which is comparative, thematic and places politics in its historical, social and international contexts. Our material is drawn from Africa, Latin America and the Middle East, three important and historically contrasting regions. We wanted an approach which was comparative and yet was not pitched at such a general level that our intended audience, relative newcomers to non-Western politics and political systems, would be unable to assess contending theories for lack of basic knowledge. We hope to have avoided the deep sea of general theory and the devil of too detailed a regional specialisation, while at the same time presenting the distinctive aspects of the historical and social development of the three regions.

Our comparative introduction fills a gap between modernisation and dependency, the two broad approaches which have taken so central a place in analyses of the Third World over the last three decades. There already exists a plentiful literature dealing with the pros and cons of various modernisation and dependency theories and there is a wide range of single-theme studies which reel off scores of illustrative examples from around the globe but provide little depth or context for the examples. It seemed to us that the time had come to integrate a comparative approach with one that was both thematic and historical. It was almost thirty years ago that a comparative text which examined the Third World from a modernisation perspective was published: Almond and Coleman's *The Politics of the Developing Areas* (Princeton: Princeton University Press, 1960). It was the first serious attempt to account systematically for patterns of political development. It had a lengthy theoretical introduction followed by chapters on

1

several regions of the world, and the comparative framework was provided by a theory of **modernisation**, which drew on processes largely abstracted from Western political patterns. One of the major criticisms of this work was the gulf between the theoretical introduction and the chapters by the area specialists who did not, probably because they could not, link social and political change in their areas to the theoretical concerns of the introduction. This first work was followed by a set of companion volumes treating themes like communications and political development and political culture and political development. The last in the series was *Crises and Sequences in Political Development*, a title symptomatic of the tension between the process of modernisation laid out in the original introduction and the actual pattern of political change. The comparative effort was hampered by problems inherent in modernisation theory and many of those involved in this 'school' turned to case studies of particular themes or analyses of particular states. The venture to compare globally was set aside.

The modernisation approach stimulated the growth of the more internationally diverse **dependency** school, in which there were very different emphases. At the core of dependency theory is the view that the character and economic situation of the Third World cannot be understood unless it is placed in the context of the development of the international capitalist economy. It sees the underdevelopment of the Third World as a product of the same process which generated development in the Western industrialised world and stresses the unequal relationship between these worlds. In its crudest formulations it suggests that the integration of the Third World into the international economy created and sustained a relationship of dependency in which Third World regimes acted as either the agents or passive accomplices of international capital. Scant attention was paid to politics. There are, of course, more sophisticated versions of the dependency perspective, which suggest that regional specificity is as important as global similarity, that changes in the character of the evolving world economy make static models suspect and that capitalism can play a progressive role in developing productive forces. We have attempted to incorporate some of the insights of dependency theory in our work but have avoided a direct discussion of competing theoretical approaches. A useful account of these can be found in Vicky Randall and Robin Theobald's *Political Change* *and Underdevelopment: A Critical Introduction to Third World Politics* (London: Macmillan, 1985). Our aim is to focus on selected themes, organise our discussion around them, and to place the substance of Third World politics in a historical context.

Our first two chapters present an account of the historical origins of the contemporary Third World and an analysis of the social context and social bases of politics. We emphasise the social, economic and political repercussions of the integration of Africa, Latin America and the Middle East into a global economy, and the different mechanisms by which this was undertaken. In Latin America, it was the establishment of the export economy; in Africa, colonialism; and in the Middle East, the social restructuring and eventual disintegration of the Ottoman Empire under the impact of the West, together with a short period of direct European rule. Our view is that under the aegis of a broadly comparable process, differences in the timing, intensity and mechanisms of Western capitalist expansion (and differences in the nature and response of existing indigenous societies, political systems and cultures) provide a framework for understanding the contrasting political experiences of the Third World. Such a framework allows us to explain variations both between regions and between states within regions as a function of different levels of economic and political penetration and interaction with widely different constellations of local factors.

We have organised our subsequent chapters around themes which illustrate the way in which contemporary Third World states (and their institutions) have been shaped by their pasts and have attempted to reshape their present, a dialectic which has produced deep social tensions and considerable political violence.

Four chapters look at issues linked to the state and to power and powerlessness: parties and participation, the military, revolution and women. They were chosen for their intrinsic interest, their comparability and their illumination of contrasts. Two further chapters examine the international milieu in which Third World states function. One analyses the role of superpower influence, regional co-operation and the role of multinational corporations, and the other the international political economy of oil, famine and debt. Our analysis of the selected themes allows comparison across regions and between states within regions and allows us to examine the continuing impact of capitalist penetration in the nineteenth and early twentieth century. Our chapter concerned with state and society is of particular importance here, since it sketches in the broad social characteristics established by the impact of external forces (colonialism, the mandates or the creation of an export economy), and presents the distinctive social characteristics of Africa, Latin America and the Middle East preparatory to our comparative thematic chapters. It is clear that Africa and the Middle East share certain social and political problems resultant from the imposition of colonial boundaries on multicommunal and regionally differentiated societies: the process of establishing the power and authority of the new state and its institutions, and creating, expanding and diversifying a new national economy. As new classes were formed – particularly the middle strata, a small bourgeoisie and an urban proletariat – a rather complex and varying relationship came into existence between communal groups (religious sects, nationalities, ethnic groups and tribes), these new classes and institutions like the army, bureaucracy, political parties and trade unions. Because the state was so central for social and political change, competition for scarce resources (employment opportunities, budgetary allocations, development projects, business contracts, etc.) often resulted in social and economic demands being channelled into communal and regional demands. In Africa and the Middle East, the political process became frequently characterised by a dual tendency toward authoritarian control of political conflict and the eruption of conflict into tragic civil wars, as in Lebanon, Nigeria and Uganda. Although many states in Africa and the Middle East have this sociopolitical process in common, one distinctive feature of Middle Eastern society and politics is the political salience of a class of large landowners, a group largely absent from African society. Even though at independence many Middle Eastern states were controlled by such a class, the politics of land reform became entwined with **communalism**, the main Middle Eastern forms of which were sectarianism and ethnicity. In the Middle East and Africa, states vary as to their capacity to maintain stable rule through combinations of patronage, authoritarianism and repression. On the one hand, there are states which manage social change and communalism and on the other states which disintegrate under the pressure of social, ethnic, sectarian and regional tensions. The ability of some states to overcome the forces of disintegration is linked to their capacity to establish institutions of a coercive, distributional or representative nature. Of particular significance are the army and the party, on which we focus in our comparative chapters.

The distinct historical development of Latin America provides a contrast to Africa and the Middle East. Very different societies emerged there, because of their much earlier and more intensive history of capitalist development, and the associated class structures created. And yet similar political processes have occurred in Latin America: high levels of military involvement in politics and a limited role for political parties. We explore the factors which make the region as vulnerable to instability and conflict as Africa and the Middle East.

The role of the **political party** in Third World political systems is like the ghost in Hamlet: on the periphery of the action but the play cannot do without it. It has frequently been argued that the more developed a state – and the more pluralist its society and array of interest groups – the easier it will be to constrain authoritarianism and produce the intergroup competition necessary to sustain a liberal democratic system. At the core of such a system, it is further argued, there will be a range of political parties providing for participation. A contrasting form of organising participation is the single party, the ideal type of which is internally democratic. In each of our three regions autonomous political parties and competitive political systems have been weak or non-existent, except for brief periods. Their authority and powers have been eroded by presidents or they have been banned or dissolved by military regimes and with the same *diktat* have been resurrected or created by them. Where parties have existed they have been instruments of control – frequently paralleling the bureaucracy – rather than vehicles for participation. Why should such patterns be so common? Why should military regimes or personalistic and autocratic leaders appear so frequently in Third World politics? Different levels of development do not seem to offer a convincing explanation since the more highly developed states of Latin America (with their more advanced economies and urban class structures) have produced regimes as anti-party as any of the lesser developed states of Africa and the Middle East. The answer appears to lie more with the nature of the Third World state which – whether controlled by a military or a civilian regime – mediates, controls and represses social discontent and social conflict and functions as the horn of plenty, access to which accords wealth, privilege and power. The Third World state is also at the fulcrum of international political and economic forces and the domestic constellation of political groupings, classes and strata. In most cases it is the motor for economic development and has to manage (or at least digest) economic changes and crises induced by external forces. Control of the state and its patronage is more crucial for the nurturing and establishment of parties than is participation through party as some 'natural' expression of interest.

The role of the **military** helps to account for the weakness of parties and limited popular participation. Military intervention, military rule and the withdrawal of the military from politics are processes common to all three regions, if not to all states within the regions we examine. The very salience of the military and the military regimes invites comparison and raises the question of the extent to which the motivations, roles and goals of the military transcend those variations in history, culture and different patterns of economic development and social organisation which have been presented in our first two chapters. Our approach – based on regional comparisons and comparisons within regions – permits an analysis which can assess the relative weight to be attributed to a set of multiple factors. It also permits us to compare military regimes and to explain variations between them.

If the plethora of military interventions allow some greater comparison between and within the three regions, the comparative experience of revolution in the Third World can be set against a stronger theoretical framework than exists for the military. Our emphasis on the heritage of the past as a means of grasping the distinctiveness of the three regions' historical development stands in contrast to the essence of what revolutions are about: a systemic break with the past.

The integration of the Third World into the **international capitalist economy** was the most decisive and formative factor shaping it, and the continuation of such deep ties throughout the twentieth century make revolutions which break those connections immensely difficult to achieve. Trade relations, credit for capital requirements, markets for exports, foreign currency for import financing and foreign aid have perpetuated this dependency relationship. In principle, the less integrated a state is into the **international economy**, the more such a state would appear susceptible to revolutionary outbreaks; however, in such under-developed societies the strata able to generate protracted revolutionary movements are often absent. Furthermore, prospects for socialist revolutions would seem unlikely, for although the Third World state is weak in the sense that it is permeable by external economic and political forces, dominant social classes and institutions (like the officer corps) are powerful and generally anti-socialist. In addition, in the contemporary world, the coercive and repressive capacity of internal security forces is very well developed. On the other hand, both external domination and internal repression are factors which can engender large-scale political mobilisation. In particular, foreign political and economic control has frequently caused nationalist uprisings, and nationalism has often gone along with revolutionary upheavals. Then again, because nationalism generally lacks a social content nationalist movements are frequently led by an eclectic set of classes and class alliances, and these can produce movements ranging from socialist through reformist to conservative. It would seem that only a rare and infrequent conjuncture of circumstances creates a revolutionary situation – as when alienated classes formed in a revolutionary movement confront a weakened state in a favourable international context. Even then a revolutionary movement – particularly one that is avowedly socialist – which seizes or edges toward power is vulnerable to internal and external subversion. The nature of the internal and external obstacles that revolutionary regimes face depends on multiple factors, the geographic position and strategic importance of the revolutionary state being of particular importance.

Our chapters on the military, political parties and revolution deal with political power and the state. Our chapter on **women** looks at a group which lacks power. Whatever the level of development in the three regions women are in inferior positions, be they employed in agriculture or manufacturing industry or confined to domestic roles. In the Middle East, an ideological justification – based on a particular interpretation of Islam – is advanced for the secondary position of women. Despite cultural variations between the Middle East, Africa and Latin America (and whatever the nature of development or modernisation that has taken place) such autonomous areas as **women** have occupied in the past have mostly been eroded. Through an examination of women's roles in three regions of widely varying cultures and histories we are able to assess the relative weight of history and culture and the impact of social and economic development on women's subordination.

In many respects the last two chapters follow from (and link back to) the themes of our first chapter, in that they examine the continuing impact of external factors on Third World politics. We concentrate on the post-Second World War period of post-colonialism, and the struggle for economic and political independence, on the differential impact of superpower rivalry in the three different regions, on attempts to institutionalise regional co-operation and on the role of multinational corporations. Although Third World states have attained legal sovereignty, regional conflicts and continuing economic dependence provide the opportunity for superpowers to exert influence and the greater the strategic and economic interests at stake the greater superpower involvement and intervention in a particular region. Since the Second World War, the emergence of the **Soviet Union** as a world power has provided newly independent states of the Third World with an alternative source of political and diplomatic support and economic aid. However, Soviet caution and a shortage of foreign exchange, the commitment of the majority of Third World states to a capitalist development path and the economic power of the **United States** and the international financial institutions in which it has the major voice have limited the Soviet role in the Third World to one of forming political alliances, supplemented in some cases by substantial military assistance.

Increased economic and political independence through higher levels of regional co-operation in the Third World has proved less than might have been expected. In the political sphere certain crises have produced regional solidarities: the Palestine problem for the Arabs, the Malvinas/Falklands crisis for Latin America, and South Africa for the African states. But attempts to establish (and expand) political unity, economic integration and regional trade and financial links have not been very successful in Latin America and the Middle East and have been only moderately successful in Africa. Indicative of the problems facing Third World states is their greater stress on relations with the advanced capitalist states through the North–South dialogue and the New International Economic Order (NIEO), rather than on development through regional co-operation.

Although dependence is still the order of the day, there have been some changes in the economic sphere. In some Latin American states a significant manufacturing base has been established, and in the Middle East the oil-producing states reversed their previously supine relationship with the massive oil conglomerates and gained control of production and supply, even if the ability to set prices has proved a somewhat transitory phenomenon. Such changes as these, however, are placed in context in the final chapter when we examine three aspects of the international economy: oil, famine and debt. In this chapter, we see the legacy of the past as it has been sustained to the present. The roots of African famine are traced back to colonial agricultural policies which began the neglect of food production, particularly of subsistence agriculture. The impact of the rise (and subsequent fall) in the price of oil is traced for the oil producers themselves, and for international financial markets where it set in motion the complex sequence of events which gave rise to the debt crisis. This has mainly affected those Latin American states with a developed industrial base but hungry for capital and too successful, in some ways, in attracting it.

We have not sought to make reference to all the Third World, nor all the states in Africa, Latin America and the Middle East. We have set out to produce a broad introduction to Third World politics which is built around systematic comparisons between three large, diverse and important regions. Our underlying framework is one which emphasises the importance of the past for understanding the present, of social and economic relationships for understanding politics and of international political and economic forces in shaping the Third World. We hope it will lead readers on to more detailed and specialised studies of the individual countries and regions discussed, and to a greater understanding of issues and areas of historical and topical interest.

Although the book has been a truly co-operative venture, there has been a division of labour: Paul Cammack has been responsible for Latin America and the drafts of the chapter dealing with women; David Pool for the Middle East, the final revisions and the compilation of the text; and William Tordoff for suggesting the project and the sections on Africa. William Tordoff and David Pool would also like to thank Karen Hall and Marilyn Dunn for their secretarial assistance, and Hannah Pool for her help with the index.

1

The Heritage of the Past

1. Introduction

The world as we know it today has been shaped by two developments of global significance: the spread of the **capitalist** world
economy through conquest, colonisation, and economic penetration overseas, and the emergence of a socialist bloc in the
wake of the Russian Revolution and the division of Europe after
the Second World War. As we shall see in our fifth chapter, the
second of those developments has had a substantial impact upon
the shaping and perception of conflicts in the Third World. In
this chapter, we are concerned with the part played in the creation
of a capitalist world economy in a context of rivalry between the
'Great Powers' by colonisation, the formal occupation and rule of
overseas territories by the European powers from the sixteenth
century onwards.

The focus, here and throughout the book, is on three areas:
Africa, Latin America, and the Middle East. In some aspects, as
we shall see, the impact of colonial rule was uniform; but in
others it differed greatly from area to area. Broadly speaking, we
may say that the similarities from region to region arise from
similarities in the purposes engaged (primarily economic and
strategic) and the resources deployed (generally scanty, consider-
ing the magnitude of the enterprise), while the contrasts result
from differences in timing (the colonial period in Latin America
was virtually over before its counterpart in Africa had begun), in
the nature of the indigenous society encountered, and in the
administrative practices favoured by the colonising power.

We shall draw these themes together at the close of the chapter.
Before embarking upon case studies of the three areas examined,

however, we draw attention to the broad contrasts that can be made between them. With Africa, colonial rule comes late, mostly toward the end of the nineteenth century, and endures for six decades into the twentieth – and longer in the case of the Portuguese possessions. Great Power rivalry plays an important part in explaining the timing and dynamic of colonisation, and differences in the way in which those powers organised themselves administratively in Africa have vital consequences for the nature of post-colonial society and politics. For Africa, therefore, our emphasis is squarely upon colonial rule and its consequences. Latin America provides a sharp contrast. On mainland South America colonial rule has been over for 150 years. New élites – largely the descendants of the original Spanish and Portuguese settlers – won independence from their distant colonial rulers in the first decades of the nineteenth century. Along with early independence, however, came a particular role within the emerging world capitalist economy which was to differentiate the region sharply from the developing centres of industrial capitalism in Europe and North America. Latin America became (haltingly at first) a supplier of minerals, foodstuffs, and other raw materials to the hungry industrial centres of the advanced nations. It was this phenomenon – rather than the direct impact of recent colonial rule – which was to shape the region. When looking at Latin America, therefore, we focus upon the twin experience of early independence and the development of the export economy. The Middle East, in contrast again, falls somewhere between the virtually total Western colonisation of Africa on the one hand, and the early political independence of Latin America on the other. Our focus is on the prior impact of the rise and fall of the Turkish Ottoman Empire, and the 'mandate period' which followed it. We pay particular attention to the attempt by the mandate powers to create a class capable of ruling on their behalf once they withdrew from direct rule. We expand also upon the consequences of the clash between two highly sophisticated cultures, Christianity and Islam. Within our general focus on colonisation, then, we seek to differentiate, where appropriate, between the three regions studied.

2. Africa: the colonial legacy[1]

Many different forms of sociopolitical organisation existed in pre-colonial Africa, ranging from centralised kingdoms to state-less societies. Some of the kingdoms, such as Ashanti (Asante) and Benin in West Africa, extended at the height of their power over wide areas and were often underpinned by centralised bureaucracies. Urban communities existed in parts of pre-European Africa and particularly in the western Sudan, where Gao, Jenne, Kano, Timbuktu, and Walata had been established many centuries before the advent of colonial rule; indeed, by the eleventh century Kano (now in northern Nigeria) had already become a prosperous trans-Saharan trading centre. Most Africans, however, lived in the rural areas and especially in stateless societies organised around the family, kinship group and clan, though this did not necessarily mean that they were more backward. They were engaged in a constant struggle with a harsh environment and migrated frequently from one area to another in the face of war, disease, drought and economic need.[2]

European contact with Africa long preceded the establishment of European rule – the Portuguese began to trade to the West Coast in the fifteenth century. They, together with rival European seafarers, established a pattern of coastal trading (in gold and ivory, and – especially from the seventeenth century – in slaves) which had the effect of diverting African trade away from the trans-Saharan route, linking West Africa with the Maghreb. In the nineteenth century, this pattern began to change: the slave trade (which over a period of 300 years had resulted in the trans-portation of millions of Africans to the Americas) was supplanted by legitimate commerce, and the interior of the continent was gradually penetrated by explorers and missionaries, culminating in the period of European empire building, especially following the Berlin Conference of 1884–5 (see Map 1). The various European powers – France and Britain, Belgium and Portugal, Germany, Italy and Spain – established (or were confirmed in possession of) colonies and protectorates, mostly drawing the boundaries between them arbitrarily and with scant regard for the pattern of traditional allegiances. Though it was the northern boundary separating the Gold Coast from Upper Volta which cut the Mossi kingdom in two, it was the demarcation of boundaries at right angles to the coast which caused most social dislocation in West Africa – the Akan, Ewe and Yoruba peoples, for example, were split between different colonies. The map of Africa came to

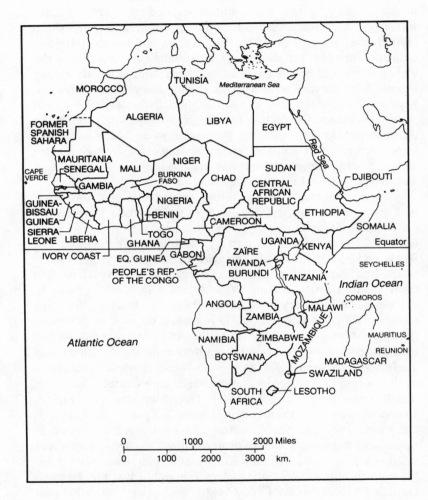

Map 1 *Africa*

resemble a patchwork quilt; it was changed slightly after the First World War when Germany, following its defeat, was stripped of its colonies and the latter became 'mandated territories' administered by other European powers (notably Britain and France) on behalf of the League of Nations (after the Second World War, they became trusteeship territories of the United Nations).

Though strategic considerations were sometimes important and 'civilising' and other altruistic – if arrogant – motives on the part of some colonisers cannot be entirely discounted, the prime motive for the establishment of colonies was economic – the European powers were anxious to secure easy access to the raw materials needed to fuel the manufacturing industries established in Europe following the industrial revolution and to obtain a protected market for their manufactured goods; moreover – as the British showed in 1900 in Ashanti and the Germans a few years later in Tanganyika – they were prepared if necessary to fight in order to gain these objectives. Africa became locked into the international capitalist economy, leading Walter Rodney to claim that colonialism entailed 'the development of Europe as part of the same dialectical process in which Africa was underdeveloped'.[3] In fact, the impact of colonialism was not entirely negative – it was significant that African leaders, who had often been educated overseas and nurtured in the Western political tradition, accepted not only the colonial state as the focus of their aspirations but also many of the changes which colonialism had introduced. Its beneficial effects included checking intercommunal fighting and establishing a framework of territorial unity out of disparate social elements; introducing a common colonial language and administrative structure; creating an essential infrastructure of railways, roads and harbours; providing schools, churches and hospitals; introducing new food plants, such as cassava, maize and sweet potato; and controlling disease among cattle through the use of veterinary skills. Colonialism also had less wholesome aspects: for example, the rule of different colonial powers in neighbouring territories created linguistic and administrative barriers that were difficult to overcome; communication links were designed to facilitate the export of cash crops to European markets rather than to stimulate internal production and trade; African cash crop cultivation was controlled, as in Kenya, in the interest of European settlers and led to the neglect of food production, with devastating long-term effects; forced labour, in one form or another, was practised by all the colonial powers, most persistently by Portugal; and the very extensive knowledge of local conditions possessed by the rural people themselves was too often ignored by expatriate agricultural officers. Perhaps above all, colonialism entailed dependence on foreign private capital and enabled foreign trading companies, such as the United Africa Company (UAC) in British Africa, the Compagnie Française de l'Afrique Occidentale (CFAO) in French Africa, and subsidiaries of the Companhia União Fabril (CUF) in Portuguese Africa to monopolise the import–export trade and the purchase of farmers' produce. A pattern of external economic dependence was thus established that was to persist after political independence was achieved.

Though colonial rule, until the Second World War and beyond, was everywhere authoritarian, bureaucratic and paternalist, and rested ultimately on superior force and technology, the colonial powers differed (often widely) in their specific policies and overall approach to colonial development. Common features included the small number of European administrators in relation to the size of the population being administered, the paucity of the resources made available to them by the colonial powers (especially before the 1940s), and the sense of European superiority which they were able to instil in the subject (especially rural) people, with the result that the hold of colonial rule came to be more psychological than military. The Second World War helped to shatter this myth of superiority.

Policies of the powers

Following the Berlin conference of 1884–5, the French eventually established eight colonies in Afrique Occidentale Française (AOF), with headquarters in Dakar, and four in Afrique Equatoriale Française (AEF), based on Brazzaville.[4] Each colony had its own governer and budget and (from 1946) its own elected assembly; it acquired substantial territorial autonomy under the *loi cadre* reforms of 1956. A colony was divided for administrative purposes into *cercles*, a *cercle* being administered by a political officer, the *commandant de cercle*, who was assisted at the lower levels of administration by *chefs de canton* and *chefs de village* –

frequently old soldiers and retired government clerks appointed as 'straw chiefs' in place of the traditional rulers. The governors were subject to the overall direction and authority of a governor-general (there was one for AOF and one for AEF), who controlled a general budget and was advised by a 'grand council', made up of elected territorial representatives. Ultimate control over what was, overall, a highly centralised system, characterised by parallel administrative structures in each territory and staffed by a remarkably mobile public service, was vested in the Minister for Colonies in Paris. Unique features of the French system, in the wake of the Brazzaville conference of 1944, were first that African political parties and trade unions tended to be either linked with (or to function within the orbit of) metropolitan parties and unions; secondly, that some of the political parties – notably, the Rassemblement Démocratique Africain (RDA) – were interterritorial parties with sections in individual territories; and thirdly, that Africans were allowed to send representatives to the French National Assembly and the Council of the Republic in Paris (a right long enjoyed by inhabitants of the *'quatre communes'* of Senegal).

British colonial policy was more pragmatic than the French, and British rule was also less centralised. There was no counterpart to the 'metropolitan axis' of French colonial policy and, within the framework of policy laid down by the Colonial Office in London, British colonial governors (in the pre-1939 period especially) were allowed greater discretion than their French counterparts in initiating policy deemed suitable for their individual territories. The governors were assisted, in each case, by legislative and executive councils, though these bodies were limited both in composition and competence until after the Second World War. Up to that time, the cornerstone of British policy was 'indirect rule'. This approach entailed the British administration (and the District Commissioner in particular) ruling through indigenous political institutions; these were the chiefs and their councils, who were constituted into native authorities and supported by native courts and, eventually, by native treasuries. The system made limited demands on expatriate manpower and worked best in areas such as Northern Nigeria where chieftaincy was strongly entrenched; it proved least satisfactory in areas (such as south-eastern Nigeria) where traditional institutions were weak or non-existent and use had to be made of government-created chiefs. Disadvantages of indirect rule were that it largely excluded the educated élite from power-sharing and accentuated existing communal divisions.

By contrast with British colonial rule, Belgian rule was extremely centralised and subject to close European supervision, with executive power remaining firmly in the hands of the administration; chiefs were absorbed into the administrative organisation at the lower levels. Belgian rule was also strongly paternalist, and sought to arrest social and political change through the creation of a materially prosperous and contented people, educated (mainly by missions – Protestant as well as Catholic) to the primary level. The formation in October 1958 of the radical Mouvement National Congolais and the outbreak of riots in Léopoldville in January 1959 showed that this attempt had failed. The central government of the Congo was not strong enough to overcome the ethnic and regional separatism that surfaced when independence was granted precipitately in 1960 and the secession of the copper-rich province of Katanga plunged the country into civil war.

Portugal was the only other European power with an extensive African empire – Germany was stripped of its colonies after the First World War; Italy was ousted from Ethiopia during the Second World War and had no colonies of its own, though it administered Libya and part of Somaliland on behalf of the United Nations until December 1951 and July 1960 respectively; while Spain was under little pressure to grant independence to Spanish Guinea and Spanish Sahara, both of which were very thinly populated. Portugal claimed to be undertaking in Africa a non-racial, Christian civilising mission, but in fact it exploited its colonies economically and subjected them (in the educational sphere, for example) to long years of neglect; racial discrimination and tight bureaucratic control were key features of Portugal's highly authoritarian rule. In the post-war period – and especially after the outbreak of the African colonial wars in 1961 – Portugal, still an underdeveloped country in European terms, looked to its colonies to supply it with cheap raw materials and to import more than a third of its cotton manufactures.

Nowhere in colonial Africa was there any sustained and meaningful preparation for independence. The Belgians resisted independence until a very late hour; the French fought a bloody colonial war in order to 'keep Algeria French' and, in the mid-1950s, accepted territorial autonomy as a means of preventing independence in AOF and AEF; in the 1950s also Britain battled against a Kikuyu-based nationalist movement, known as 'Mau Mau', in Kenya; and Portugal fought a bitter and protracted war in a bid to retain its African colonies. Britain did more to prepare its non-settler colonies for independence than any of the other European powers, but preparation began very late, and, as Bernard Schaffer pointed out, was 'all along rivalled and hindered by other values, which were predominantly bureaucratic'.[5] Moreover, the wrong people were 'trained', since those who came to power following national elections held under an ex-panded franchise in the 1950s and early 1960s were, in most colonies, radically-minded young men rather than the professional and traditional élites who had hitherto served as unofficial members of their countries' legislative and executive councils.

In British (and possibly also in French) Africa more might have been achieved in the way of preparation if the transition to independence had been longer in the post-Second World War period. The experience of many Africans as soldiers during the war in south-east Asia and elsewhere and the scarcity of jobs and rampant inflation after it heightened resentment against European rule and exploitation. Anti-colonial nationalism spread quickly and was canalised into political parties and interest groups led in most colonies by a thrusting petty-bourgeoisie of teachers, clerks and small businessmen who often indulged in socialist rhetoric and were impatient to change places with the colonial élite. In some cases – in areas of substantial white settlement such as Algeria and Southern Rhodesia, and above all in Portuguese Africa – African demands for constitutional change went un-heeded and violent conflict followed. In the majority of cases, however, even to talk of an independence 'struggle' is somewhat misleading. In the 1950s, successive British governments seemed to be all too ready to shed themselves of the burden of African empire, stilling the imperial conscience by incorporating in the independence constitutions (for example, of Ghana, Kenya and Uganda) unworkable provisions designed to protect minority interests. French-speaking Africans only raised the issue of independence (as distinct from equal status with Frenchmen) towards the end of the decade, when President Charles de Gaulle realised that he could best preserve French economic and other interests in Africa by granting political independence. In both French- and English-speaking Africa, most nationalist movements were willing to enter into power-sharing arrangements with the regimes which they aimed to displace and brought their countries peacefully to independence under the tutelage of the colonial government itself.[6]

The colonial legacy

Since Africa was subject to rule by several powers, the colonial legacy has varied from one part of the continent to another. Generalising, therefore, one can say in the first place that the economies and communication networks of the African colonies were largely developed in accordance with the needs of the colonial power. Primary products – whether cash crops such as cocoa and coffee or minerals such as copper and bauxite – were exported to European markets in their raw state at prices which fluctuated widely and sometimes (in the 1930s and 1940s) fell dramatically; in return, the colony imported manufactured goods from abroad, mainly from the 'mother country', at prices subject to the inflationary pressures of the European domestic economies. As we noted above, trade was monopolised by large European companies; resentment of their monopoly and of the often low prices which they paid for produce led farmers on the Gold Coast (in 1931 and 1937) and elsewhere to hold up their produce in order to force up the price and caused the colonial state itself to establish the cocoa, coffee and other marketing boards which were retained and extended in the post-independence period. Not that the ordinary farmers benefited directly from the introduction of these boards since the latter retained (ostensibly for price stabilisation and development purposes) a large part of the money realised from the high commodity prices prevailing in the 1950s and early 1960s; in this way, and through taxation, the rural population carried the main burden of state expansion. Moreover, European import–export houses continued to operate on a substantial scale and Asians in East Africa and Lebanese in West Africa tended to monopolise distribution; the result was that the great majority of indigenous (African) entrepreneurs had scope only at the lowest levels of business activity. Nevertheless, an African middle-class was beginning to emerge in Nigeria, Senegal and a few other colonies, though (as we shall see in the next chapter) its main growth took place after independence.

Secondly, the imposition of colonial rule integrated the African territories more fully into the international economy, but it did not necessarily alter fundamentally the domestic economic structure.[7] In countries with predominantly agricultural economies (a feature of the vast majority), disruption was greatest where (as in Portuguese Africa and parts of French Africa) plantation agriculture was introduced and least where (as in the Northern Territories of the Gold Coast and much of Upper Volta) peasant farmers grew yams, millet and other crops to meet the needs of their extended families and to market any surplus. The smallholder production of cash crops – undertaken, for example, by cocoa farmers in the Gold Coast Colony and Ashanti and in the Western Region of Nigeria – was potentially more disruptive of the domestic economic structure than predominantly subsistence agriculture in so far as, in certain contexts, it stimulated the emergence of the rural capitalist farmer who employed wage labour, invested his profits in urban property and even (as in the Akwapim district of the Gold Coast) bought land. The picture was different again in those few colonies which had developed a sizable manufacturing industry; these were mainly colonies (such as Southern Rhodesia) where there was extensive European settlement. Substantial mining was undertaken in a large number of countries – for example, bauxite in Guinea, iron ore in Sierra Leone, copper in the Belgian Congo and Northern Rhodesia – though ownership, production and control were vested in European- (or South African-based) companies. The more radical pre-independence political parties were committed to ending foreign control over the economy, but on coming to power found themselves hampered by the lack of trained and experienced managers. Until new state governments began to adopt nationalisation measures in the 1960s, there was one slight, temporary advantage in the persistence of foreign ownership: the foreign company served to an extent as a buffer insulating the political leadership from the substantial wage claims put forward by what, in a state such as Zambia, had become a well-organised trade union movement. The governments were determined not to be held to ransom by a predominantly urban workforce that was already well paid in relation to the peasant majority and whose demands, if granted, would have an inflationary effect on the economy as a whole. They therefore moved quickly (though not always, as in Zambia, entirely successfully) to reduce trade union autonomy.

Thirdly, colonialism – through its handmaiden, capitalism – had a differential impact on African countries, accentuating differences caused by geography and geological good fortune. It resulted in the juxtaposition within the modern state of advanced economic regions, characterised perhaps by the mining of bauxite, copper and iron ore, or the growing of cash crops such as cocoa, coffee and tea, and deprived areas where the people eked out a meagre living on marginal, badly irrigated land. In these latter areas educational and health provision was inadequate, often for understandable reasons – in West Africa, for example, the northward expansion of Christian missions had been checked by the shortage of funds following the economic depression of 1929–31 and by colonial governments anxious not to offend the susceptibilities of Muslim rulers and their subjects. There was also a sharp urban–rural divide, and this was accentuated as more and more rural dwellers migrated to the towns in search of jobs. By independence in states such as Zambia large and volatile urban electorates already existed and accounted for the urban bias of much government policy in the post-independence period.

Fourthly, traditional social values and institutions were undermined during colonialism; this was a universal phenomenon, though the erosion was uneven. It was probably least severe in non-colonial Ethiopia and hardly less so in such 'semi-colonial monarchies' (to use Christopher Clapham's phrase) as Libya, Morocco, Swaziland and Zanzibar, where the ruler's territory was coterminous with that of the colonial administration. In most cases, the French broke up the old political units, as they did in Guinea's Fouta Djalon; however, they occasionally retained and worked through established traditional leaders, such as the Mossi chiefs in Upper Volta, the Fulani Emirs in the northern provinces of the Cameroons, and the Muslim brotherhoods of Senegal. French political officers believed in France's civilising mission and the thrust of their assimilationist policy was to substitute French language, culture and nationality for indigenous social and cultural systems. The British system of indirect rule resulted in the preservation of certain wholesome African traditions and customs, but exacerbated existing communal divisions and often drove a wedge between chiefs and those of their people who joined mass-based political parties. Christianity introduced values (not only of course in British Africa) which were at variance with traditional ones and occasionally – as in Uganda – gave a religious dimension to intergroup conflict. In the (Belgian) Congo, the legacy of Belgian colonial policy was that the *évolués* acquired a desire for material wealth more obviously than they accepted other Belgian middle-class values, while the struggle for independence in Portuguese Africa under a leadership committed to Marxist–Leninist principles and organisation undermined the traditional social system in most of Guinea–Bissau outside the Fula areas and in those provinces of Angola and Mozambique which were subject to guerrilla warfare.

Ruth Collier has drawn attention to differences in the post-independence political pattern of Francophone and Anglophone Africa which stem from the contrasting attitude of France and Britain towards traditional authorities in their colonies. She points out that the French reduced the power of chiefs and traditional institutions and thus fostered élite cohesion, while the British policy of indirect rule sponsored two systems of authority and legitimacy (the traditional and the modern) and thereby heightened élite differentiation. Moreover, because the provision of education was more extensive in British than in French Africa, the modern élite in British Africa split between an older, predominantly urban élite of doctors, lawyers and merchants and a petty-bourgeoisie of teachers, clerks and small traders which had emerged in the nationalist ferment of the post-Second World War period. This élite differentiation, coupled with the more gradual introduction of electoral politics and the longer period of de-colonisation, meant that the party system was more fragmented in British Africa than in French Africa. The generally higher levels of party dominance in the latter resulted in the more rapid transition to one-party rule in French-speaking states after independence.[8]

However, we must not exaggerate the extent of the erosion of tradition, marked as it undoubtedly was. While it is true that chiefs and their elders were largely (or entirely) excluded from participation in 'modern' local government, much of the traditional social and economic organisation remained intact, especially in predominantly agricultural communities, with important consequences for political behaviour in the post-independence period. Nigeria, Senegal and Zambia were among the many states where both central and local politicians continued to win popular support by appealing to those ethnic, regional–linguistic and other vertical divisions in society which linked the new states of Africa to their colonial past. Industrialisation – in the form of extractive and manufacturing industry – did shake up the traditional social and economic organisation, but it was the advent of a booming oil industry in a country like Nigeria (where production reached two million barrels a day by 1973) that was to prove especially disruptive.

A final colonial legacy that might be mentioned was constitutional and political. In the terminal phase of colonial rule, Britain and France introduced ministerial systems and other features of modern democratic government under constitutions modelled substantially on those of the metropolitan countries. The constitution of the French Fifth Republic, which was tailor-made for General de Gaulle, was fairly easily adapted to the needs of the new Francophone states: it facilitated the transition to an executive presidency, with the president supported by a dominant or single party and unencumbered by a strong legislature. In Anglophone Africa the Westminster-style constitution, with its stress on parliamentary government and the two-party system, fitted less easily the aspirations of political leaders who had led their countries to independence. For example, in relation to newly-established and independent public service commissions, these leaders were expected to forego some of the powers over the civil service which the colonial governors had enjoyed. Both Kwame Nkrumah in Ghana and Julius Nyerere in Tanganyika had, at independence, to assume the office of prime minister under a monarchical system topped by a governor-general representing the Queen; they had to wait for three years and one year respectively before the relevant constitutional changes could be made enabling them to assume the presidential mantle. This arrangement was subsequently relaxed: at independence in 1964, Northern Rhodesia immediately became the Republic of Zambia under an executive president and Bechuanaland (which became the Republic of Botswana) followed suit two years later.

Constitutional provisions restricting political control over the civil service were removed and in Tanzania from 1963 and Zambia from 1969, a number of senior political and administrative posts became interchangeable. (While South Africa's domestic politics are not considered in this volume, it is interesting to note that the white-ruled Republic moved further away from the Westminster system of government through the adoption in 1983 of a new constitution. Cardinal features of this constitution are the shift to an executive presidency, the adoption of a national legislature divided into three separate chambers, one each for Whites, Coloureds and Indians, and the exclusion from any semblance of power-sharing of the Black (African) majority.)[9]

There was continuity as well as change in the post-independence governmental arrangements in Black Africa: thus, the pyramidal type of ministerial structure persisted in much of Anglophone Africa, while French-speaking states retained the essential features of the inherited prefectoral system. The old structures were certainly extended – notably, by the almost universal creation of a large number of parastatal bodies – but were rarely trans-formed. This was even true of ex-Portuguese Africa, despite governmental commitments to socioeconomic transformation on Marxist–Leninist lines; in practice many of the policies pursued – in relation to private trading and peasant farming in Mozambique, for example – were pragmatically based. As far as most African leaders were concerned, their attitude was understandable: they had sought to take over rather than dismantle the inherited insti-tutions of state, and they were content for the most part to operate within the framework of control which the colonial powers had established.

3. Latin America: early independence and the export economy

In Latin America, as in Africa and the Middle East, levels of social and political organisation varied widely from area to area at the time of colonisation. In contrast to the experience of other regions, however, Latin America saw the early subjugation of the indigenous population in the most advanced and densely settled areas, and a long process of intermixing and assimilation which left the Catholic religion of the Spanish and Portuguese colonists dominant, and rendered ethnicity relatively weak as a basis for collective identity and resistance to colonial rule. Liberal–Conservative conflicts in which religion and the Church played a major part were significant in the late nineteenth and early twentieth century in some areas, but neither religion nor ethnicity have played a major role in social and political conflict in the area in the contemporary period. A further striking contrast is provided by the early independence achieved by those areas under Spanish and Portuguese rule. In the early decades of the nineteenth century – well before the systematic colonisation of Africa had even begun – independent states had emerged in all the territory in mainland Central and South America previously ruled by the Iberian powers. Some of the major sources of political identity and political conflict in much of Africa and the Middle East during recent decades – ethnicity, tribalism, religion, and opposition to colonial rule – have thus been weak in Latin America. Despite this, Latin America is recognisably a part of the Third World today. In order to understand the strong parallels between Latin America and the other regions considered here, one needs to examine the way in which the economy of the region developed during and after the colonial period, and the distinctive part it played in shaping societies quite different from those of the developed world, and structurally similar to those whose experience of colonial rule generally stretched well into the present century (see Map 2).[10]

Significant variations existed in population density and levels of social organisation throughout the region at the time of the first contacts with Spanish and Portuguese colonists (around the end of the fifteenth century). Two distinct and well-developed civilisations existed in what is today Mexico (the Aztecs in the central region, and the Maya in the Yucatan peninsula), while the Inca had built up an extensive empire in the Andean region, centred upon the magnificent cities of Cuzco and Macchu Picchu. In contrast, the dense forests which covered much of tropical and central Brazil sheltered thousands of largely separate groups, living a far more rudimentary life. The remnants of these groups still inhabit the Amazon region, and fight a hopeless battle against the continuing encroachment of 'Western civilisation'. Further south, in Chile and Argentina, the indigenous inhabitants quickly adopted the implements of Spanish warfare, and kept the European colonists at

Map 2 *Latin America*

bay until well into the nineteenth century. The result was that they were in the end largely exterminated rather than assimilated, and Chile's small Mapuche community is the last remnant of these proud and powerful peoples.[11]

Even in the areas of densest settlement and earliest contact, where present-day societies reflect the survival and numerical dominance of the indigenous inhabitants, the demographic impact of colonisation was catastrophic. Recent estimates suggest that a population perhaps numbering 25 million in Mexico and Central America was reduced to 1 million within a century of contact, partly as a result of war, but primarily as a consequence of the fatal impact of Western diseases to which the indigenous peoples of the Americas lacked immunity.[12]

The primary purpose of colonisation (in the sixteenth century as always) was economic gain. The fortunes of the colonists and the impact of colonisation varied in accordance with the availability of exploitable resources, both natural and human. If the finely worked gold seized from the Incas and Aztecs first aroused the avarice of the Spanish adventurers in the early sixteenth century, it was the fabulous silver mines of Mexico and of Potosí (in present-day Bolivia), which proved the greatest source of wealth in the colonial period. They were equally a source of misery, as the populations of the surrounding regions were forced to render increasingly onerous tribute in the form of labour in the mines. With the passage of time, complex economies arose – centred upon the mining areas, but also involving surrounding regions as suppliers of foodstuffs and other essential goods to the mines themselves and to the expanding urban centres where commercial and bureaucratic activities multiplied. In due course similar developments occurred in Brazil, initially with the development of an extremely prosperous sugar-exporting plantation economy in the north east of the country (around the settlements of Salvador and Recife), and in the eighteenth century with the shift of the centre of gravity of the economy southward to the central-southern state of Minas Gerais, where gold and diamonds were discovered at the end of the seventeenth century. In Brazil, however, initial economic exploitation on any appreciable scale was delayed by rival Portuguese interests in Africa and the Far East, and the absence (at the point of contact) of any lucrative opportunities for trade. It was only in the later sixteenth century that a minor trade in 'brazil wood' (a source of natural dye-stuffs) gave way to sugar production in the north east to supply the expanding European market. A further contrast with Spanish America which was to prove a development of major significance was the early abandonment of attempts (spearheaded by settlers in the struggling southern colony of São Vicente, today São Paulo) to capture and enslave the indigenous inhabitants of the country, and the switch to negro slavery. This was made possible by Portugal's extensive African trade, and the endurance of slavery (successively in the production of sugar, gold, and coffee) to 1888 had a social and political impact which was matched only in Cuba, where slavery spread dramatically in the nineteenth century with the rapid extension of sugar production on the island.[13]

It was thus during the colonial period, over three centuries, that the present-day nations of Latin America adopted the role of suppliers of primary commodities to already industrialising Europe. Even so, Latin America owes its present character not primarily to its colonial experience but to developments which took place in the nineteenth century. The first of these was the coming of political independence. The second was the development of the 'export economy' on a much extended scale, as the industrial revolution in Europe gathered pace and transformed the international economy of which Latin America was already an integral part.

Early independence and its consequences

With the minor exceptions of British Honduras (Belize) in Central America and three small British, French and Dutch colonies on the Caribbean coast of South America (today Guyana, French Guiana and Suriname), the whole of Central and South America fell under the rule of either Spain or Portugal. Among the most significant consequences were the early development of commercial exploitation, the establishment of a common language throughout the area (with the exception of Portuguese-speaking Brazil), the unchallenged ascendancy of the Catholic Church, and the reproduction throughout the region of élitist and absolutist conceptions of social organisation and rule. Overriding all these in importance, however, was the early departure of the Spanish and Portuguese, and its manifold consequences. The early mercantile development of Spain and Portugal had given them an initial advantage over other European powers in the area of trade and colonisation, but by the end of the eighteenth century the combined effect of economic backwardness and military overextension resulting from the dogged attempt to sustain the Hapsburg empire across Europe had greatly weakened Spain, while the extent of Portugal's overseas empire masked a chronic weakness at home. In the later eighteenth century, both Spain and Portugal were seeking to reorganise the administration and exploitation of their colonial possessions, but in the period of the Napoleonic Wars both countries suffered occupation and invasion, the temporary triumph of the Liberals over the monarchy, and the loss of their American possessions. In the case of the Spanish possessions, the four separate viceroyalties of the late colonial period split further to produce fourteen independent states by the 1830s; in the case of Brazil (the only Portuguese possession), the flight of the Portuguese royal family to Rio de Janeiro in 1807 and the subsequent declaration of Brazilian independence by the Portuguese prince Pedro I in 1822 were factors in the survival of the territory as a single independent state. The overall impact of early independence was the coming into being across the Atlantic of a new group of distant, relatively impoverished and underpopulated states, just at the moment that the industrial revolution was gathering pace in Western Europe.[14] For fifty years, (during which momentous changes took place in Europe), the primary concern in the majority of these states was the restoration of order and authority in the wake of wars which began over the issue of independence, and continued as the succession to power was disputed. Across most of the continent the resulting destruction (along with the disruption of colonial patterns of production and trade) undid much of the relatively modest economic development achieved during the colonial period.[15] And where a relatively rapid and peaceful transition to independence and stability was achieved, as in Chile and Brazil, the new élites (generally based upon the land) saw the rapid development of the export economy as the key to prosperity. Nowhere could a pattern of industrial revolution parallel to that under way in Europe be set in motion, and early experiments with protectionism were soon abandoned.[16]

The export economy

It is the virtually unique combination of early and uninterrupted political independence and early and substantial incorporation into the international capitalist economy through the production and export of primary commodities which gives Latin American political development its distinctive character within the Third World. The development of the region under independent political rule as a supplier of primary commodities was part of a single global process dominated successively by the rise of Great Britain to industrial pre-eminence, rivalry between the leading capitalist economies from the late nineteenth century on, two World Wars centred on Europe and the subsequent emergence of the United States in a position of unrivalled supremacy within the capitalist world. Naturally, no understanding of Latin America or the development of the Third World in general can be gained without reference to that global process. At the same time, the complementary development of each region of the Third World has its own complex internal dynamic. In the case of Latin America, where (as we have seen) some of the complicating factors present elsewhere – ethnicity, tribalism, religious conflict, Great Power rivalry and colonial rule in the modern period – were weak, this internal dynamic arose primarily out of the secular struggle during the process of export-led development between the different class forces which it spawned.

In Western Europe, the process of rapid industrialisation weakened the formerly dominant landed élites, and generally subordinated them (in one way or another) to the rising industrial bourgeoisie. The complementary process of export-led development (experienced to one degree or another throughout the Third World, but most strongly in Latin America) gave new strength to the traditional landed classes. The first problem they faced (as we have seen) was to restore order and reassert their authority in the wake of the gaining of independence. The second was to organise production for export. Even where order was rapidly restored, there were significant discontinuities with the colonial period. The products which became the basis of expanded export economies in the nineteenth century were rarely the ones which had dominated colonial trade. Brazil's steadily declining mining economy was eclipsed by coffee and plantation labour; in

Chile, a varied export structure of wheat, copper and silver was submerged after the War of the Pacific (1879–82) by the development in the newly-acquired northern territories of nitrate mining; Argentina, a poorly-developed source of hides, tallow and other products of a primitive free-ranging cattle economy at the end of the colonial period, eventually prospered as a result of the highly organised production of wheat and beef; Uruguay developed a modern and prosperous wool industry which also displaced a poorly-organised cattle-ranching economy. In each of these cases the development of new products in new areas meant the rise of new élites, and necessitated the forging of alliances in which previous élite groups were either divided, incorporated, or deposed. As the types of production undertaken varied, so did the relations of production involved. For example, the development of coastal plantation agriculture in Ecuador (for cocoa) and Peru (for sugar and cotton) made coastal entrepreneurs dependent upon reserves of labour in the highlands, while the continued reliance in Brazil upon slavery made the powerful coffee élites of the centre-south dependent upon the support of the sugar barons of the north east, for without it the monarchy and the system of slave labour it upheld could not have been maintained. One consequence in Brazil (which persisted after the end of slavery in 1888 and the fall of the monarchy in 1889) was the sharing of national power between a number of regional élites. This was reflected in the adoption of a federal system in 1891. In contrast, the absence of major centres of regional power in Argentina after independence allowed an early process of centralisation, leading to the unchallenged supremacy of Buenos Aires and the cattle and wheat economy by the end of the nineteenth century.[17]

Although the general picture across Latin America was the emergence of powerful groups associated with new or expanded export sectors, there were considerable regional differences. The greatest of them was between the agricultural or land-based export sectors on the one hand and the mineral-based sectors on the other. Where the export products came from the land, rural production was generally modernised, and the landed élite combined economic and political power. Where export-led development was based primarily on minerals – as in Chile, in Mexico, and in Venezuela after the belated discovery of petroleum – traditional élites tended to preserve power by acting as allies of foreign investors, rather than by taking direct control of the export sectors. A second consequence of this pattern of development was the relative backwardness of agriculture, neglected in view of the flow of foreign exchange from the exploitation of minerals. This has had considerable significance in the present century.[18]

Export-led development brought relative peace, stability and prosperity to Latin America. But it did so at the cost of introducing a pattern of development which had serious internal and external drawbacks. Internally, it condemned the majority of the population to a level of exploitation which threatened stability in the longer term. This was particularly so where the most dynamic expansion was taking place, for the dynamic expansion of the export sector frequently meant the destruction of peasant communities as the land was taken over by large-scale commercial agriculture, or the imposition of harsh regimes in mining camps drawing their labour from displaced peasantries.[19] Externally, it meant the entrenchment everywhere of a pattern of development complementary to (and dependent upon) the industrial development of Western Europe and the United States. The problems arising out of the internal tensions generated were seen most dramatically in the Mexican revolution of 1910, in which some two decades of intermittent warfare saw first the overthrow of the old élite based upon the Diaz dictatorship and (at a cost of over a million lives) the victory of a newly consolidated northern bourgeoisie over the peasant armies of Emiliano Zapata and Francisco 'Pancho' Villa. Similar tensions (though on a less dramatic scale) were everywhere apparent after the First World War, which disrupted patterns of trade and growth, and provoked considerable unrest. Rising urban groups were peacefully assimilated in Argentina, and were challenging for power elsewhere, when the external dependence of the export economies was ruthlessly exposed in the wake of the 'crash' of 1929 and the ensuing depression. After 1930 the export-based economies and the ruling groups they had sustained could never be reconstituted on a stable footing. The dividing line which comes in Africa with decolonisation and in the Middle East with the withdrawal of the European powers from direct control comes in Latin America with the collapse of the export economies in 1930 and the emergence of new social forces and alliances, bringing with them the pursuit of a markedly different pattern of growth, based now upon attempted industrialisation.

4. The Middle East: from empires to states

The contemporary Middle East emerged from the Ottoman Empire after the First World War when the mandatory system was established and the states of the area took their current form. Social and economic structures of the independent countries were formed through a lengthy process of change in the nineteenth century, as the Empire crumbled, and through the impact of the mandatory form of government, a disguised and short-lived colonialism. Of the Arab states, the Arabian peninsula and North Yemen remained free of imperial and colonial rule, the Gulf states had British advisers but not direct rule and Iran (or Persia, as it was sometimes called) was an Empire in its own right.

The Ottoman Empire extended across the Middle East to the Persian Empire in the east, Ethiopia and Sudan in East Africa, into the Balkans and across North Africa.[20] It was an Empire based on relations of tribute rather than fixed territorial unity with tribal leaders, provincial governors and military commanders paying regular tribute to Istanbul, the centre of the Empire and seat of the Ottoman sultans. Pre-colonial society had elements of both hierarchical and communal organisation. The village, the clans of pastoralists, the craft and merchant guilds in the towns had their heads theoretically responsible to the local representatives of the Ottoman state but frequently not responsive to the demand for tax and dues.

In the nineteenth century, an expanding Europe qualitatively transformed the nature of the tributary state, its territorial extent, political form and economic base (see Map 3). Constant military pressure from Russia, recipient of new western technology, and nationalism in the Balkans had cut off one of the main sources of Ottoman military strength: the levy of slaves from the Caucasus who were converted to Islam and trained to serve the Ottoman dynasty as soldiers, governors and bureaucrats. Originally they were insulated from society and owed allegiance to the state. The demise of this institution had a weakening effect on the army in particular. The spread of Western trading companies and the

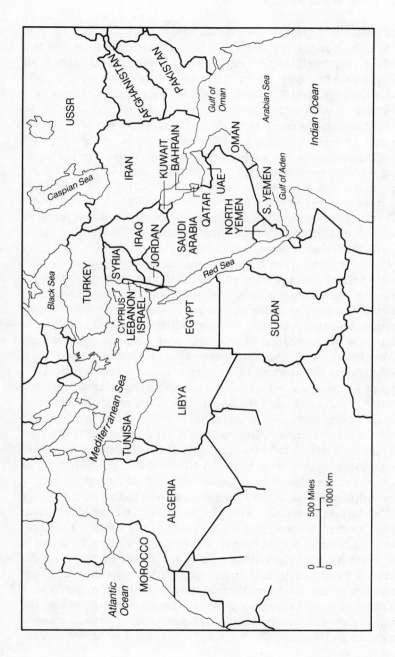

Map 3 *The Middle East*

establishment of European colonial rule in Africa eroded the grip of Middle Eastern merchants on long distance trade across this trading crossroads of the world. Furthermore, traditional craft and manufacture were hit by the influx of goods from the rapidly industrialising West. These developments seriously weakened the economic base of the state, and consequently its capacity to combat external military pressure and centrifugal forces organised around provincial military commanders, local governors with dynastic ambitions and well-armed tribal groupings. At the beginning of the nineteenth century Muhammad Ali asserted his autonomy in Egypt, and most of North Africa was effectively controlled by ruling families from the local Ottoman military and administrative establishment. These autonomies marked not only the territorial shrinking of the Empire but also (through the denial of tribute) further eroded its financial base.

However, during the nineteenth century, the Ottoman Empire – and formally component parts like Egypt – attempted to re-structure state organisation with the goal of strengthening it against predatory colonising powers which were establishing colonies and protectorates, bringing settlers to North Africa and competing for influence in Palestine and Lebanon. The reform effort began with the introduction of educational and legal measures for the purpose of creating a modern army, generating greater revenue and establishing a more efficient system of central control. Both Egypt and the Ottoman Empire sank into debt and the European embassies changed their role from advice to direction. In the Ottoman Empire and Egypt the development of private property in land was probably the most politically significant change in the long term. In the Empire, the beneficiaries were the urban-based merchants, officials and soldiers and in Egypt the members of the ruling dynasty and their allies.

The Ottoman alliance with Germany in the First World War and Egyptian indebtedness and nationalist rebellion against foreign advisers brought France and Britain into direct control in the Arab Middle East. Britain occupied Egypt in 1882 and declared a Protectorate and Britain and France divided the Arab provinces of the Ottoman Empire during the First World War, a division of spoils recognised by the League of Nations as the 'mandate system'. In the latter arrangement Iraq, Syria, Lebanon, Palestine and Transjordan were to be prepared for independence under the benevolent tutelage of Europe. The mandatory system was aimed at preparing the inhabitants for self-rule. The underlying social and economic effects of colonial rule, however, were more important than the 'training' given to politicians and civil servants.

The mandatory powers succeeded to the Ottoman Empire, and these newly-created states (which had previously been a collection of provinces connected only by rule from Istanbul and a dominant Arabo-Islamic culture) were the heirs to massive areas of land, title to which had been vested in the Sultan or the Ottoman state. Although the process of privatisation had begun in the mid-nineteenth century, it continued in the colonial and post-colonial periods. The major beneficiaries were the tribal chiefs, the urban notables and merchants, the top bureaucrats and members of the ruling dynasties.

Colonial rule in the Middle East and North Africa divided into two types: direct colonial rule by Italy in Libya and the French in Tunisia and Algeria; indirect colonial rule in Egypt and the mandated states of the Fertile Crescent. One of the major effects of colonial rule was the establishment of colonial boundaries, with the attendant creation of new centres of power and national economies grafted on to the existing social structures. For the colonised it was the Ottoman Empire that was divided, for the incipient Arab nationalist movement it was the Arab nation. Nationalities were left straddling boundaries. The Kurds, for example, were divided between Iraq, Iran and Turkey. When Lebanon was formed Arab Sunni Muslims were attached to Mount Lebanon with its multiplicity of Christian and Muslim sects. Pastoral nomads accustomed to shifting across the deserts of the Middle East were increasingly entrapped within a new state boundary. Traditional trading routes like those of Mosul–Aleppo and Damascus–Baghdad were disrupted. Egypt (with its longer history as a political entity) was less affected in this respect by the coming of colonial rule.

More broadly, the colonial period hastened the integration of the states of the region into the international economy, subjugating them economically to the coloniser. Dependency was created not simply by the export of a single product to Western markets (cotton from Egypt, phosphates from Tunisia and Morocco, oil from Iraq, wine from Algeria) but by the direct grip of Western trading companies on these key exports. Prices were determined by Western market forces, over which the local producer had no control. There were some successful attempts to break this economic stranglehold: in Egypt some of the largest landowners and nationalists were behind the independent Misr Bank and attempted to use this institution as a vehicle for indigenous industrialisation.[21]

The colonial state established the social basis for the post-colonial regimes. The monarchies of Jordan and Iraq were created by the British and the social forces recruited to the 'façade' of political institutions were the urban notables, the former Ottoman officers and the leading families of the tribes. The economic basis of their wealth lay in land ownership and the colonial state (as a successor to the Ottoman Empire) inherited state land.

One further effect of the colonial period was the strengthening of the state. Armies, ministries, police and local government were established, along with a limited educational system to supply the necessary personnel. The poverty of these societies and the limited number of primary and secondary schools combined to provide access to the educational system for a limited number of students; it was typically an access confined to the areas surrounding the urban centres.

The expansion of the state carried with it the political thrust to erode the autonomies of the leading village heads and tribal leaders. The expansion of police posts, the establishment of a standing army and a secular judiciary impinged on customary tribal authority and the authority and status of the Muslim religious men. The irrigation engineer and local government official stood juxtaposed to the prominent local landowners. The village primary school teacher threatened the values, status (and indeed financial position) of the traditional village teacher of the Koran. The salience of agriculture in the economy, the limited industrialisation and lack of absorptive capacity of the economy tied the graduates of educational institutions to a career within the state apparatus, either the army or bureaucracy. At the same time the political power of the landed and mercantile sectors blocked agriculture as a significant source of state revenue: those who became salaried officials were better off than the peasantry and landless, but considerably worse off than the large landed and big merchant families.

In certain cases the particular combination of social forces enabled such autonomies to be perpetuated. In Iraq, the tribal leaders were aligned with central politicians and had strong representation within parliament and thus secured their interests in land with their local political power: they had their own armed bodyguards and exercised judicial authority over their tribesmen through the Tribal Disputes Regulation. In Lebanon, the rural *zu'ama* (*s. za'im*: landowners and local leaders) combined with import–export merchants and Beirut financiers to establish a state which was powerless. Most Lebanese provided votes for the *zu'ama* who gave services and protection in return. In Syria and Egypt, the landowners predominated, although in the latter geography and history combined to diminish the power of provincial autonomies: the Egyptian peasantry was highly concentrated along the Nile, organised for production for the market and ethnically homogenous. This pattern is different from Syria, Lebanon and Iraq where minority sects and ethnic groups lived in mountainous zones and followed cultural imperatives (deriving from a history of persecution) to maintain solidarities against an expanding state.

One general pattern, then, was a dominance of landlords within a new context of parliaments and cabinets, the operation of which helped to preserve and expand their power. The social base of the new regimes brought about major political conflicts in the post-colonial period. Landlords with massive concentrations of land determined policy, a consequence of which was very limited industrialisation. The establishment of the state apparatus, the expansion of schools, the creation of a small working class and the burgeoning numbers of landless in the rural areas provided the counter forces to the domination of the landed.

The graduates of the educational institutions found limited opportunities for employment. The frustration of this strata was compounded by the great difficulties in actually graduating. The low level of industrialisation provided only limited opportunities in the non-government sector. The primitive conditions of the small working-class enhanced the appeal of the Middle Eastern Communist parties. The landless labourers and poor peasants (many of whom had previously owned land) migrated to the towns where they eked out a living in the margins of urban life: selling chewing gum, biros or cigarettes. With the students they became the nucleus of the urban demonstration mobilised by various shades of socialist and nationalist parties and organisations.

Within these general patterns, however, Middle Eastern societies are marked by divisions which are not wholly economic. As the centre for the emergence of three world religions these political, social and economic developments which have set the framework for contemporary political patterns have had various effects on religious and ethnic politics.[22]

A few examples will suffice to illustrate the complex interaction of minorities in the Middle East and the historical, social, economic and political developments outlined above. During the nineteenth century, the Maronites of Mount Lebanon were the beneficiaries of two developments related to European expansion.[23] First, the development of Beirut as a port and the related expansion of mulberry bushes and silkworm-rearing took place largely in the Maronite areas of Mount Lebanon. Although the largest factories were initially French-owned, by the third quarter of the century silk was an important source of wealth for merchant families as it was for the peasant-workers. The factories employed women and, it seems, it was easier for Maronite than Muslim women to work in such factories. Peasant cultivators became increasingly involved in mulberry growing. The population of the mountain developed into a relatively wealthy peasantry and in the process overthrew the traditional feudal system in an uprising in 1859–60 which, rather like contemporary Lebanese politics, took on a communal form. The second set of developments which took place concerned education.[24] Although the Maronite church was linked to Rome it was not until the second and third decades of the nineteenth century that missionary activity became of importance in Lebanon, and then it was through Protestant and American missions stimulating French Roman Catholic ones. The result was that, by the time of the French mandate, the Christian communities, Greek Orthodox, Greek Catholic and Maronite, had far higher levels of education and modern skills than other communities. Colonial competition, trade and the disintegration of the Ottoman Empire through the nineteenth century facilitated this differentiation of communities although it should be added that certain leading families of the Druze and Sunni Muslim communities were beneficiaries of mission education and economic development.

The establishment of the French mandate enhanced the general position of the French Catholic-educated Maronite community. Mount Lebanon, the Maronite heartland, was united with the Sunni coastal towns and the Shi'a Beqa valley. Despite tensions between Maronite Lebanese nationalists and the French authorities, the political institutions of presidency and confessional parliamentarianism ensured a dominant political role for Christians in general and Maronites in particular.

The relationship between the historical developments of the nineteenth century, the combination of alliances established and the particular preferences of colonial administrators can be observed in Iraq.[25] There, members of the Shi'a community were not appointed to positions within the Ottoman bureaucracy, nor recruited to the military schools because of the intolerance of the orthodox Sunni Empire for the heterodox Shi'i. The level of secular education among the Shi'i was generally lower than the Sunni community and thus when the British established the Iraqi mandate the Shi'a were rarely recruited into the new state institutions. While Sunni Arabs who were nationalists were branded as 'extremists' by the British authorities, Shi'a nationalists were invariably tagged as 'fanatics'. This sectarian preference, however, operated within a framework where landlords of whatever persuasion were encouraged.

Iran, a multiethnic empire, underwent a process of change similar to that of the Ottoman Empire.[26] Until the middle of the nineteenth century Iran's tribes, villages and towns were relatively isolated from each other and because the Qajar dynasty failed to establish a centralised bureaucracy, they had a high degree of administrative autonomy. The Qajar shahs had no standing army, and depended for coercive power on tribal levies who owed more allegiance to their tribal leaders than they did to the rulers. Royal power inhered in the ability of the Shah to manipulate and mediate between the different segments of Iranian society.

Western economic and cultural penetration were the main agents of change. In the last half of the nineteenth century, the shahs were forced to grant economic concessions to foreign commercial concerns, the way for which was prepared by military defeats and humiliating treaties earlier in the century. Toward the end of the century, the dynasty was increasingly squeezed between foreign powers and companies and the traditional commercial and trading classes. The new intelligentsia, which was created through the impact of the West, although animated by secular ideas was alienated from the Qajars because of their subservience to Western interests. These two forces played an important role in the 1905–9 Constitutional Revolution which placed further limits on the power of the Qajars. It was not until 1926 that the Iranian state asserted itself through the person of Reza Khan, a colonel in the Russian-officered Cossack brigade. Reza founded the Pahlavi dynasty in 1926 when he became Shah and set about establishing a strong centralised state based on a standing army and a modern bureaucracy. He introduced secular reforms in law and education and launched a programme to modernise the economy; increased oil revenues helped pay for the modernisation.

Although Iran was never directly colonised, it had a lengthy history of foreign interference and periods of military occupation. During the nineteenth century there were the imposed treaties and the concessions. The concession for tobacco caused an uprising after a British Major Talbot gave the Shah a £25 000 personal gift and 25 per cent of the profits to the state in return for a 50-year monopoly for distributing and exporting Iran's tobacco. In the early twentieth century Iran was effectively partitioned into two zones of influence by the Anglo-Russian Agreement of 1907 with the Shah left a swathe of central Iran. In 1911 Britain and Russia occupied Iran and again in 1941 invaded it, removed Reza Shah because of his pro-German sympathies and remained in occupation until after the war. If the legacy of Reza Shah was a stronger, centralised state, the legacy of foreign intervention was an anti-Western nationalism (at times dormant) which unified the broad range of Iranian classes.

One aspect of Middle Eastern history and politics merits separate attention: the Islamic and nationalist response to the spread of imperialism and foreign influence. Although Turkish, Arab and Iranian nationalisms developed during the late nineteenth and twentieth centuries they never wholly superseded the appeal of Islam. Indeed, as a more secular set of nationalisms developed nationalists frequently drew on Islam as a source of cultural authenticity to oppose an encroaching West, which had inflicted military defeat, debt, and finally, the humiliation of direct political control. It was a massive reversal of history for peoples proud of their past and the achievements of successive Islamic empires. The Arabs had carried Islam from the Arabian peninsula, through the Middle East and across North Africa into Spain. The Ottomans had pressed into the Balkans and Eastern Europe. The march of Islam established great civilisations, the palaces and mosques still evident today in places as far apart as Granada, Cairo, Damascus, Shiraz, Istanbul and Samarkand. Achievements in conquest and conversion were as great in science, medicine, mathematics, art and architecture. Although the Muslim empires had been long in decline, the developments of the nineteenth and twentieth centuries were earth shattering. A wide range of solutions were sought, but the most popular were those which drew on solidarities of the past to confront this shift from victor to vanquished. Muslim fundamentalism and Islamic modernism, secular Arab and Iranian nationalism and a less coherent but nevertheless popular entwining of nationalisms and Islam can (and do) mobilise the populations of the Middle East. Such consciousness of the past, both national and religious, (even when manipulated by political leaders) has been a significant factor in limiting the level of cultural penetration by the West. The contemporary power of these indigenous sources of political mobilisation were very evident in the combination of Islam and nationalism in overthrowing the Shah of Iran.

The economic, political and ideological developments of the nineteenth and early twentieth centuries are crucial for understanding the course of Middle Eastern politics after the Second World War. The nineteenth century was of particular importance: Egypt and the Ottoman and Persian Empires sank into debt, this fostered the expansion of private property in land and it was the great landed proprietors who took the reins of power in most of the new states of the Middle East on independence. The colonial period was relatively short, but began a process which was to continue in the post-colonial period: the assertion of control by new states over areas and peoples that had gained considerable autonomy during the period of Ottoman decline. Colonial institutional arrangements, in some cases, hampered the development of strong states, which confronted tribes and minorities, many of which were well-armed and inhabited mountainous terrain. One issue which touched many Middle Easterners was the land question. It emerged into politics at different times in the post-independence period and frequently became entangled with other divisions and conflicts such as those between the urban and rural populations and between the minorities and majority religious and ethnic groups.

5. Conclusion

As even this brief review shows, the history of the emergence of the contemporary Third World is extremely varied and complex. While it does make sense in some ways to see it as a single global process, this should not be allowed to obliterate the specificity of each region and each country. The 'global' processes that can be identified may be translated at local level into very different outcomes as a consequence of differences in intensity and timing, and interaction with different constellations of local factors. Given this inescapable complexity, the focus on three contrasting regions makes a useful starting point, making meaningful comparison possible without descending so far into minute local detail as to make it impossible to grasp the broader significance of events.

Our survey of the 'making' of the Third World in Africa, Latin America and the Middle East suggests that at least three broad issues have to be distinguished for analytical purposes, even though they may be closely entwined, in different ways, in practice. These are the development of an international economy, the pattern of rivalry between states in the world system, and the direct impact of colonial rule. In each of the regions studied, the balance between these factors has been different; and variety in (and between) each region in matters such as natural resource endowment, climate, demography, and previous economic, social and political history have generated widely varying outcomes. In the end, there is no substitute for a detailed and intimate knowledge of such matters. What we propose here is a broad framework within which they can be approached. The first essential, we feel, is to recognise that we are concerned with a single complex historical process – that the shaping of the Third World, in other words, is part of the same story as the shaping of the modern industrialised world. This does not mean at all that every development in the regions we study should be seen as being imposed from outside, but it does mean that due weight has to be given to external military, technological, economic and political factors. Secondly, the central process involved is the expansion of a vigorous and dynamic international capitalist economy outwards, over centuries, from a core in Western Europe (and later the United States). Thirdly, although the pattern of conflict between states is partly an outcome of this process, it has had a dynamic of its own which cannot be discounted. And, finally, although direct colonial rule has in one sense only been a specific outcome in certain parts of the world of these other broader processes, its impact has been such that it merits separate treatment.

Viewed from this perspective, it is clear that the term 'Third World' is somewhat imprecise and potentially misleading. It should not suggest isolation and separateness from the developed world, nor a shared history which is uniform in character. We retain it as a useful and all-embracing descriptive term, without attaching to it any great analytical value. The framework we adopt allows us to compare and contrast three major areas of the world outside the core capitalist economies and the Socialist bloc in a common historical context, and it is this exercise which is our primary concern.

In Africa, direct colonial rule has left an indelible mark. In Latin America, in contrast, it is distant in time, and whatever view one takes of its impact, the subsequent transformation of the region under the impact of incorporation into the international economy from the mid-nineteenth century onwards has a far greater claim to our attention. Africa and Latin America have in common, however, the fact that they have been thoroughly reshaped by penetration from the 'West'. In this respect, the comparison with the Middle East is of great value, as it provides a salutary reminder (brought home most forcibly in recent years by the re-emergence of militant Islamic fundamentalism) that for all the vigour of the forces for change unleashed from Europe since the Middle Ages, they have not carried all before them. The combination of the sheltering effect of the Ottoman Empire (the 'Eastern bloc' of its day), and the internal vitality of the Arab world, limited 'Western' incursions until the time of the First World War, and the halfway house of mandate rule similarly mitigated the effect of British and French involvement, tending to produce a greater level of alliance and compromise with local élites. The failure of the Middle East to fit easily into the set of 'global' processes we have traced is no accident. It is a faithful reflection of the relative separateness and cultural strength of the Arab world. In due course, oil was to draw the region fully into the world economy, with consequences that are discussed at length in later chapters, but in the period considered here there is no doubt that the extent of Western political and economic penetration was limited in comparison with that experienced in Africa and Latin America. And even where the extent of economic penetration was substantial (as in Egypt), the political and cultural impact was much less marked.

If one of the remarkable features of colonial rule has been the achievement of large effects from the deployment of small resources, this is partly because direct colonial rule has been just one local manifestation of the broader global processes of change discussed above. Colonial rulers have never lacked allies, from the first Spanish incursions into the Americas to the mandate period in the Middle East. In large part, these allies have been conservative, and we shall discuss one of the consequences of this below; but perhaps the most striking testimony to the power of the forces driving the process forward is the imprint of the colonial legacy on its fiercest opponents. The opponents of colonial rule in Africa were for the most part the direct products of colonial penetration and rule in either its political or economic manifestations. As pointed out above, they sought not to destroy but to take over the new regime. In general, there has been no going back from colonial rule to an earlier age of innocence. The same is true for Latin America, where in many countries virtually the entire population is European in origin. In Latin America (as we shall see later), political traditions and aspirations are thoroughly Western; liberal democracy has not fared well, but it remains the central point of reference; equally, in Africa, competitive democratic regimes have not generally long survived independence. Then again, they had not long preceded it either, and the types of regime consolidated in post-colonial Africa bear a close enough resemblance to colonial systems of rule to suggest that there is a degree of continuity that is not accidental. Colonial rule was not liberal democratic, and if liberal democracy has not flourished in Africa it is more because it was not planted or tended than because it has been violently uprooted since independence.

The 'colonial legacy' is strongest, then, where it has been carried forward by its adherents and its opponents alike, taking on a momentum of its own beyond the immediate intentions and goals of the colonisers themselves. Much of the instability of the contemporary Third World can be traced back directly to periods and practices of colonial rule. But the most intractable conflicts are often the unforeseen outcome in the longer term of modest, short-term solutions to immediate problems. The French authorities who introduced silk farming into the Maronite areas of Mount Lebanon did not intend to bring about the conflicts that have engulfed the area since the middle 1970s, any more than the British authorities who devised indirect rule as a means of governing in Africa intended to make Nigeria ungovernable after independence. But the connections are there. It is a mistake to attribute too great a capacity to bring about particular ends to any actor in the Third World, and one only has to reflect upon the global catastrophes of the depression and the current economic crisis to realise that the 'Great Powers' have signally failed to control their own destinies, let alone those of other peoples. We address some of the issues that this perspective raises in our final chapter, which explores the politics and the political economy of famine, petrodollars, and debt.

To an extent, however, the European nations can be held responsible for instability in the Third World. It may in part be seen as a necessary counterpart of poverty and inequality. But it can also be attributed to the contradictions between the social and political strategies of the European nations and their citizens, and the dynamic economic forces which they represented and carried with them. Marx drew attention well over a century ago to the progressive side of capitalism and even of colonial rule, and there have been dynamic forces at work whose effects have ranged far beyond the intentions of their human agents. But at the same time the social and political strategies of colonial rulers and of entrepreneurs, merchants and traders abroad have been deeply conservative. While colonial rulers and the advanced guards of Western industrial society can be said to have introduced progressive forces into the Third World, they also created conservative alliances which blocked the possible progressive effects of those forces. Indeed, the satisfaction of their own interests depended upon their doing so. In Latin America conservative landowning groups were strengthened in the course of the nineteenth century, often as a result of direct alliances with foreign interests; in Africa the colonial authorities looked to amenable traditional rulers and to minorities to shore up their control; in the Middle East a decaying landowning class was resuscitated as a suitable instrument for the purposes of the mandate powers. It is not sufficient, therefore, to see turmoil in the Lebanon, instability in Nigeria and revolution in Iran simply as unpredictable long-term consequences of humdrum decisions made by harassed and pragmatic officials, merchants and adventurers abroad. There is a deeper logic underlying them, which can be traced ultimately to the distinction made here at the outset between the global dynamism of expanding capitalism, and the attempts of particular individuals and nations to control, direct and benefit from it.

2

State and Society

1. Introduction

Whereas the Spanish and Portuguese colonies in Latin America had achieved political independence by 1830, the contemporary state system in Africa and the Middle East (with the main exceptions of Ethiopia and Egypt) is of relatively recent creation. In the post-Second World War period new state governments in Africa and the Middle East tackled the problem which had faced Latin American rulers over 100 years earlier – that of welding together a variety of different people, who were divided along ethnic, regional and other cultural lines and who were at different stages of educational development. Spanish was the *lingua franca* of Latin America (outside Portuguese-speaking Brazil) and Christianity, almost exclusively in its Roman Catholic form, was the main religion. Most people in the Middle East were Arabic-speaking and predominantly Muslim. Africans, however, were divided by a myriad of vernacular languages and (as a colonial legacy) by seven European languages – English, French, German, Belgian, Italian, Portuguese and Spanish; the African people were Christians (Protestant and Catholic), Muslim and animist. Moreover, African states were also divided by artificial boundaries which resulted in the eventual creation of 51 states – more than twice the number of states that existed in each of the other two regions; not surprisingly, some of the smallest of these states (such as the Gambia and Lesotho) were hardly viable.

This chapter examines the relations between state and society in each of the three regions and identifies the factors which make some states (such as Egypt and Brazil) strong and other states (such as Lebanon and Chad) weak. Among these factors are the

49

length of time that the state has existed, its political heritage and institutions, and its social complexity and economic base.

Political leaders in the Third World are not immune from the pressures of the societies to which they belong. Their escape route lay in their control of the machinery of state which they used to achieve often contradictory goals – on the one hand to foster (through social change) a sense of national identity and, on the other, to advance their own interests by means of factional appeals. They also used their public offices to strengthen the state's diplomatic, economic and military links with the international community. This meant, in most cases, allowing multinational corporations (MNCs) to play an important role in their countries' economies and accepting the aid conditions imposed by the World Bank and the International Monetary Fund (IMF). The corollary of political independence was therefore often external economic dependence.

In looking at the state in the light of the social context within which it operates, we note how that context changes under the impact of urbanisation, the provision of educational and other services, and industrialisation. Can one say, for example, that the state which is socially homogeneous will necessarily be stronger than the state which is socially pluralistic or that there is a direct correlation between social sophistication and state stability? We shall consider the salience of horizontal and vertical divisions in society in order to identify the determinants of political behaviour in each region. Among the questions to be asked are: where classes exist, why do politicians recruit support on a class basis in some states, but not in others? In the latter, are they afraid that such an appeal will undermine their élite position or are communalism, religious sectarianism and other vertical divisions in society more important than class considerations? The sections on Africa and the Middle East give considerable attention to communalism, by which is meant the competition between communal or sectional groups for a share of state resources. It is important to note that though politicians may play upon the regional–linguistic, ethnic and religious identifications of their followers in order to gain support, their motivation may be rational and economic rather than primordial. The section on Latin America draws attention to significant social bonds which cut across class differences and which have played an important role in the politics of the region. Clientelist ties also exist in Africa and the Middle East, though their social roots differ. In each region, we point therefore to a 'patronage' kind of politics, whereby those in control of the state reward their supporters and these supporters (the 'clients') themselves act as patrons to dependants at lower state levels, and we consider whether clientelism reduces the significance of class as an organising and explanatory factor.

The distinction has been made between empirical statehood and juridical statehood, and the argument has been advanced that the latter has contributed to the survival of certain weak Third World states.[1] We concede that membership of the United Nations and of other international organisations may serve to guarantee the continued political independence of such states. However, we make two points: first, a politically independent state may be economically dependent on a stronger state within the international community, and secondly a state which is strong juridically may be woefully weak in political and indeed sociological terms. This chapter discusses the second of these issues but leaves consideration of the first to subsequent chapters.

2. State and society in Africa

The anti-colonial African nationalists of the post-Second World War era achieved independence for their states within artificial, colonial-imposed boundaries. Some of these states (notably Sudan and Zaire) were immense in area, Nigeria was huge in population, while others including the Gambia in West Africa, Ruanda and Burundi in East Africa, and Lesotho and Swaziland in southern Africa, were so small in both size and population as to be hardly viable as independent states. With the exception of Egypt (which for most purposes can be classified as part of the Middle East) and Ethiopia, the new African states therefore lacked the deep historical roots of states in south and south-east Asia. Several of them, however, including Dahomey (now Benin), Ghana and Nigeria in West Africa, contained within their borders what had once been powerful centralised kingdoms. The survival of a traditional unit such as Buganda within modern Uganda often fanned sub-national loyalties, while the absence of such units facilitated (as in Tanganyika) the process of nation-building. However, sub-national loyalties might also flourish where, as among the Ibo in Eastern Nigeria and the Kikuyu in Kenya, there was no centralised traditional unit upon which they could build. In short, communalism in Africa took various forms and was widespread; it constituted a formidable challenge to the leaders of the newly independent states.

A vitally important question was whether these rulers – who had next to no experience of operating a governmental system on a national scale – would be able to adapt to their own purposes the structures of power established within the former colonial state. Their inheritance normally included the essential machinery of government (notably a legislature, executive and judiciary at the centre and – in Anglophone Africa above all – the rudiments of a representative local government system at the base). As we pointed out in Chapter 1, adaptation generally proved easier in Francophone African states (which followed the Gaullist constitutional model with its stress on firm executive leadership) than in Anglophone countries which initially adopted Westminster-type constitutions. However, within ten years at most of independence, the latter had been discarded in favour of executive presidential systems. Though Anglophone countries retained 'residual' legislatures and pyramid-shaped ministerial structures as a legacy of the colonial past, the one-party state became a well-nigh universal feature of the African scene (Nigeria was an important exception in the period before and after the first phase of military rule, both in this respect and in its adoption of a federal constitution). Within this framework, the national president exercised extensive (and often dictatorial) powers.

Unfortunately, the new state rulers did not also inherit the state capacity needed to work either these institutions or the new institutions (such as a large number of parastatal bodies) which they themselves created. Trained and experienced manpower was in short supply, and in some cases the shortage was critical. In Zambia, at independence in 1964, few of the country's 109 African graduates possessed administrative experience at a senior level, and a number of chief clerks became permanent secretaries overnight. In Mozambique, the exodus of expatriate managers in 1974–5 and the dearth of Africans with managerial skills meant that the extensive measures of nationalisation undertaken by

Samora Machel's government floundered and flagging industrial output was not revived. This acute manpower shortage was partly the result of the slowness with which colonial regimes had adopted Africanisation policies, and reflected above all the inadequacy (or sometimes the irrelevance) of the colonial educational provision. In the Belgian Congo, for example, the primary educational net was spread very wide, but secondary and higher education was badly neglected – in 1960, when the Belgian Congo became the newly independent state of Congo–Léopoldville (now Zaire), there were only sixteen graduates out of a population of over 13 million; in Northern Rhodesia (which, like the Belgian Congo, had a large copper industry), next to no attention was given to technical education. In Portuguese Africa, the record was abysmal: according to official government statistics, the illiteracy rate in 1959 (after some 500 years of Portuguese presence) was over 95 per cent in Mozambique, Angola and Guinea–Bissau and nearly 80 per cent in Cape Verde.

The governments of the independent African states accorded education a high priority, as the following statistics reveal. In Zambia, educational expenditure rose from K13 million in 1963–4 to K85 million in 1973; primary education doubled during this period and secondary, technical and university education expanded even faster. In 1974 Tanzania, one of Africa's poorest countries, set the end of 1977 as the date for the achievement of universal primary education (UPE); though this target proved unrealistic, it was well within sight by the scheduled date. In Nigeria, educational objectives changed several times. At independence the emphasis was on secondary, tertiary and vocational rather than primary education. The number of universities increased from 1 (at Ibadan) before independence to 13 by 1975 and 21 by 1985. During the 1970s the military (mainly for political reasons) shifted the emphasis to primary education, and in 1974 launched a plan to phase in UPE from 1976. In 1976–7 UPE accounted for 55 per cent of federal capital expenditure on education (much of it went on teacher training institutions) and for well over 40 per cent of total federal recurrent expenditure. The enrolment of children was up from 3.5 million in 1970 to 13 million by 1980.[2] While the results achieved by this educational expansion were mostly to be welcomed, they had certain negative consequences. In Nigeria especially, the number of children entering primary schools outstripped the state's ability to supply trained teachers and, inevitably, there was some fall-off in the quality of the education provided. Moreover, the educational measures themselves (and corresponding initiatives in health and the other social services) were adopted at the expense of investment in more directly productive, job-creating sectors. In view of the downturn of their economies in recent years, most states have had to cut capital expenditure and have been hard put to maintain high levels of recurrent expenditure on the social services generally.

This is serious because urban migration (which was already marked in the colonial period) has proceeded apace since independence: in 1960 no tropical African city had a population of over 1 million; in 1985 there were 28 such cities. Today, the urban population of many states (including Cameroon, the Central African Republic, the Congo, Ghana, the Ivory Coast, Zambia and Zaire) is approaching (or already exceeds) 40 per cent. The consequences of this urban drift are manifold. One is the reduction in the number of able-bodied men to work the land, thus contributing to a fall in food production: whereas in 1970 Africa's population was increasing at a slower rate than food production, since 1975 population growth (at about 3 per cent a year) has overtaken the rate of increase in food production; moreover, it is a very young population – about a half consists of children. Other consequences are urban problems of housing, sanitation and unemployment, and rising crime rates; and – through subsidies to keep the price of food and other produce artificially low – the distortion of government policy in favour of often politically volatile urban dwellers who (as in Zambia in 1974 and 1986, and Morocco and the Sudan in 1984) demonstrate angrily when these subsidies are removed or threatened. Rural producers are disadvantaged, and often react to the prevailing low prices by ceasing to produce for the market, merely growing enough food for themselves and their extended families, or by smuggling their harvest across the state borders (the reaction of Senegalese peanut-producing peasants in 1969–70). Both these practices have serious consequences for the state economy since the need to import grain and other essential foodstuff from abroad increases the already high level of external debt.

Most African states are dependent for foreign exchange on the

agricultural crops (including cocoa, coffee, sugar, tea and tobacco) which they export, as well as, in some cases, mineral products ranging from oil (for the fortunate minority) to chrome, copper and diamonds. New state leaders, anxious to end their dependence on primary produce, sought to diversify their economies, with industrialisation as a favoured strategy. Unfortunately, the new manufacturing industries that were established in many states (mostly in the towns) tended to be capital-intensive and dependent on the importation of costly machinery from abroad; they therefore created only a limited number of jobs. Urban migration and high levels of urban unemployment militated against trade union organisation and effectiveness. Moreover, as Michael Lofchie has pointed out, industrialisation in Africa (as distinct from the West) did not have healthy social pluralistic effects through the creation of new interest groups. On the contrary, the prevailing pattern of social inequality was deepened and increased social conflict resulted.[3] Deceptively, this conflict was expressed in ethnic or regional–linguistic terms, though the real competition was over educational opportunity, jobs and government contracts, and the provision of roads, bridges and hospitals. Severe developmental imbalances existed in most countries (including Uganda, especially between the 'heartland' of Buganda and the neglected northern areas of the country) and Ghana, the Ivory Coast and Nigeria where, too, the northern part of each country had benefited much less from economic and social change than the southern parts. The differential impact of colonialism was felt not only between areas, but also within them, and these differences were often accentuated under successor, post-colonial regimes. A case in point was the Copperbelt Province of Zambia, where the bustling Copperbelt towns were ringed by depressed rural areas.

This ethnic competition – both between one area and another and within a particular area – tended to obscure the growing importance of class inequalities in Africa, though such inequalities (as might be expected) were more marked in some countries than in others, and were in most cases more a feature of the urban than of the rural scene. As John Iliffe has pointed out, it was not until the first twenty to thirty years of this century that pioneer capitalism penetrated the rural areas of Africa on any scale.[4] In the Gold Coast, cocoa- farmers purchased land in the Akwapim district, while further inland in Ashanti, many of the early leading cocoa farmers were chiefs and rich merchants. On the other side of the continent, in Buganda, the effect of the 1900 Agreement with the British was to create a new system of private landowner-ship, under which some of the landowning chiefs acquired large rubber and coffee plantations. Though rural capitalism emerged in different forms and had varying consequences throughout the continent, what Iliffe has called 'the synthesis of capitalist and pre-capitalist elements' was a widespread feature. An important reason for the persistence of pre-capitalist relations was the fact that though there were instances of substantial African land-ownership (in Uganda and Ethiopia, for example) and though large foreign-owned estates requiring African labour did exist in certain territories (including Portuguese-ruled Angola and southern Ethiopia) land remained abundant over most of the continent and labour still tended to be migratory.

Despite isolated peasant protests against the spread of rural capitalism (as in Buganda in the 1920s), there was little organised resistance to early African capitalism, one explanation being the part played by religion (both indigenous and imported) in easing the transition to capitalism. Cases in point were the Christian ministry which Albert Atcho, healer and entrepreneur, established in 1948 at Bregbo near Abidjan in the Ivory Coast and the work of the Mouride brotherhood of Senegal among their peanut-growing Wolof followers.[5] In the subsequent period, thorough-going capitalism sometimes provoked a sharper response – as occurred in Kenya from 1952, Zanzibar in 1964, and Ethiopia in 1974, when southern tenants and labourers seized the land from their (predominantly) Amharic landlords. In Tanzania, govern-ment policy adopted in the wake of the Arusha Declaration of 1967 checked the further spread of rural capitalism, but the latter made headway among (for example) big African cattle-owners in Botswana and large farmers in Zimbabwe.

From an early date, rural capitalists – prosperous Gold Coast cocoa-farmers and Ivorian coffee-planters among them – invested their profits in urban property. In Accra and Abidjan (as in Lagos and Nairobi) they then rented their houses to foreign embassies and commercial companies. Just as the migrant labourer (working on the Zambian Copperbelt for example) retained his links with his home village, so there were often links between urban and rural capital. The post-1945 period, however, saw the burgeoning of African urban capitalism in its own right in a number of colonies. Following the achievement of political independence, the growth of manufacturing industry (mainly of an import substitution variety) was marked in most of the richer countries of tropical Africa, and was especially rapid in Nigeria during the oil-boom years of the 1970s. Most of the early manufacturing enterprises were started by foreign firms, though state participation became increasingly common from the mid-1960s. Given the relative weakness of domestic private capitalism, such participation was inevitable if the new state governments were to end foreign control of the economy; however, this has rarely been achieved. Prime examples of state participation were the Zambian government's assumption of majority ownership of Zambia's copper industry in 1969–70 and the Nigerian federal government's acquisition (on an instrumental scale) of part-ownership of the Nigerian operations of the foreign oil-producing companies in the 1970s. These and other cases reveal how, after as before nationalisation, foreign-based MNCs were able to uphold substantially their own interests by using a variety of devices; these included transfer pricing, patents, and management and sale contracts.[6]

State participation in the economy was accompanied by the creation of a large number of semi-public ('parastatal') enterprises which were made responsible for running these industrial ventures, either on their own account or jointly with foreign companies. The Nigerian National Oil Corporation (NNOC) was thus established in May 1971 to engage in all phases of the oil industry from exploration to marketing.[7] Such parastatals mushroomed in all states, irrespective of their governments' ideological leanings, but had, for the most part, a poor record of performance. Capitalist-oriented regimes (such as Cameroon, the Ivory Coast, Kenya and Nigeria) also encouraged private entrepreneurial activity, thus enabling local businessmen to obtain a growing share in the development of urban enterprise; many of them worked closely with the MNCs. Virtually everywhere, the state has played a vital role in stimulating the growth of African capitalism and the ruling élite has benefited enormously, as the Zambian experience reveals.

In the colonial period, conditions in Northern Rhodesia were not conducive to the emergence of an indigenous bourgeoisie.[8] Independence, however, enabled top members of the United

National Independence Party (UNIP) and the government, as well as senior public officers, to buy farms along the line of rail, become directors and shareholders in private companies, and launch businesses on their own account. This process was greatly facilitated by the economic reforms of 1968–72 which resulted in an enormous expansion of the parastatal sector (and therefore of the bureaucracy), and opened up massive new opportunities for citizen entrepreneurs. While former ministers, permanent secretaries and parastatal directors were among those who entered the private sector on a full-time basis, many others defied the country's leadership code and, as in Kenya and Nigeria, combined public office-holding with the pursuit of private business interests. A substantial middle-class emerged and the political members of it articulated class interests in their capacities as members of the bourgeoisie. But it is important to note that they continued also to play upon the regional–linguistic divisions in society in order to win popular support. Such communal appeals proved less politically destabilising in the Second Republic (created in December 1972) than they had done in the First Republic (1964–72).[9]

Extrapolating from Zambian experience, we can say that in most of sub-Saharan Africa class consciousness is most highly developed among the emergent middle class. The latter, being closely associated with the state apparatus, is now a feature of virtually all African states, though its advance has been fastest in urbanised and industrialised states which have adopted a capitalist (or state capitalist) strategy of development. However, the middle-class is internally divided, and class identifications have not yet emerged sufficiently to structure political conflict. This statement also applies to Africa's other identifiable classes – the peasantry and what may loosely be called the urban proletariat.

Though elements of the peasantry in individual states may (as was suggested earlier) react to the exploitation of urban élites by either ceasing to produce for the market or by smuggling their produce across the state borders, they are too scattered and disunited a force to be able to organise and sustain concerted resistance. They tend to be divided by particularistic loyalties and do not yet see themselves as an obviously or directly exploited class.[10] For their part, urban workers earn high wages by comparison with the great majority of the rural people, but often retain close social links with them. Despite a relatively high level of cohesion, organised labour has (in the words of Baylies and Szeftel) 'represented a reformist and economistic, rather than radical, voice' in most countries.[11] Among the reasons for this limited ability to show political solidarity as a class are the continuing practice of seasonal migration in most states (though in both Zambia and Zaire the copper industry has for some time attracted a settled labour force) and the prospect of upward mobility, the effect of which is to dampen class polarisation, even when differences of status and wealth among the workforce are well perceived. Moreover, the fact that factional politics have (as in Kenya) penetrated labour organisations and other modern interest groups also militates against the development of class consciousness.

Predominantly in Africa, therefore, we are dealing with a kind of 'patronage politics', with economic resources used as political currency to enable the leadership to buy support for their policies.[12] In these circumstances, patron–client linkages may reflect the intense communalism to which many states are subject; but they may also serve as a cement – the cement of material interest – holding a weak state together.

3. State and society in Latin America

Three factors discussed in Chapter 1 in relation to Latin America – the early achievement of political independence, the development of export-oriented economies from the mid-nineteenth century, and the relative insignificance of potential complicating factors such as ethnicity, tribalism and religious conflict – combine to give a particular stamp to the theme of state and society in this region. The shaping impact of export-led development (and its breakdown after 1930) has been considerable, and its impact has not been diluted either by the impact of recent decolonisation or by conflicts provoked by tribal, ethnic or religious rivalries. In the circumstances the nature of the state in contemporary Latin America and the dynamics of change from country to country are best understood in the context of the changing relationship through the twentieth century between the countries of the region and the international economy, the development of internal social forces, and the resulting political conflicts.

This can best be seen in terms of three quite different phases.

The first (that of the export-dominated economy) extends to 1930. The second (characterised throughout most of South America by a turn to a form of industrialisation) continues into the 1950s or beyond. The third phase (dominated by the 'internationalisation of capital', or the movement into the region of manufacturing multinational firms, and its impact upon the rest of the local economy) has endured to the present, in the countries where it has been reached. It may be succeeded, in one or two of the most advanced countries of the region, by a 'mature' phase, in which relatively powerful economies emerge with a capacity to compete internationally across a diverse range of export goods. The long history of political independence in the region, the early incorporation of its economies into the international market, and the relatively advanced degree of development achieved make this perspective fruitful where Latin America is concerned.

The state and the period of export-led growth

As pointed out in Chapter 1, the export-led economy did not emerge immediately in the wake of political independence. The collapse of the colonial economy was generally followed (with Chile and Brazil being the obvious exceptions) by a scramble for power among contending groups, during which revenues collapsed and control of the machinery of state was hotly disputed. The struggles typical of the 'age of the caudillos' represented more than the simple pursuit of power for its own sake, with the aim of personal enrichment through the partisan use of state power. The most characteristic caudillos (such as Rosas in Argentina and Garcia Moreno in Ecuador) managed to secure the ascendancy of a particular set of economic interests, linked in a particular way into the international economy, and to create a relatively enduring political regime to underpin them. They represented, in Argentina and Ecuador respectively, moments in the transition to modern export-oriented economies. When these economies did finally emerge, usually toward the end of the nineteenth century, they brought distinctive new élites to power, sometimes incorporating and sometimes excluding their predecessors. In Argentina, a new élite arose around 1880, displacing its rivals and centralising power at a particularly early stage; in Brazil, the new coffee élites of the centre-south, dependent on the slave economy for their development and socially a part of the ruling élite of the empire, were obliged to share power with a north eastern landed élite whose sugar-based economy was in decline, and the result was a complex pattern of regional alliances; in Chile, the acquisition of new territories to the north after the War of the Pacific (1879–82) reduced the economic ascendancy of the landed élites of the central valley, but with nitrate mining dominated by foreign interests they were able to preserve their political influence as brokers for these foreign concerns. Such differences as these had significant consequences, both before and after 1930. Beyond them, however, there were equally decisive similarities, which can be taken as defining the state in an export-oriented economy.

First, these states generally ran an open *laissez-faire* economy, and embraced enthusiastically the role of suppliers of raw materials and purchasers of manufactured goods. Secondly, they depended upon exports of primary commodities not only for economic growth, but also for the generation of revenues to finance the limited activities of the state itself. In the absence of well-established income or land taxes, the bulk of revenues were drawn either directly from exports, or from the imports which exports financed. Thirdly, the increasing complexity of economic administration and social change brought with it the rise of an urban professional class, often directly employed by the state or tied to the export sector, which became an important factor in national politics. Fourthly, the working-class in town and countryside was excluded, repressed or ignored. States of this kind generally reached maturity around 1910, were shaken by severe economic fluctuations and increasing social and political unrest during and after the First World War, and prospered again during the middle 1920s, only to be toppled in the wake of the depression beginning in 1929.

The economic impact of the depression of the 1930s was severe in Latin America, reducing export revenues by 50–80 per cent across the region, and causing sharp falls in GNP. Its impact went far beyond this economic setback, however, for three reasons. First of all, it changed the nature of the international economy. The central capitalist countries reversed policies in the areas of investment, finance and trade, thus removing the conditions which had made export-oriented development possible. This meant that there could be no return to the previous pattern of growth. Secondly, the definitive demise of purely export-led growth robbed the élites associated with it of their legitimacy, and their ability to rule by consent. They became the targets of broad oppositional movements which either led directly to their removal from power, or to the reconstitution of existing regimes on a narrower and more repressive basis. Thirdly, given the structure of the export-led state, the drop in foreign exchange revenues led directly to a fiscal crisis. This was particularly severe in its political implications where the regime had been broadened, as in Argentina, to give new middle-class élites a share in power through the medium of expanded public employment.[13]

The depression gave rise to a period of instability in Latin America similar to that experienced after independence. Throughout the region, control of the state was disputed between badly weakened old élites and new forces aiming to steer economic development in new directions, or even to overthrow old regimes entirely. In some cases (notably in Central America but also in Peru and Argentina) the old élites were able to reassert control, generally on the basis of repression. Where radical reform was attempted – as in Chile's brief 'socialist republic' of 1932, Grau's revolutionary nationalist administration of 1933–4 in Cuba, or the three-year rule of *Acción Democrática* in Venezuela between 1945 and 1948 after the belated departure of the military successors of the dictator Gomez – it generally proved fragile.[14] The classic case of unsustainable reform was El Salvador, where brief reform-oriented experiments in 1930, 1944, 1960–1 and 1979–80 were succeeded by the swift reimposition of authoritarian rule. Reform was carried furthest in Guatemala for a decade after 1944 (to be cut off by United States' intervention) and Bolivia, where the old regime (restored in the 1940s after a period of hectic experiment) was toppled in 1952 by a revolution which had largely lost its initially considerable reforming content by 1956.[15] Until the Cuban revolution of 1959 introduced a new alternative, new and relatively stable state forms appeared only where counter-élites (clearly differentiated from the old exporting sectors, but committed to capitalist industrialisation rather than more radical reform) were able to rally an urban and largely working-class following but at the same time to control its mobilisation.

The styles of political mobilisation combined with state control adopted by these counter-élites gave rise to the term 'populist' to describe them. It has been so widely used that attempts to give it precise meaning have generally foundered, but for our comparative purpose here we can identify 'populism' (broadly conceived) as the most successful political strategy of the post-depression period in Latin America. The policies and politics of 'populism' make most sense if seen as a direct contrast to those of the period of export-led development: export-led development itself gave way to a process of 'import-substituting' industrialisation, based upon the local manufacture of the most easily produced of formerly imported goods – textiles, processed foods and beverages – and complementary state investment in selected infrastructural and heavy industrial projects. The greater involvement of the state in the promotion of industrialisation entailed the abandonment of *laissez-faire* principles. The promotion of industrial production and the simultaneous need to enlarge the internal market made for a temporary alliance between an industrial bourgeoisie dependent upon the state and a working-class newly mobilised through the state itself. At the same time, the expanded role of the state allowed it to build a considerable base among the professional classes. To tie workers to the regime, they were organised in state-controlled unions (and to a lesser extent in pro-regime parties) while autonomous alternatives were crushed. Finally, the old élites were either excluded from the regime, or incorporated in minor and subordinate roles.[16]

The 'classic' case of political mobilisation of the urban working-class behind a project for import-substituting industrialisation came under Perón in Argentina. Perón cultivated a backing among workers while Secretary of Labour in the 1943–6 military government which ousted the old regime. He destroyed independent challenges to his leadership and set out deliberately to channel the loyalties of his followers towards himself and his wife Evita personally. Peronism may be taken as a reference point for other populist experiments. In Brazil under Vargas the landed élites were retained as an important (though subordinate) element in the populist alliance, and the workers never played so dominant a part; in Mexico, exceptionally, the previous defeat of the landed élites in the revolution meant that land reform and the incorporation of the peasantry had to be a part of the 'populist' settlement of the 1930s, though Cardenas was careful to keep peasants and workers separate, and equally tied to the state.[17] In Peru rival civilian and military populists clashed around 1930, and the return of the old regime allowed the civilian populist party APRA (American Popular Revolutionary Alliance) to survive only as an opposition force; and in Ecuador the scope for the development of an urban coalition was too slight to allow the indefatigable Velasco Ibarra to do more than seize and lose power on five successive occasions. The appeal of populism can be gauged from the fact that it was essayed (generally with limited success) in countries where unstable processes of reform and conservative reaction had developed: Ibañez in Chile, Rojas Pinilla in Colombia, Perez Jimenez in Venezuela and even Batista in Cuba provide examples of this tendency.

In the long run, states organised along these lines suffered a number of serious weaknesses. Their leaders were vulnerable to attack from direct representatives of capitalist interests wary of state intervention and working-class mobilisation. In addition, it became increasingly difficult to combine policies of investment with improvements in the living standards of the urban population. Export sectors could be taxed heavily, but in the end declining production meant shortages of all-important foreign exchange. Equally, it proved difficult in the long run to contain the ambitions of the organised working-class within the bounds laid down by populist regimes. There was a tendency therefore for populist regimes to find growth flagging, state investment subordinated to boosting consumption, capitalist allies withdrawing their support, and lower-class constituencies turning to more radical solutions. Only in Mexico was this outcome avoided, as a result of the greater strength of the state, its successful incorporation of the peasantry, and its more comprehensive co-optation of the working-class.[18]

In the larger Latin American states at least, populism was successful in creating a temporary stability and a reorientation of economic development. As economic development proceeded, however (and particularly as foreign multinationals began to invest on a large scale in these countries), it became a victim of its own success. Given the unequal distribution of income and the widespread poverty, such goods as cars and domestic appliances were available initially only to a relatively small proportion of the population; at the same time, the introduction of their manufacture required large capital investments, and drew domestic manu-facturers into complementary sectors where start-up costs were also high. Opportunities for new investment in the production of widely consumed wage goods were reduced as 'import-substitution' in these areas became virtually complete. There was therefore a need to channel funds more towards investment than towards consumption, to increase the rate of accumulation both for private industry and within the productive state sector itself. This coin-cided with a political crisis provoked by the radicalisation of groups initially mobilised from above, the emergence of challenges from excluded groups, and the incapacity of élites outside the 'populist' alliance to generate an electorally viable alternative. It was this political crisis – reflected in the end in the inability of populist leaders to govern and the equal inability of their civilian opponents to take over from them – which brought the military to power for protracted periods in both Brazil and Argentina. The emergence of these military regimes can thus be traced back to the political and economic crisis set in train by the depression.[19]

Other Latin American states, also among the most highly developed of the region, have reached the same situation – mili-tary rule for protracted periods in recent years – by a different route. In both Chile and Uruguay, pressure for reform eventually overwhelmed the forces of conservatism, but provoked a highly authoritarian response, bringing particularly murderous military regimes to power. Each country had reached a state of political crisis. In Uruguay, the traditional *Blanco* and *Colorado* parties had been unable to find an answer to economic stagnation after the middle fifties and mounting social unrest, while the leftist *Frente Amplio* (Broad Front) gained adherents and the young turned increasingly toward the urban guerrilla movement of the Tupamaros; in Chile, the apparent continuity of civilian rule had masked a cycle of exhaustion of successive political alternatives, reaching a first peak with the popular front government of the late 1930s, and a second (after a succession of Radical, 'populist', conservative and Christian Democratic regimes) with Allende's election on a socialist platform in 1970. The process of polar-isation along class lines went further in Chile than it had else-where, and in 1973 Allende's civilian opponents themselves called upon the military to intervene.

These militarised 'bureaucratic authoritarian' regimes have

been seen by one influential analyst, the Argentine social scientist Guillermo O'Donnell, as representing foreign capital in alliance with the largest national monopolies and oligopolies, ruling through technocracies, both military and economic, rather than through representative civilians, seeking to remove key policy issues from the 'political' arena and to demobilise the previously mobilised working-classes, and excluding the latter (both politically and economically) from participation in the regime.[20] This is a fair description, so long as it is remembered that the origins of these regimes differ, and that there have been major differences in economic policy. Whereas Brazil has pursued industrialisation along lines very similar to those followed in Mexico, the deliberate stimulation of industry through widespread government intervention has been reversed, with catastrophic consequences, in Chile, Uruguay and Argentina. Also, O'Donnell and others were initially inclined to overestimate the ability of such regimes to provide a basis for long-term rule.[21]

If the proliferation of military rule in the most advanced states of the region was the most striking characteristic of the 1960s and the 1970s, the contemporary picture is one of their withdrawal. This is discussed in more detail in the relevant chapter below. It appears to be leading to a restoration of civilian politics of a cautiously social democratic character, as in Argentina (1983), Brazil (1985) and Uruguay (1985), and this in turn brings the countries concerned into line with a trend first apparent in Colombia and Venezuela after 1958, and subsequently experienced in Ecuador, Bolivia, and Peru: the emergence (after a period of sometimes severe upheaval terminating in a period of protracted military rule) of a 'self-limiting' party political system dominated by parties committed to a moderate consensus and prepared to discipline their own forces in order to maintain it. This theme is explored further in the following chapter.

Class and clientelism in Latin America

As we have seen, communalism, religious sectarianism and other forms of primordial attachment are relatively insignificant in Latin America. Even so, there are significant social bonds which cut across class differences, and they have played an important role in the politics of the region. Ties linking lower-class individuals as clients to higher-class individuals as patrons (typically involving peasants and landowners), can be seen as weakening (and at times obliterating) any tendency for horizontal bonds of class loyalty or solidarity to develop. It is possible to trace the impact of clientelism in urban settings as well. Networks of contacts based upon common regional origins, kinship and the like play an important part in integrating migrants, for example, into city life and work. The most significant aspect of clientelism, with regard to relations between the state and society, is the part it plays today in the organisation and the activities of the state itself. Patronage practised through the ability of the state to reward (in conjunction with its equal ability to punish) plays a vital part in Latin American state and party politics, and at times this is seen as weakening the significance of class as an organising and explanatory factor in politics in the area. This is a mistake. In Latin America, as elsewhere (in the Lebanon, for example), clientelism – viewed from a social rather than an individual perspective – is a means by which one class perpetuates its domination over another; at the level of the state, it is a means by which a political project favouring one set of class interests over another is advanced. It owes its prevalence to the particular nature of 'dependent development' in Latin America: the survival and strengthening of the landed classes; the existence of a numerous peasantry; the weakness of the urban bourgeoisie, its dependence upon the state and its need to create a political base through expansion of the bureaucracy; the weakness of urban workers; and finally the divisions within the dominant élites. The fact that political loyalties do not neatly echo horizontal class distinctions may weaken class as an indicator of political attachment, but it does not rule out an explanation rooted in class practices.

For an example, we may return briefly to Brazilian 'populism' after 1945.[22] The coalition of the PSD (Social Democratic Party) and the PTB (Brazilian Labour Party) which dominated Brazilian politics during the 1950s brought together one party (the PSD) based upon the authorities of the Vargas dictatorship terminated in 1945, substantial sectors of conservative rural élites, and urban middle-class elements attached to the regime, and another (the PTB) dominated by the official trade union bureaucracy and the workers enrolled in official unions. The opposition UDN (National Democratic Union) drew on a rural constituency similar in profile to that of the PSD, and also enjoyed considerable support among the urban middle-classes. On the face of it, political alignments cut so strikingly across class boundaries that an explanation based on class appears impossible. However, if we take as a starting point the failure of export-led development after 1930, and the commitment, by Vargas and his allies, to a process of industrialisation, a 'class logic' can be perceived. Given the weight of rural population and the need to draw for industrialisation on resources generated by the export sector, Vargas could not break entirely with the landed élites. The outcome of the 1930 revolution was to provide him with an opportunity to make an alliance with a section of those élites, while the departure of others into opposition meant that (in the short term at least) the split within the landed classes gave him a degree of freedom to impose policies oriented toward industrialisation. The granting of patronage based on the utilisation of state resources was an important part of his strategy for securing the continuing support of his rural allies. A second (and even more important) element was a tacit agreement not to extend the organisation of the working-class into the countryside, or to challenge existing social and economic relations there through initiatives aiming at land reform. For the project for state-led industrialisation to succeed, the urban working-class had to be organised as a support base, while the rural élites were given guarantees that their own situation would not be challenged. In addition, a welcome (if unexpected) outcome of the division of the rural élite into opposing factions, each seeking electoral victory at local level in order to gain access to state patronage, was to provide an extra incentive for electoral participation and mobilisation. This tended to swell the rural vote as a whole, and to lessen the impact the urban working-class and the PTB could exert in national politics. While it lasted, then, this peculiar political alliance put together by Vargas divided the rural élites, at the same time guaranteeing their survival, and tied the urban working-class to a more conservative ally, making a process of industrialisation possible and rendering a radicalisation of the process less likely. There was a clear 'class' project behind the apparently chaotic alignment of class forces. This example suggests that in Latin America, at least, class domination may be secured and maintained through what appear to be clientelistic practices; it suggests also, that a focus upon the state is essential if the link between class and clientelism is to be perceived.

State and society in the Middle East

The Arab Middle East has a range of states which share a common historical heritage and whose populations are largely Muslim and Arabic-speaking. Despite this commonality, the contemporary state system is a relatively recent creation, dating from the division of the Ottoman Empire into French and British mandates at the end of the Second World War. Egypt is an exception: it had established autonomy from the Empire by the beginning of the nineteenth century.[23] It has had a history as an established political entity longer than Germany or Italy, and an historic seat of power in Cairo from where rulers have taxed and administered a stable population living in a limited area along the Nile delta and valley. Egypt is also relatively homogenous: a 15 per cent Christian Coptic minority, geographically spread and socially integrated, with a majority of Sunni Muslims. These are some of the factors which have made Egypt a strong state: it has undergone three succession crises and dramatic shifts in policy without significant domestic political turmoil.

At the other end of the spectrum is Lebanon, a state which is extremely weak, where regimes have been sustained by inertia and where power has inhered in society.[24] The lack of either an integrative or coercive capacity has brought more than ten years of civil strife, numerous foreign invasions and interventions and created what is essentially a stateless society. In between these two poles are Syria and Iraq which are heterogeneous but have nevertheless been able to assert the power of the state in a context of intense social and political conflict in the 1950s and 1960s and ethnic and regional rebellions and uprisings.[35] It is quite clear from the Syrian and Iraqi examples that heterogeneity is not the only factor leading to a weak state. There are other contributory factors. Of particular importance is the evolution of class forces and the way in which these have interacted with communalism, ethnicity and sectarianism.

Communalism

One of the major problems facing Middle Eastern governments has been the welding together of different ethnic and sectarian groups into a cohesive society. It is not simply that these groups were held together by a positive sense of communal solidarity; they had been communally organised in the past. Prior to the creation of the contemporary state system, religious communities had organised their own affairs: Jews, Muslims and Christians had their own legal system and were communally responsible for the payment of special taxes to the Sultan. Compounding this legal separation was the geographic isolation of some minorities, particularly the non-Sunni Muslim sets. With some exceptions, ethnic groups and minority sects tended to live in particular regions: the Kurds in the mountainous north east of Iraq; the Alawites in the eponymous mountains of north west Syria; the Druze in the mountains of southern Syria and the Lebanese Shuf district; and Shi'a Muslims in southern Iraq and the southern parts of Lebanon and the Beqa valley. Since Sunni Islam was the orthodoxy of the Arab and Ottoman Empires, Sunni Muslims tended to predominate in the urban provincial centres of administration and their environs. Even though rural migration has altered this balance, newcomers to the towns have tended to settle together in urban quarters.

One further legacy of the past is that non-Sunni Muslim minorities like the Alawites, Shi'a and the Druze were generally excluded from the establishment and expansion of the new Ottoman educational and administrative systems and the officer corps during the nineteenth century. As a result, members of the minorities were less educated, lacked experience in civil administration and were hardly represented in the officer corps. Such an imbalance was perpetuated in the period of European control as the mandatory authorities recruited those with experience and education. Within this general pattern, it is necessary to point out two exceptions. Firstly, the French authorities in Syria consciously recruited minorities into the Syrian army because urban Sunni Muslims were identified with nationalism. Secondly, Mount Lebanon had acquired a high degree of autonomy during the nineteenth century and both Maronite and Druze leaders, religious and civil, participated in administration in their own particular areas. With these exceptions, communities were to some extent politically stratified: orthodox Sunni Muslims had greater representation in (and access to) administration, government and the officer corps.

Economic development has also served to differentiate the communities of the Middle East because economic development has affected regions differently, and communal groups tend to live in particular regions. The more peripheral any community to the urban centres of trade and commerce, the less traditional patterns of stratification have been changed. It is possible to identify two processes: social relations within communal and sectarian groups have been changed and the relative socio-economic positions of communal groups has been affected. This is not to say that all social and economic exchange was communalised, but that until quite recently they were highly localised. We have mentioned how the establishment of Beirut as an important port and the growth of a silk industry (sponsored by French entrepreneurs in Mount Lebanon) increased the economic opportunities of the Maronites in the Lebanese mountains and began a diversification of the Maronite community which was enhanced by Christian educational mission activity and favour shown to the Maronite Catholics during the French mandate. By the middle of the twentieth century the Maronites ranged from millionaire bankers and businessmen through an educated and middle- and lower-middle class to a relatively prosperous peasantry.[26] The Shi'a of southern Lebanon were divided between a handful of large landlords and a poor subsistence peasantry. The Alawites of Syria (inhabiting an inhospitable mountain area) were middle and poor peasants and landless labourers working the land of absentee urban Christian and Sunni Muslim landowners. One writer has called the Alawites a 'class-sect' because their position in Syrian social structure has correlated with sect membership.[27]

It is then a combination of the political legacy of the past and the process of economic development and its regional impact which has given a social content to the present communalism of Middle Eastern societies, and influenced its reflection in national politics. To analyse Middle Eastern societies wholly from this perspective is, however, misleading because whatever the levels of disadvantage, discrimination and privilege from which the different sects have suffered or benefited since independence they have functioned within a new national, social, economic and political system which has restructured these societies. Social change and class formation between and within these communities have dramatically altered the nineteenth-century pattern of communal separateness.

Class

Any discussion of class in the Middle East has to begin with the first class which had national power: the landowners.[28] In Iraq, Syria, Egypt and (to an extent) in Lebanon, this class was not only very wealthy but controlled the political system. They dominated the parliaments of these states and thereby maintained the economic and political privileges of the big landowners. Landownership was highly concentrated. In Egypt, before the 1952 land reform, the top 1 per cent of landowners controlled 72 per cent of Egypt's cultivated area. The position was similar in Syria up to 1963 and Iraq up to 1958. The peasantry were generally owners of small plots or sharecroppers, and were usually indebted to the landlord.

At independence, there was very little industry. Egypt (the most advanced of the Arab states) had only 9 per cent of the labour force employed in industry as late as 1960. As a result, rural migrants and the graduates of the expanding post-independence educational system found little opportunity for employment outside of either agriculture or the state. These were the two new social groups which were to emerge in the post-independence period.

Varying combinations of rural overpopulation and pressure on the land, rural poverty, the mechanisation of agriculture, landlord oppression and the possibility of slightly better employment prospects in the towns led to a large-scale migration from the countryside. The twelve major cities of Syria increased their population by 57 per cent between 1960 and 1970 and between 1927 and 1966 the population of Cairo increased threefold. In Lebanon, Beirut became encircled by what was called the 'belt of misery' as the rural poor joined the Palestinians in the shanty towns around the outskirts. Although the Middle Eastern states became more urbanised the process involved the translation of rural deprivation into visible urban poverty. Most of the new migrants were underemployed or employed in casual or menial tasks. For example, 20 per cent of employed urban dwellers in Egypt were servants. It has been estimated that 48 per cent of Egypt's population is living in absolute poverty.[29] The position of rural migrants in Syria is somewhat less stark, and in Iraq has been ameliorated with the flow of oil revenues. The migration of labour to the oil-producing states has not radically altered the position of the urban poor. Iran's oil revenues only increased the flow of migrants from the rural areas and although casual work in construction provided employment the urban infrastructure was not sufficient to absorb the inflow: in 1977 45 per cent of urban families in Iran lived in one room and Teheran (a city of 4 million people) had no proper sewage system. Those living on the margins of urban life found little time for politics, but when they have their participation has been violent. The burning of Cairo before the 1952 revolution and the mass support for the fundamentalist clergy in Iran came from this underclass.

Another marked change in Middle Eastern societies is the numbers in education and state employment. The radical and reformist parties and groups; which were the main opposition to the dominance of the landowners; sprang from this class and it was their military counterparts in Egypt, Syria and Iraq which ended landowners' rule. In Egypt, primary school enrolment increased from 1.5 to 4.2 million between 1952 and 1977, secondary from 182 000 to 796 000 and further education from 51 000 to 453 000.[30] In Iran, between 1963 and 1977 enrolment in primary schools increased from 1.6 to over 4 million, in secondary from 370 000 to 740 000 and in colleges (at home and abroad) from 42 000 to 230 000.[31] Far greater expansion has taken place in the towns than in the countryside, and (except in Lebanon where private schools predominate) the state has been the engine behind these developments. Most of the secondary and further education graduates have been employed by the state, in part because of the absence of any other opportunities, and in part because of governments' desire to placate this stratum which has produced opposition leaders and parties. Despite such co-optation, only the upper echelons of this stratum receive a salary anything like commensurate with their education and expectations.

Although there has been a substantial shift in employment

patterns, large numbers are still employed in agriculture. In 1978 the percentage share of the labour force in agriculture was as follows: Egypt 51, Iran 40, Iraq 42, Syria 49. In Lebanon the share was only 12 per cent.[30] Small peasants who are owners and tenants are the largest proportion, and about 80 per cent of these are subsistence or near-subsistence farmers. Despite the expansion of education, most are illiterate. The countryside, however, is highly diversified with significant differences of income. A recent International Labour Organisation (ILO) report on Egypt has pointed to the impossibility of delineating income groups in rural Egypt because of the diversity: landownership, agricultural and urban wage labour, crafts and services, government employment. Like the middle strata, then, the peasantry is not monolithic: there are prosperous peasant owners subsidised by the state selling their produce to the overpopulated towns, urban absentee, small but highly capitalised farmers exporting produce to Europe, subsistence peasants scraping a living, peasants who have to work because their landholding is not sufficient, and landless labourers. In Egypt, despite extensive land reform, the ILO report has asserted that the incidence of rural poverty is high, 'affecting 35 per cent of the households and 41 per cent of the population in 1977', and that poverty has not diminished over the past 15 years.[33]

Class, communalism and politics

There has been quite significant social and political change in the Middle East. In some states like Iraq and Syria, upper levels of the middle strata have seized power from the landowners, and have been able to assert the power of the state over entrenched autonomies of political leaders of communal groups. Where the dominant landowning group was multicommunal, this process has been somewhat easier. In Iraq, where the biggest landlords were Sunni and Shi'a, there have been less communalist political repercussions, although Kurdish demands for autonomy and national rights have resulted in civil strife as the post-1958 regimes have struggled to establish a strong centralised state. In Syria, where the landlords were overwhelmingly Sunni Muslim and urban, the architects of the land reform (the Ba'th party and Ba'thist military officers) were preponderantly of the rural minorities, particularly

Alawite. The result has been a series of urban uprisings spear-headed by the Muslim Brothers, a fundamentalist political move-ment drawing its support from Sunni Muslims. Insofar as the urban landlords and merchants exploited their rural hinterlands and were generally Sunni Muslim, political conflict in Syria has taken on aspects of both a communal and social struggle. Such violence has led the political leadership to recruit only those who can be trusted into strategic military, security and political posi-tions, and these have often been friends and relatives who have generally been members of the same sect. Even though the policies of the post-1970 regime in Syria have not been aimed at the minorities in general or the Alawite community in particular (and, indeed, from the early 1970s have sought to conciliate the urban merchants), the regime is perceived as one based on narrow sectarianism.

Little reference has so far been made to Lebanon. But it is here that the most complex relationship between communalism and class has been reflected in politics. The political system was organised on a religious basis. Seats in parliament were allocated on a 6:5 ratio of Christian to Muslim, the president had to be a Christian and state employment was distributed proportionately between the sects. It is something of a distortion to see Lebanon as a wholly Christian-dominated state. For every six Christian deputies there were five Muslim, and although the president was a Christian and had extensive powers the prime minister was a Muslim. Cross-sectarian alliances were built into the system: because the president was elected by the Assembly it was incum-bent on aspiring candidates to gain support from a number of Muslim deputies and mixed sect multimember constituencies promoted electoral co-operation between Muslim and Christian candidates. Factional alliances between members of the political élite and the exchange of electoral votes for patronage were as significant as sectarianism. It was the control of patronage which sustained the dominance of the political leaders, known in Lebanon as the *zu'ama*. Most of these had more in common with each other than they did with their co-religionists; they came from old-established families, were generally wealthy and attended the best schools and universities.

At base, it was a class alliance which underpinned the political structure. Businessmen, bankers and import-export merchants (with a vested interest in an open *laissez-faire* economy) and traditional landlords (with a vested interest in maintaining their power over their peasantry and diminishing the legal and security powers of the state) combined to establish a state which did not intervene in the economy, and provided minimal welfare and social security. Health care, social welfare, housing and employment existed almost wholly in the private domain, and the deputies provided these goods in exchange for votes. A job transfer, a teaching position, a hospital bed and even burial services were offered by the *zu'ama* in exchange for political support. Although the Lebanese system was formerly based on confessionalism, in essence it was one in which a class alliance perpetuated a social and economic order which sustained a small ruling group's powers of patronage thus defusing any threat to that order.

In the Lebanese system, the Christian communities were generally more prosperous, better educated and greater beneficiaries of the *laissez-faire* economy. The Muslim communities did less well. The Shi'a were generally rural, poor and under the dominion of large landowners, many of whom went into commercial mechanised farming during the 1960s and forced their peasants into seasonal labour. Lebanon, then, had a social system wherein Christians were better off than Muslims but at the apex of the system was a religiously mixed group of businessmen, merchants, bankers, landowners and politicians.

Underlying the political crises which led to the 1975 civil war was the breakdown of the patronage system. Large numbers migrated to the urban areas as a result of the expansion of commercialised farming and Israeli air raids on southern Lebanon in reprisal for Palestinian attacks. With a quarter of a million Lebanese arriving in the coastal cities the patronage system (orientated to providing services and favours on an individualistic basis) ceased to cope with much broader social demands. Demands for welfare, housing, education and employment, as well as for an army which could defend the state, were converted by the Muslim leadership into a demand for a change in the confessional allocation of political and bureaucratic positions. Their solution was greater Muslim representation. What was at base a social crisis became a political crisis with a sectarian face. The more privileged Christian communities saw these demands as a threat to their advantaged position and to a system out of which they had done relatively well. The Phalange party (representing the less opulent Maronites and ideologically committed to a strong state and Christian hegemony) became the vehicle for the Maronite response to the crisis. The civil war, with all its barbarities and criminality, brought an overt sectarianism to a deep social crisis which a weak state (built on the privilege of a few) could not manage. There was not even the coercive capacity: that inhered in localised sectarian and political militias – and, at times, criminal gangs.

In conclusion, the Middle East exhibits a range of state–society relations. In certain cases the centre holds (as in Egypt and Iran) although the political upheaval resulting in the overthrow of the Shah saw considerable ethnic-cum-regional unrest. In other states like Syria and Iraq although social change has exacerbated domestic conflicts with ethnic and sectarian dimensions, strata and sections of classes have emerged supportive of a central state against fissiparous tendencies. These post-independence developments have taken place within the context of large-scale social and political upheaval: the overthrow of landlords and monarchies, the beginnings of industrialisation, a rapidly expanding urban society, the decline of agricultural production and rapid population growth. Only Lebanon, based on the formal acceptance of religious division as an essential component of the political system, has dissolved.

5. Conclusion

In Africa and the Middle East, which are both mainly agricultural regions, political leaders invoke communal differences that are readily understandable to the rural people in their competition for power and access to economic resources. However, the writ of the central government has never run fully throughout Chad, a vast, landlocked and mostly arid country in central Africa, while political crisis has wracked the small, mountainous and formerly prosperous Middle Eastern state of Lebanon as the patronage system revolving around the *za'im* has broken down; in juridical terms, these are sovereign states, even if broken-backed, but in most other respects they are stateless societies at the mercy of rival, warring leaders. In Latin America, the collapse of the

colonial economy following the achievement of political independence resulted in a scramble for power among the competing
groups, though in general ethnic and religious conflict has been
less significant here than in the other two regions. This 'age of
the caudillos' heralded the development, from the mid-nineteenth
century, of export-oriented economies, whereby the state economy rested upon the export of raw materials and the import of
manufactured goods. This, predominantly, was the characteristic
pattern of the colonial economy in Africa and the Middle East,
but it was a pattern which the new state rulers, far from embracing
enthusiastically as in Latin America, sought to end through the
development of manufacturing industry. At independence, neither
region had much industry other than of an extractive kind, and
the educated element had little opportunity of employment outside agriculture and the state sector. These are some of the considerations which have led Richard L. Sklar to advance, in respect
of Africa, the controversial proposition that 'class relations, at
bottom, are determined by relations of power, not production'.[34]

In Latin America, the depression of 1929 ushered in a period
of political instability, resembling that experienced after independence a century or more earlier. This led (during the time that
nationalist forces were beginning to challenge colonial rule in
Africa and foreign rule in the Middle East) to the emergence of
populism as the post-depression strategy and to the replacement
of export-led development by import-substituting industrialisation,
and (from the 1950s) to the movement into the region of multinational manufacturing firms. Capitalist interests opposed the
widespread state intervention and working-class mobilisation
which Peron-style populism entailed, and created a climate
favourable to military takeovers in Brazil, Argentina and other
states in the 1960s and 1970s, though some military rulers subsequently withdrew in favour of social democratic regimes. On
the social front, the process of polarisation along class lines
proceeded apace, going further in Chile than elsewhere. An increasing proportion of the rapidly expanding populations moved
to the towns, giving rise to acute urban problems of unemployment and overcrowding that were beyond the capacity of the
urban authorities to handle.

Such urban problems also characterised states in Africa and the
Middle East. Here, too (though to a lesser extent in Africa than

in Latin America and the Middle East) class has become increasingly important as a determinant of political behaviour. In Africa landlordism, which has been a prominent feature of the Latin American and Middle Eastern scenes, is largely absent and there is plenty of land to cultivate in most states (though not in all – land shortage is pronounced in central Kenya and the eastern area of Botswana, for example). Class consciousness among urban workers is limited in most African states – perhaps because the prospect of upward mobility has dampened class polarisation – and is most developed among the emergent middle-class, which is closely associated with the state apparatus. In the Middle East, though class formation has proceeded further than in Africa, the extent to which class identification structures political conflict is still limited. One can certainly point to examples of class action – for example, the seizure of power from the landlords by upper levels of the middle strata in Iraq and Syria – but the bourgeoisie is, in general, hardly any more monolithic than the peasantry.

Class, then, constitutes a more important basis for interest-group appeals and for political cleavage in the industrialised countries of Latin America than in the predominantly agricultural societies of Africa and the Middle East; in Africa especially, only the middle-class is well-developed and there is not yet in the great majority of states a strong sense of urban or rural exploitation. Despite Latin America's greater social sophistication, strong parallels exist between the three regions, in so far as the ruling class in each of them uses clientelism to strengthen its hold over state power and thus to perpetuate its dominance over other classes in society. There is, in short, no incompatibility between class and a patronage system of politics. In social terms, the convergence between the three regions can be expected to increase as the further development of a national market economy in Africa and the Middle East gives rise to a more nationwide pattern of social stratification; class considerations will then increasingly determine political behaviour. This does not necessarily mean that communalism will cease to be important for, as Melson and Wolpe conclude, an individual's 'acquisition of a new socio-economic identity need not mean the elimination of his prior communal point of reference'.[35]

Two final points might be mentioned. The first is that there is not only considerable variation between our three regions, but also between states and societies *within* each region – between, for example, Chile and Nicaragua in Latin America, Kenya and Chad in Africa, and Egypt and Lebanon in the Middle East. Secondly, the importance of the external dimension to states in the three regions (which is elaborated upon in subsequent chapters) needs to be stressed. Their economies have been penetrated by the activities of multinational companies, resulting in the reduction of state autonomy in some cases, though not in others. The regions have also become the cockpit of Great Power rivalry. Because of their geographical position, Latin American states especially have been subject to frequent United States interference in their domestic affairs, delivering a deathblow to the Allende regime in Chile and affording a serious challenge to the central authority in Nicaragua. Of the three regions, Africa has suffered least from external interference, though Great Power involvement has increased over the past decade in both the Horn of Africa and southern Africa.

3

Political Parties and Participation

1. Introduction

The extent to which newly independent Third World states have adopted the formal institutions of liberal democracy has varied from area to area. In terms of political traditions and practices, Latin America is perhaps the most thoroughly 'Westernised' of the areas we examine in this volume. In Africa, the colonial powers generally attempted to establish institutions shaped in their own image before departing the scene, but these institutions did not long outlive their departure. In the Middle East, the degree of penetration of Western political institutions and practices was even less substantial.

It is generally argued that where the institutions of liberal democracy have failed to take root, it is because the substance of politics as it is practised where liberal democracy has thrived is absent. This can in turn be traced back to different patterns of social and economic development, as Chapter 2 made clear. Here, though, we wish to concentrate more squarely on political institutions, and particularly upon political parties.

The record of party politics in the Third World is not impressive. Civilian rule has proved frail, and where civilians have exercised power it has been for the most part in the shadow of the military or through non-democratic agencies such as personalist movements or single parties closely tied to the state. Our focus here, therefore, is on the origins and nature of parties in Africa, Latin America, and the Middle East, the sources of their weakness, the implications of their close links (for the most part) with the state, and the prospects for the emergence in the Third World of competitive systems of the type familiar in Western Europe today.

81

2. Political parties and participation in Africa

With the main exception of Liberia's True Whig Party (which was founded in 1860 as the Whig Party) modern political parties in Africa were essentially post-1945 creations. They were preceded by loosely structured and mostly urban-centred organisations with a limited appeal, led by middle-class elements among whom doctors and lawyers predominated; early examples were the Aborigines Rights' Protection Society founded in the Gold Coast in 1897, and the National Congress of British West Africa, which came into being in 1920. Better organised and more broadly-based associations – known variously as youth movements, congresses and leagues – emerged in British West Africa in the 1930s to put forward programmes of moderate reform. Despite the radicalising effect of the Second World War, the congress-type organisation, with its loosely knit, federal-type structure, continued in the main to dominate the scene in British and French Africa in the early post-war years. Notable examples of such congresses were the National Council of Nigeria and the Cameroons (NCNC), formed in August 1944 and made up of a large number of affiliated organisations (some 180 in 1945), and the Rassemblement Démocratique Africain (RDA), an inter-territorial party with the character of a 'national front' established in French Africa in 1946. Some of these congresses proved short-lived, while others gave birth to political parties. In 1951 the NCNC adopted an individual-member basis of organisation in order to fight a general election, while France's emphasis in the 1950s on greater territorial autonomy meant that the strength of the RDA came to be increasingly located in its individual sections, such as the Parti Démocratique de Cote d'Ivoire (PDCI) and the Parti Démocratique de Guinée (PDG).[1]

Of course, not all the political parties which came into being in the post-war period emerged out of 'parent' congresses. Others were breakaways from existing parties, or resulted from a merger between minor parties and groups. Others again were nurtured by metropolitan parties or were strongly backed by the administration (both were common phenomena in French Africa), or grew out of cultural or other voluntary associations (two of Nigeria's leading parties in the First Republic came into being in this way). In nearly every case, their origin was extra-parliamentary, though in other respects they often differed sharply from each other – for example, in leadership, structure and the social basis of support. While some parties – like the Convention People's Party (CPP) in the Gold Coast and the PDG in Guinea – sought to appeal to the lower-middle strata of the population, others – such as the Northern People's Congress (NPC) in Nigeria and the Parti Progressiste Nigérien (PPN) in Niger – had a narrower appeal, the NPC being at the outset the mouthpiece of the native authorities. Typologically, the former type of party – strongly articulated in its democratic structure, with leaders elected for their political ability, and with ideological pretensions – was characterised as a 'mass' party. The latter was dubbed an 'élite' or 'cadre' party and was built up out of associations affiliated to it; it had a weakly articulated structure and its leadership enjoyed ascriptive status. This categorisation was, however, always inexact and the divisions between the parties were never clearcut. Moreover, in quantitative terms, the designation 'mass' was often ill-deserved, even in the case of a party which, at election time, was as vibrant as the CPP. This was revealed by the pre-independence general election in the Gold Coast in 1956, when the CPP emerged with 71 (later 72) out of the 104 National Assembly seats, but was both outseated and outvoted by regionally-based opposition parties in Ashanti and the North. The number voting for the CPP in the country as a whole represented 57 per cent of those who cast a ballot, but only 28.5 per cent of the registered electorate and 15 per cent of the eligible electorate (i.e., adults aged 21 and over who were entitled to register).[2] True, these figures are deflated by the indifference towards the election shown by people living in areas (mostly in the Gold Coast Colony) where the CPP was so dominant as to render any contest superfluous and by the British (as distinct from the French) practice of excluding uncontested constituencies from the calculation (there were five such CPP-held seats in 1956). Nevertheless, the number voting for 'mass' parties in French Africa was considerably higher than in British Africa. This was because the different electoral system and type of franchise in use in French Africa favoured the strongest party and tended to eliminate weak parties, and because the greater coherence of the modern élite in French colonies meant that there was less opportunity to politicise ethnic and other intermediate groups.[3]

Again, 'mass' parties, when it suited them, looked to traditional secular (and sometimes religious) leaders for support, and manipulated local issues, as a further example from the 1956 general election in the Gold Coast reveals. The electoral slogan of the CPP in the Brong areas of western and northern Ashanti was 'vote CPP, vote Independence; vote CPP, vote Brong-Ahafo' – the meaning was clear: only if the ruling party was returned to power would the campaign led by Nana Agyeman Badu, the Dormaahene, to create a separate Brong-Ahafo Region, with its own Assembly and House of Chiefs, be successful.[4] Elite parties, on their side, attempted to create a basic branch organisation; thus in Nigeria the NPC, when confronted with the need to mount a general election campaign in 1951, developed many of the structural features and organisational techniques of the mass party. Moreover, some parties were difficult to categorise, and none more so than the National Liberation Movement (NLM) in the Ashanti region of the Gold Coast. The NLM had all the characteristics of a mass popular party, but it was a movement that throughout its brief existence (1954–7) rested on a strong traditional base. It owed its origin to the farmers' anger at the CPP government's pegging of the cocoa price at a level well below the world price, and its rapid spread to an emotional appeal to Ashanti nationalism. The belief that Nkrumah's government was discriminating unfairly against Ashanti interests and individuals brought together in one hybrid organisation cocoa farmers and traders, the Asantehene and the great majority of Ashanti chiefs, wealthy businessmen and ex-CPP leaders, and (Ashanti) townsmen and villagers. The traditional organisation powerfully reinforced the modern party organisation. Bafuor Osei Akoto, senior linguist of the Asantehene and a prosperous cocoa farmer, was chairman of the NLM. The Kumasi chiefs backed the new party and the Asantehene gave it his blessing. Bafuor Akoto and the outlying paramount chiefs swore the Great Oath of Ashanti (or their own state oaths) in support of a movement that was also underpinned by paramilitary 'Action-Groupers' (the equivalent of the CPP's Action Troopers) who were bedecked in NLM colours and armed with soda-water bottles, cudgels and guns.[5]

The PDCI in the Ivory Coast and the two main mass-type political parties in Sierra Leone – the Sierra Leone People's Party (SLPP) and the African People's Congress (APC) – also defied easy categorisation. The PDCI, noted Zolberg, 'emerged as an organization for the masses rather than as a mass organization' and made formal use of ethnic bases of support in its organisation. The SLPP and the APC competed for power until a one-party state was legally established in 1977, but were 'weak and febrile bodies not possessing much of an organization at the local level'. Tangri added that 'They therefore courted chiefdom factions seeking alliances in order to establish a firm organizational base in the local communities'.[6]

The categorisation into 'mass' and 'élite' parties persisted after independence, but became even more meaningless as power came to be concentrated in the hands of a single, ruling party and (very often) in the party leader who became state president. There were often sharp differences between one single party and another, according (for example) to whether they rested on a *de facto* or a *de jure* basis, on the amount of intraparty competition which each allowed, and on the quality of their leadership. However, the Coleman–Rosberg distinction between one-party states of the pragmatic–pluralist pattern and those of the revolutionary–centralising trend was of doubtful validity.[7] For at the time these authors wrote (1964), the great majority of African states were reformist rather than revolutionary and, like Tanzania, were ideologically weak, without any firm commitment to socialism. There was no certainty (then or later) that even a protracted war of independence would result in the emergence of a revolutionary regime, as the cases of Algeria, Zimbabwe and (to an extent) Kenya illustrate. The missing element – most obvious in the third of these cases – was the leadership's commitment to Marxism–Leninism. By contrast, this commitment was strong in the former Portuguese colonies of Angola, Guinea-Bissau and Mozambique, giving rise in the 1970s to regimes which embraced a more scientific form of socialism than any that had previously existed; this commitment was shared by a number of military regimes, notably Somalia and Ethiopia following coups in 1969 and 1974 respectively.

It is clear that the political party, whatever its ideological basis and whether enjoying a monopoly of power or (as continuously in Botswana, the Gambia and Mauritius) competing for power with other parties, is a most resilient political structure. Though in many instances political parties were swept away by incoming military regimes, in others the same party that led the pre-independence nationalist movement is still in power – for example, Neo-Destour in Tunisia, the PDCI in the Ivory Coast, the Malawi Congress Party (MCP) in Malawi, the Tanganyika African National Union in Tanzania (though now under a different name) and UNIP in Zambia. In Uganda, after a military interregnum of nine years (1971–80), the two former leading parties – the Uganda People's Congress (UPC) and the Democratic Party (DP) – were revived; the UPC again formed the government and its leader, Milton Obote, was reinstalled as state president (he was removed in a second military coup in July 1985 and his party was officially disbanded). In other instances, a military regime itself created a political party, frequently in Francophone Africa. Thus, though individual political parties might disappear, institutionally the African political party has a high survival rate, suggesting that it still has a useful role to play. The fact that most African states are ruled by single – or occasionally, as in Botswana, by dominant – parties means that, as a generalisation, the political party in Africa is much more closely tied to the state than would be acceptable in a liberal democracy. From time to time – as in Ghana in 1969, and Nigeria in 1979 – new constitutions have been adopted which sought to break this pattern, but in each case they have proved short-lived. In Senegal, under the revised constitution of 1976, opposition parties have been allowed to emerge and register; they competed in legislative and presidential elections in both 1978 and 1983. However, electoral conflict in Senegal is still subject to tight governmental control and the monopoly of the ruling party, the Parti Socialiste Sénégalais (PSS), has not been seriously challenged – the PSS won 111 of the 120 Assembly seats in the February 1983 elections. Senegal has certainly acquired the trappings of a multi-party democracy, but Abdou Diouf's regime remains presidential in all essentials.[8]

Party functions

In order to determine whether African political parties retain the vitality which most of them displayed in the pre-independence period, we examine a number of party functions, paying most attention to policy-making. We begin with the integrative function. In Nigeria the makers of the 1979 constitution looked to the registered political parties to inculcate national values in place of communal or parochial values, while in post-independence Mozambique the Frente de Libertaçao de Mozambique (FRELIMO) mounted an intensive political education campaign in areas which had been barely penetrated by guerrilla activity during the liberation struggle. In neither case has the attempt been notably successful, thereby reflecting the difficulty which virtually all parties face in the post-independence period of winning sustained support for issues and causes which lack the obvious appeal of anticolonialism.

Secondly, the party has a legitimising role. In a multiparty context, each party seeks to win maximum support at a general election. Provided that the election is free and fair and allows the country's adult citizens to play (however briefly) a full part in the political process, the winning party will confer legitimacy on the successor government. This condition was largely satisfied in Ghana and Nigeria in 1979, but much less so in Nigeria in 1983 and not at all in Sierra Leone in 1973 and 1977, when the opposition SLPP was prevented from nominating candidates, and in Uganda in 1980, where the blatant rigging of the election gravely weakened the moral authority of President Obote's second administration. In the one-party context, elections are used by the ruling party to demonstrate that it has a mandate for its continuance in office, and for its policies. This tends to be easily achieved in most of Francophone Africa where elections are essentially of a 'plebiscitary' kind and a massive vote is recorded in favour of an approved list of party candidates; thus in Guinea in 1980, 2.4 out of 2.5 million voters endorsed the PDG list. In English-speaking Africa the presidential election – in which electors vote 'Yes' or 'No' for a single candidate put forward by the party – is more meaningful in this respect than the parliamentary elections which revolve round local rather than national issues. There have been occasions when a substantial 'No' vote has been registered by a section of a country's electorate – for example, by the Ila-Tonga people of Zambia's Southern Province in 1978. Even the parliamentary elections, in the form pioneered by Tanzania in 1965, offer the electorate an opportunity to participate in the political process (by choosing between rival candidates of the single party) in a way that was not possible when interparty competition was allowed – in the Tanganyikan general election of

August 1960 TANU's dominance was such that 58 out of the 71 constituencies were uncontested. In Tanzania in successive five-year elections since 1965, and subsequently in Kenya, Zambia and (in Francophone Africa) the Ivory Coast, many sitting MPs (often including a number of ministers) were not returned.

A third potential role for the political party is the formulation and execution of policy; this is an important but sensitive area, on which it is difficult to obtain precise information. For a variety of reasons – including the subordination of the party to the state, the indifferent quality of its personnel, the dominant position of the state president, and the increasingly technical nature of economic activity – it is tempting to conclude that the party's role in policy-making, including the drawing up of development plans, is limited to that of ratifying decisions taken elsewhere. However, a number of points need to be made, of which the most important is to stress that policy-making is a complex and composite process. We take the cases of Tanzania and (more briefly) of Zambia. The working of the Westminster system of government, which Tanganyika (mainland Tanzania) adopted at independence in December 1961, was not at first radically changed with the inauguration of the Republic a year later. However, in 1964 President Nyerere acted without the concurrence of his cabinet in handling a number of crises that arose, especially in the foreign field. The union of Tanganyika and Zanzibar in 1964 and the creation of the one-party state the next year effectively increased his powers. At a time when social values were not yet fixed, but there were clear signs of acquisitive trends among senior civil servants and party leaders, he was responsible for a number of important policy initiatives, particularly the Arusha Declaration of January 1967. However, Nyerere's proposals were by no means automatically accepted. There was a great deal of discontent over the leadership rules embodied in the Arusha Declaration since they seriously restricted the leaders' income-earning activities and he experienced considerable difficulty in persuading the National Executive Committee (NEC), TANU's main policy-making body, to accept them (by contrast, the nationalisation aspects of the Declaration were welcomed enthusiastically).[9]

For some years after 1967, the president, party and cabinet worked out together the policy implications of the democratic socialist path which the president had mapped out. Jeannette

Hartmann argues that from the mid-1970s the party and government showed a tendency to pursue policies independently of each other, with the president sometimes acting as initiator, sometimes as mediator, and sometimes in support of one side or the other.[10] The extent of this divergence of viewpoint between party and government is possibly exaggerated in that it takes insufficient account of the risk-avoiding behaviour of the Tanzanian leadership and of President Nyerere's dominance of both these institutions. In so far as it occurred, it had little, if anything, to do with the adoption of a new constitution in 1977; this constitution recognised the formal supremacy of Chama cha Mapinduzi (CCM), Tanzania's ruling party following a merger between TANU and the Afro-Shirazi Party (ASP) of Zanzibar. Any divergence was more the result of Tanzania's poor economic performance, the apparent failure of the experiment in communal farming (*ujamaa vijijini*), leading to a switch of emphasis from communal production to enforced villagisation, and the shortage of foodstuffs and essential household goods. The party was at its weakest in facing up to the harsh economic realities with which the cabinet had to grapple.

One must not, however, dwell too much upon policy differences between government and party since there were overlapping links between them – in 1983 10 cabinet ministers also served on the NEC (there was no incompatibility rule equivalent to that in Zambia, the effect of which supposedly, though not in practice invariably, was to prohibit such overlapping). Most senior office-holders were reluctant to become identified with a particular policy lest it should fail, thereby underlining the consensual nature of Tanzania's political culture.[11] (The late Mr Edward Sokoine was one exception to this pattern during his second term of office as prime minister, when he introduced a number of measures designed to liberalise the economy.) Moreover, neither cabinet nor NEC were monolithic bodies, and each contained a diversity of viewpoints. Though a number in each institution had served for long periods – prime examples were Rashidi Kawawa and Amir Jamal – many others had held office for only one to three years. Cabinet ministers were also subject to frequent reshuffles, making it difficult for them to master a particular subject, while the fact that a growing number of them were appointed by the president (10 out of 29 in 1983 as against 1 out of 18 in 1965) increased their dependence upon him. However, very few even of the elected ministers sought to strengthen their position by courting grass-roots popularity, perhaps because of the absence in Tanzania of Zambian-type factional politics, and the ability of ministers on vacating office to acquire a prestigious job in another sphere – they might, for example, enter the parastatal sector (only very rarely did an ex-minister embark on a private business career, though this occurred frequently in Zambia). The distinction between politics, administration and even university is blurred in Tanzania at senior levels and President Nyerere moved individuals freely from one sphere of activity to another in an attempt to make optimum use of scarce manpower. This mobility between jobs and the presence in the presidential entourage of men (and a few women) drawn from a wide variety of institutional backgrounds – the party, cabinet, administration, university, defence forces, trade union and co-operative movements, and the Bank of Tanzania, among others – makes it extremely difficult to say whose influence on policy-making is dominant at any one time.

In Zambia, as in Tanzania, government is characterised by executive dominance. The Second Republican constitution of 1973 defined the respective roles of party and government in the recently instituted one-party state. The central committee was established on a full-time basis, recognised as superior to the cabinet by a constitutional amendment in 1975, and assigned the overall direction of policy. It works through a series of sub-committees and, following the second general election in 1978, was made responsible for supervising all central government ministries. The cabinet was relegated to the subordinate role of policy implementation and administrative decision-making. This was a constitutional fiction: the effectiveness of the central committee was by no means commensurate with its increased formal power, and its direct impact on policy was limited. It is wrong to assume that the central committee and cabinet are necessarily at loggerheads since several channels of communication exist between them both to help remove potential conflict and to facilitate joint decision-making, which is said to occur (for example) over the setting of agricultural producer prices. Though President Kaunda himself and his advisers in State House formulate policy on most major, and many minor, issues, they have to accommodate demands from UNIP, the cabinet, the state bureaucracy, the business community (in the wake of the economic reforms of 1968–72), and the IMF. Kaunda is known, for example, to consult the cabinet on a wide range of issues, including some aspects of general policy, budget proposals, and draft legislation. In 1986 he bowed to IMF pressure to remove certain state subsidies, but reinstated the subsidy on corn meal when food riots resulted in the death of 15 people and the arrest of at least 450 others. He has instituted in Zambia a regime which combines socialist, populist and state capitalist strands. The president himself embodies the socialist strand – the desire for greater social equality – while the populist strand is uppermost within UNIP, and the two together moderate the starkness of state capitalism. The party's voice is not dominant in policy-making, above all at a time of economic hardship, but account of it is normally taken in shaping Zambia's development strategy. It may also be significant that in Zambia, as in Tanzania under Nyerere, the president is careful to associate the party with major policy pronouncements, thus ensuring at least formal party support.[12]

In Afro-Marxist states vanguard-type parties may exercise more important policy-making functions, though this is doubtful given the high concentration of power in the hands of the ruling élite; these parties, too, face the challenge of burgeoning state bureaucracies. Here, and in African states generally, the initiative in the execution of policy has passed increasingly to the latter. One reason for this is often the run-down of the local party. In Tanzania, ex-President Nyerere is working hard to revive the party branch, but is everywhere met with a request from office-holders for more remuneration. Another reason is the inability of local party officials with limited formal education to understand complex development plans and to implement decisions of a technical nature.

A fourth party role may be to mobilise the people for economic development through self-help; this was a task for which, in those states which became independent in (or about) 1960, the party was believed to be pre-eminently suited. In fact, the party tended to be a weak mobilisation agent in these states and the initiative passed to the central government – for example, in rural Tanzania from 1972 to regional and district directors of development. Robin Luckham, however, is right to argue that mass mobilisation and the existence of powerful and authoritative central structures are not necessarily incompatible and may be positively related.[13] Certainly, mobilisation remains important for the socialist regimes which came into being in the 1970s, as witness the 'dynamising groups' established by FRELIMO in Mozambique soon after independence. Such regimes place a higher premium on grass-roots popular participation than on representative democracy of, say, the Nigerian type, though in practice the dialectical relation-ship between the vanguard and the people tends to tilt heavily towards the former. All parties, whatever their origin and ideo-logical orientation, can also be expected to play a reconciliation role by accommodating different interests and mediating conflict, as UNIP has frequently done in Zambia. However, in this sphere, too, the initiative in many states has passed to the president and his personal representatives at regional and district levels.

The patronage functions of political parties remain important in nearly all states. This was shown very clearly in the Nigerian general elections of 1979 and 1983. Despite the requirement in the 1979 constitution that political parties had to be national in character, Chief Obafemi Awolowo's Unity Party of Nigeria (UPN) assumed the mantle of the former Action Group and all but swept the board in 1979 in the overwhelmingly Yoruba-speaking states of Ogun, Ondo and Oyo and the Yoruba-dominated Lagos state; it formed the government in each of them. In this way, the voters underlined their trust in Awolowo and expressed their confidence in his party's ability to extract resources from the centre, even though it did not share in the ruling coalition domi-nated by the National Party of Nigeria (NPN). In 1983, however, the UPN hegemony in the western states was breached: while a large number of people in these states (including Lagos) continued to pledge their loyalty to Awolowo and to look to him and his party for benefits, many others perceived that they would fare better by joining the NPN bandwagon.

Zambia affords another example of the patronage function at work both in the period before and after 1972, when it became a one-party state. There is plenty of evidence to show that the slogan 'It pays to belong to UNIP', which had been first used on the Copperbelt in 1965, was not an empty one. In respect of access to markets, the grant of trading licences, and the allocation of building plots, for example, UNIP members received prefer-ential treatment, and members of the African National Congress (ANC) were often discriminated against. Morris Szeftel concludes

that: 'given the relative scarcity of state resources, the monopol-
isation of patronage for UNIP members constituted a major asset
for the Party in building and maintaining support'.[14]

The final party role which we identify is that of political communication, which is a corollary of political competition and
remains, potentially, an important party function. However, the
reluctance of local party leaders to communicate unpopular mes-
sages is probably one reason why many governments often prefer
to use non-party channels of communication – the Tanzanian
government, for example, relies substantially on the bureaucracy,
while the government of Senegal, both before and after independence, has used Muslim leaders to put over its rural administration
policies.[15]

Conclusion

Judged by the functions which they now perform, African political
parties have been in decline since independence, having in most
states been run down in favour of the burgeoning state machine.
However, much more empirical work needs to be done before we
can gauge the extent of that decline. In the meantime, many of
the conclusions that we reach must necessarily be tentative.

To an extent, political participation is encouraged in one-party
states such as Tanzania and Zambia, and multiparty competition
has been revived, if sometimes only temporarily, in other states –
for example, in Ghana in 1966 and 1979, in Nigeria in 1979, and
in Senegal from 1976. In the great majority of African states,
however, key decisions are taken centrally and participation has
declined, with adverse consequences for up-country party organisation. Where, as in Tanzania in 1972, 'decentralisation' measures
have been introduced, the beneficiaries have more often been
field agents of the central government than the political party and
representative local authorities. In most states, important decisions
are taken by the state president and the group of people, drawn
from different institutional backgrounds, who surround him; the
cabinet's influence is likely to be strongest on economic and
technical questions. The ruling party may retain some say in
formulating policy, either separately or jointly with the cabinet; it
will carry most weight on broadly political questions. Of the other
party functions which we have identified, the patronage function

is probably the most meaningful, even though, with the downturn in their countries' economies, virtually all governments have today fewer resources to distribute. Perhaps more remarkable than the decline of the political party is its high survival value and, indeed, its resurrection often after a lengthy military interregnum. It may be significant, too, that an incoming military regime, having dissolved the old party(ies), has sometimes subsequently – as in Mali, Burkina Faso and Zaire – itself created a new party. This suggests that, at least in the view of the military leadership, the political party still has a legitimising function to perform.

3. Political parties and participation in Latin America

Until 1930 Latin American political parties were fairly similar to their European counterparts. There was a strong commitment (for the most part a century or so old) to the formalities at least of political practice in the Western world; legislatures were modelled on European lines, grave gentlemen in frock coats confronted each other in elaborate parliamentary rituals, volumes of learned debates were printed, and party loyalties were intense and enduring. Parties were élitist and initially loosely organised; electorates were small; nowhere did women have the vote before 1932; liberties were periodically curtailed by the oppressive hand of government; at times (as in Colombia betwen 1899 and 1902) bloody civil war interrupted the normal squabbles of party politics; here and there lengthy dictatorships appeared, while party politics and functioning congresses were a mere facade. However, all of these elements could equally well be illustrated out of the experience of Western Europe. Latin America becomes distinctive in party political terms only in the modern period. Liberal democracy as practised in Western Europe and in North America remains the ideal, the goal to which all participants in the political system claim to aspire, and in that sense Latin America falls more squarely into the Western political tradition than either Africa or the Middle East; but at the same time modern political parties fail to develop along typical 'Western' lines, or at least to move to the centre of the stage as they have done in Western Europe since the Second World War. Here we discuss why this should be so.

In a limited number of cases (such as Colombia and Paraguay) liberal and conservative parties dating back to the nineteenth century have survived to the present day; in the Colombian case, this represents a recovery after 1958 from crisis ending in civil war and a period of military rule; in Paraguay the apparent continuity conceals the dominance of the ruling *Colorado* party under the Stroessner dictatorship. Until 1973, Uruguay could have been placed alongside Colombia, and the recent ending of military rule there has restored its *Colorado* party to power and made the *Blanco* party its leading opponent; until 1979 Nicaragua, boasting a Conservative and a Liberal party but in the grip of the Somoza dictatorship, could have been placed alongside Paraguay. In Paraguay under Stroessner, as formerly in Nicaragua under Somoza, the survival of old labels concealed a dominant single party in an authoritarian regime. In Cuba, Mexico, and contemporary Nicaragua, more fundamental breaks with the past have taken place, and post-revolutionary regimes have created single or dominant parties. Only Cuba, since the revolution of 1959, has adopted a single-party state model along Soviet lines, albeit in combination with a continuing experiment in popular participation; Mexico has been governed since 1928 by a dominant party, now called the PRI, and the opposition parties, led by the *National Action Party* (PAN), have never been allowed more than a minor share of the vote; in the third case, Nicaragua since the revolution of 1979, the ruling Sandinista party remains committed to effective pluralism, but has overwhelming control of state structures and such substantial popular support that it is unlikely that it will be displaced through political competition in the near future.

The remaining countries in the region, viewed historically since 1930, have generally seen new parties emerge and displace their predecessors, but at the same time have been subject to periodic breakdowns of civilian political control and military intervention. Even here, however, the situation has not typically been one of free political competition. In Argentina and Brazil after the Second World War, in Ecuador in the period of Velasco Ibarra, in Bolivia after the 1952 revolution, and in El Salvador until 1979, a single party or coalition tended to dominate; in Chile until 1973, in Cuba until Batista's 1952 coup, and intermittently in Peru, party politics (when allowed) has largely been competitive. Venezuela, as we shall see, scarcely experienced democracy before 1958.

In summary, the record of democracy in Latin America in the modern period is not good. Apparent continuity has frequently masked *de facto* single-party rule, and even where competition has tended to be the norm, military intervention has tended to be frequent.

Two very important developments have taken place in recent years. The first was the seizure of power by the military for long periods of time, reflecting a deep crisis at the level of civilian politics, and bringing to an end two exceptional and enduring democracies in Chile and Uruguay. The second was the establishment (in the wake of the withdrawal of the military in a number of countries) of moderate and competitive systems even where they had not existed before. By 1986 – with the Radical leader Alfonsín in power in Argentina, moderate conservatives Sarney and Sanguinetti coming to power in Brazil and Uruguay, Peru governed by APRA's Alan Garcia, Ecuador in its seventh year of civilian rule, and Colombia, Costa Rica, and Venezuela celebrating more than a quarter of a century of democracy – Latin American politics appeared more comparable to contemporary North American and Western European politics than it had done for many years. In the circumstances, it could not be argued that democracy was 'impossible' in the region. Two issues suggest themselves. Why has democracy been so fragile in the region? And are the prospects better for democracy, and for stability and continuity in party politics, than they have been in the past?

The outward sign of the fragility of party systems has generally been either the unrestrained conflict of civil war, or military intervention. But these breakdowns frequently reflect in part internal weaknesses in the party systems themselves. In order to approach this topic, a clear distinction should be made between parties which have their origins within the state itself, and those which arise outside it to compete for power. Part of the explanation for the weakness of democracy in Latin America lies in the fact that the most successful parties in the region have been formed after power has been obtained by means other than electoral competition. They have therefore begun life as ruling parties. This has implications both for the ruling party itself and for the prospects for viable opposition parties (and hence for the viability of a party system making possible alternation in power and thus stable democracy in the longer term). A ruling party founded after power has been gained by other means is likely to lack the authority *vis-à-vis* the executive to set the political agenda, and the legitimacy *vis-à-vis* society at large to attract independent and principled support. As a result, it runs the danger of being subordinated to purely formal status, or being used simply as an agency to regulate state employment – or worse, to mobilise support for the regime while lacking any input into the process of policy formation. On the other hand, parties outside government seeking to compete are liable to remain weak as a result of their lack of access to public resources. Feeling unable to compete on equal terms in the electoral arena, they may be tempted to seek routes to power other than through the ballot box.

This was the case, in different ways, in Argentina under Perón, in Brazil between 1945 and 1964, and in Mexico after the revolution of 1910–17. In the latter case the Institutional Revolutionary Party (PRI), founded in 1928, established itself as the dominant party in the country primarily as a result of its monopoly on linkages between the powerful executive and the population at large, particularly as gathered into separate official workers' and peasants' unions. The party functions primarily as a channel for the distribution of public goods, with politicians at municipal, state and federal levels playing the role of intermediaries. Deputies are not allowed, under the 1917 constitution, to stand for re-election at the end of their three-year term, and the administrative and 'political' positions are closely intertwined. The norm in career terms is for individuals to move back and forth over time between appointed and 'elective' positions (the latter virtually 'appointed' in fact as a result of the overwhelming dominance of the PRI and the virtual certainty of election for official candidates). The combination of enforced mobility and dependence on the state for advancement makes party members servants of the state rather than independent representatives.[16]

In the Mexican political system overall, the legislature and the party play a relatively minor role. Two incidents in recent decades have illuminated the nature of the party, and its relationship with the executive. The first occurred in the middle 1960s, when an attempt by Carlos Madrazo to institute primaries to generate candidates for elective posts was defeated; this confirmed the centrality of the mechanism by which candidates are able to receive 'unanimous' backing from the party faithful, ensuring not only the appearance of unity, but also the survival of defeated factions and their reintegration into the party. The second incident was the attempt in 1981–2 by party leaders to take charge of the policy-making process by drawing up a manifesto to which the incoming president would be committed. The move was resisted and defeated, confirming the subordinate role of the party.[17]

For all its subordination to the executive, however, the PRI has enjoyed extraordinary success over practically six decades. At the other end of the scale of parties having their origins within the state itself lies the Peronist Justicialista Party, founded after Perón's election victory of 1946 and after the crushing of the pro-Peronist but independent *Partido Laborista*. Endowed with an ambitious ideology stressing the virtue of a 'third way' between capitalism and communism, the party was crippled from the start by Perón's refusal to allow it any organisational or political autonomy. It failed to establish itself as a coherent political force, remaining simply a convenient umbrella grouping to be activated as elections approached, and a vehicle for the distribution of state patronage dispensed by the Peróns.[18] Entirely dominated by Perón (and after his death by the union bosses), it has shown signs only in the aftermath of Alfonsín's electoral victory for the Radicals in 1983 of transforming itself into a coherent, autonomous and democratic party.[19]

The third case (that of Brazil between 1945 and 1964) is a little more complex. Both of the parties which dominated throughout the period, the Social Democratic Party (PSD) and the Brazilian Labour Party (PTB), had their origins within the authoritarian state of the *Estado Novo* (1937–45). The PSD began its life as the party of the dictatorship, in a literal sense: Vargas called together the state governors and local executives (*intendentes*) of the *Estado Novo* and formed them into the party, banking on their ability to hold on to the clienteles they had built up as monopoly suppliers of state funds during the period of dictatorship. The PSD thus began life as a party of official patronage, closely wedded to the state. The second party, also formed at Vargas's instigation, was the PTB. This was formed on the basis of the bureaucracy of the official trade union movement set up in the country after the smashing of independent (and largely Communist-influenced) workers' groups in the 1930s, and always hovered uneasily between its original role as a means of organising and controlling a minority of urban workers, and its growing tendency to press beyond these narrow limits into independent urban organisation and mobilisation in the countryside. The party system was shaped and dominated by the politics of clientelism and class alliance described in Chapter 2. Democracy finally broke down in Brazil when the PTB (rivalling the PSD in size and influence by the early 1960s) set out to achieve autonomy from the state, and raised the issue of rural recruitment and land reform to the top of its agenda. This development destroyed the delicate balance Vargas had established between the PSD (a relatively conservative party, a 'party of government' *par excellence* with many traditional landowners in its ranks) and the PTB (intended to be confined to urban areas and to enrol the workers behind a programme of state-led industrialisation). When the PTB lost its character as an 'arm of government' the ingenious system devised by Vargas rapidly broke down. In the circumstances, it would be wrong to see the 1961–64 crisis which led to military intervention as one of a simple breakdown of the party system; it was more a case of the parties threatening to break out of the artificial confines within which they had been created. The threat of the emergence of genuinely representative and independent parties was enough to bring the system down.[20]

In all three cases, the dominance of 'parties of government' had a substantial effect on the nature of opposition parties and their attitude towards electoral competition. The PAN in Mexico, the divided Radical and Intransigent Radical parties in Argentina, and the UDN in Brazil were all model liberal democratic parties in terms of the ideologies they endorsed. They all despaired, however, of gaining power through the ballot box, and attempted at some stage to ride to power on the backs of the military, either through armed rebellion, backing for coups, or acquiescence in the proscription of their rivals for power.

It is clear from this account that one of the major causes of instability in Latin America has been the creation (and ascendancy) of 'parties of government' after the acquisition of power, the tendency for such parties to sustain themselves as monopoly suppliers of state patronage and intermediaries between the executive and the bureaucracy on the one hand, and the population at large on the other, and the consequent crippling of the prospects of opposition parties, whether of the right or of the left. Where these parties have additionally been the first to mobilise new social groups they have so dominated the political arena that the prospects for opposition groupings have been bleak. It would be misleading, however, to see 'populism' in particular as a cause of political instability in Latin America. As we have seen before, it was itself a response to a loss (on the part of preceding élites) of the ability to rule by consent. It is not surprising, therefore, that where strong populist movements failed to materialise, regime followed regime in a destabilising cycle of experiment and failure: as successive attempts to recreate a viable political regime foundered, options were eliminated, and new expedients adopted.

The clearest example of this was in Chile, where between 1932 and 1970 no government succeeded in securing re-election. In the 25 years before the coup which instituted the Pinochet dictatorship, Chile was governed successively by the Radicals, the would-be populist Ibáñez, the Conservatives under Alessandri, the Christian Democrats under Frei, and the Popular Unity coalition under Allende. Each of Allende's predecessors found his political backing had evaporated by the end of his term; the rise and decline of the Christian Democrats made party alignments (particularly on the centre and the right) highly unstable, and the Alessandri–Frei–Allende sequence produced a steady shift of regimes to the left, finally precipitating the coup of 1973.[21]

The two closest parallels to the Chilean experience are found in Colombia and Venezuela. The Liberals and Conservatives continued to dominate in Colombia after 1930, but highly destabilising dynamics developed in each party, leading to increasingly authoritarian rule in the 1950s, and an eventual military takeover which led to an attempt by General Rojas Pinilla to set up a populist regime. The Liberals under Lopez Pumarejo in the early 1930s had adopted a progressive programme in which land reform featured prominently, but the party had subsequently lost its reforming zeal. In the late 1940s its character was transformed with the rise to prominence within its ranks of the radical urban populist Eliecer Gaitán, who became dominant in the party before his assassination in 1948. Over the same period, the Conservative party underwent a similar transformation, falling into the hands of the arch-conservative Laureano Gomez. Elected to office in 1952, Gomez set about reforming the constitution in order to increase the power of the executive and to reduce that of the legislature. The polarisation of political forces throughout the country had in the meantime led to a situation of virtual civil war, and the breakdown of the political system was confirmed by military intervention in 1953.[22]

Venezuela, lacking the experience of Chile or Colombia with democratic politics, experienced a similar cycle of destabilisation between 1935 and 1958. The death of the dictator Gomez in the former year produced a sequence of military-led regimes which wavered between repression and cautious reform, until a coup by reform-minded officers in 1945 was instrumental in bringing the Democratic Action party to power. This party, led by Rómulo Betancourt, proceeded to build upon its earlier mobilisation of the peasantry to launch a radical programme of social change. The consequence was the gathering of a broad conservative coalition against it, and a counter-coup in 1948 which led (after a period of military rule) to an attempt by Colonel Marcos Perez Jimenez to set up a popular-authoritarian regime.[23] Similar sequences of regimes leading to breakdowns of democratic politics can be witnessed in Peru and Bolivia. This suggests that while populism (with its authoritarian practices and its closeness to the state) was a flawed solution to the political crisis experienced across Latin America after 1930, it was more effective than any other political strategy in providing stability and promoting economic development.

In one way or another, however, with populism or without, virtually every political system in Latin America broke down in the period after the Second World War, leading to military intervention, often of a protracted nature. Paradoxically, the cycle of military interventions across the region was to make possible a reordering of civilian politics which restored the prospect – for the first time since the 1930s – of stability within a context of respect for the rule of law. As we shall see when we discuss the role of the military in power (Chapter 4), hard lessons were learnt from military rule and the shambles which resulted. The consequence (practically everywhere) was a greater willingness on the part of civilian parties to tolerate each other and to seek compromise, a greater abstention from use of state power for systematic political advantage, and a determination to make democracy succeed. It was combined with a general move toward the centre on the part of parties to right and left, and a conscious policy of exclusion of radicals, limiting of political agendas, and strengthening of discipline and hierarchy within parties. In other words, self-censorship took over from outside intervention, enabling democratic political systems to survive, at the price of slowing reform, containing radicalism, and placing the highest priority on establishing and obeying the 'rules of the game'. This general reorientation, apparent first in Venezuela and Colombia in 1958, and followed in Ecuador in 1978, in Peru in 1980, in Argentina in 1983 and in Brazil and Uruguay in 1985, has produced a range of 'self-limiting democracies' which (if they were to survive) could transform the face of politics in Latin America.

The record of the last two decades has prompted a degree of attention to the weaknesses of the democracies which gave way to military rule, and awoken interest in the 'successful' post-World War Two democracies of Colombia, Costa Rica and Venezuela.[24] The latter have tended to be dismissed as highly restricted, conservative, and élitist, and accorded little sympathy or attention. In purely descriptive terms, that picture is not altogether misleading. The competing parties have tended to become more similar (and more centrist) over time; they have often benefited from explicit agreements to share power or to exclude more radical opponents, and although the very high levels of participation and intense party loyalties of Venezuela contrast sharply with the low levels of involvement registered in Colombia, the Venezuelan system increasingly favours groups with vast financial resources, and so offers limited opportunity for independent participation.[25] It is becoming clear, however, that the limited and cautious nature of these democracies has given them a degree of durability that was lacking in the more open and polarised systems of, say, Chile and Brazil before military intervention. A comparative study by Peeler suggests that the common feature which explains the survival of democracy in each case is 'a conscious and explicit decision between élites to accommodate one another'.[26] This is helpful as far as it goes, but it begs the question of why élites were willing (and able) to co-operate here, when unable (or unwilling) to do so in other cases. This question can be answered only by first of all identifying the class nature of the élites involved (broadly, representatives of different 'bourgeois' interests), then establishing the programmes on which they co-operate (again, broadly ones aiming at excluding radical alternatives in their joint interests), and finally asking why it has been possible for such programmes to be successfully implemented. On the latter point, I suggest that the experience of deep social crises in each case (civil war in Costa Rica and Colombia, military intervention in Colombia and Venezuela, and intense political polarisation in all three cases) had the double effect of uniting previously divided bourgeois groups on a programme aimed at their common survival, and persuading a significant majority of the population at large to accept (and support) a cautious democracy promising little in the way of immediate social and economic advancement, but committed to stability and the restoration of calm and a state of law. It may be that after the traumatic events in recent years elsewhere in South America, similar developments are possible. If so, the prospects for Latin American democracy may be bright in one sense, but less so in another: there may be a strong possibility that élite co-operation will secure democracy on a more stable basis than in the past, but at the same time that democracy may be too cautious to provide the means for tac\ling the enormous social problems which are the legacy of decades of dependent development and years of harsh military rule. In the long run, those social and economic problems will have to be resolved if even the most restricted and élitist forms of democracy are to survive. In any case, the question of the prospects for democracy in Latin America is a controversial one. It has already prompted considerable debate (with the pessimists stressing the impact of severe economic crisis and the continuing power of the military), and is likely to remain the central issue in regard to party politics in the region.[27]

4. Political parties and participation in the Middle East

Political parties in the Middle East have ranged from loosely-organised cliques of notables through trans-state Pan-Arab and Pan-Islamic to the classic clandestine cell-based Communist parties which have been small but important in organising strikes and demonstrations. There seems to be no overall general pattern in the historical evolution of parties other than that in some states parties of notables have given place to radical nationalist parties (as happened in Iraq and Syria in the 1960s), or to state sponsored bureaucratic parties (like the Arab Socialist Union in Egypt and the Sudan Socialist Union). In Lebanon, alignments of notables have continued to be significant up until the mid-1970s. In the kingdoms of Jordan and Kuwait the ruling families have allowed parties or groupings to function but ensured a central role for independent pro-regime tribal representatives in the assemblies. In the Libya of Qaddafi parties are banned on the grounds that the people should represent themselves directly, and in Saudi Arabia on the grounds that the state implements Islamic law and that is all that is required in an Islamic polity.

In general, however, organised parties with some sort of ideology, structure and membership independent of the state have not flourished. Where such parties have emerged they have required an alliance with the military in order to assume power or they have been suppressed. In Iraq (1963 and 1968) and Syria (1963 and 1966) different wings of the Ba'th (Renaissance) Party came to power after military coups and have had a difficult and complex relationship with the officer corps as a result. One major factor in the development of this party–army relationship was the inability of the parties to make any political headway in an electoral system where landlords and tribal leaders held sway over the peasantry. At the same time, armies have found that they have required civilian support, and have organised party-like organisations. In Egypt, the Free Officers who came to power in 1952 banned the old political parties but attempted to form a nationwide organisation to mobilise, legitimise and control. In Lebanon, parties really came into their own only after the 1975 civil war, and that was because they had associated militias. Prior to 1975 they had never been able to assert their role against entrenched local political bosses.

The early history of political parties in the modern Middle East is reflective of the changing constellations of social and economic power. In Iraq, Syria and Lebanon parties were first established in the Mandate period. In Syria, a loose party coalition of notables spearheaded the opposition to the French, although they were in a minority to the independents. In Iraq and Lebanon, prominent individuals formed loose political groupings. In the 1930s, however, ideological, organised political parties began to form. Some, like the Lebanese Phalange and *Najjadeh* (Scouts) and Syrian Social National Party, were modelled on European fascist forms of organisation, others, like the Syrian National Action League (one of the roots of the Ba'th party) were more political clubs. They were established to mobilise various forms of nationalist opinion, and appealed to a new generation of the young and educated which the older nationalist blocs of the 1920s had ceased to attract. The Communist party was also active in this period in the French mandates as a result of the Popular Front government in Paris lifting legal restrictions. None of these new forms of political organisation was able to compete with the landowners and tribal chiefs, who were factionally divided but conscious of a shared benefit arising from their large landholdings. Indeed, in Iraq a short-lived Shaykhs' Rights party was established.

At independence, this pattern did not change. The assemblies of Iraq, Syria and Lebanon were controlled by independents or loose coalitions representing regional or local interests. Parties of this period were short-lived electoral lists controlling the peasant and tribal vote or parliamentary factions coalescing around a cabinet minister who controlled and dispensed patronage. Against this entrenched ruling group socialist, nationalist and communist parties were unable to achieve any electoral success. In both Iraq and Syria these parties sought influence and allies in the officer corps. The 1958 coup in Iraq which swept away the monarchy and landlords presented the Ba'th with no greater political opportunity since the army refused to cede power to the parties. As a result, the party sought to recruit and place supporters in the army rather than rely on sympathisers. A short period of Ba'thist rule in 1963 was followed by a further five-year period of military rule until 1968 when a fully fledged Ba'thist government was established, although again after another military coup. Though dependent on military goodwill the civilian party was able to establish a degree of civilian control over the military and Saddam Husayn, a civilian party leader, held the levers of power. In Syria, the Ba'th came to power in 1963 after a coup by a group of Ba'thist officers organised in the Military Committee, which was separate from the civilian party. As a result, party politics in Syria was essentially intertwined with the internal politics of the officer corps.

In Egypt before the 1952 coup, party politics were somewhat more developed than in the other states. The *Wafd* (delegation) was a popular nationalist party and dominated Egyptian politics from the 1920s through the 1940s and generally won majorities in parliament when the palace did not exercise control. Like other pre-1952 parties the *Wafd* was a party of the Egyptian middle- and upper-classes, but unlike the others was able to appear as the party of the nation fighting for complete independence from the British. The 1952 coup by the Free Officers brought the banning of the political parties, although it was the well-organised Society of Muslim Brothers which was more of a threat. Subsequently the regime established a series of single-party organisations, although in the 1970s (when Anwar Sadat liberalised the political system, albeit under guidelines favourable to the government party) the Muslim Brothers and the *Wafd* resurfaced, indicative of the en- grained sentiment for parties in Egypt.

Although Iran has had a distinct political history, there too parties have had only a limited role in shaping politics, at least until the rise of the clergy-dominated Islamic Republican Party. Reza Shah (1926–41) ruled through army, court patronage and bureaucracy. After his deposition in 1941 coalitions did emerge in the Assembly and a Communist party (the Tudeh) and small nationalist parties were formed. As in landlord-dominated Syria and Iraq, these parties faced severe problems in establishing any statewide support. Where members of the western educated intelligentsia did break through the entrenched power of the landlords and tribal chiefs, it was because they were sons of prominent local leaders. The role of organised parties in Iran was more one of bringing issues to the fore and mobilising popular nationalist opposition to the Shah. It was nationalist and Com- munist agitation that led the Shah to flee the country in 1953, although subsequently the CIA together with the Iranian military brought about his restoration. On his return, an 'iron curtain' fell on Iranian politics: 'It cut the opposition leaders from their followers, the militants from the general public, and the political parties from their social base'.[28] Muhammad Reza Shah's sub- sequent reign saw the establishment of state-sponsored parties for the purposes of support and control.

One distinct type of Middle Eastern political party has been that organised across state boundaries. The Ba'th party and the Arab National Movement have been orientated toward Arab unity and have been pan-Arab in structure and ideology. The Syrian Social National Party has recruited in Syria, Lebanon and Jordan with the aim of forming a Greater Syria. The Muslim Brothers have branches in most Arab states and both Iraq and Lebanon have had movements supportive of the Islamic regime in Iran. With the persistence of state boundaries such parties have tended to become based in a single state, or (as in the case of Iraq and Syria) divided into two separate Ba'th parties.

Middle Eastern politics, then, have to some extent reflected social and political change. Coalitions of landlords, urban notables and tribal leaders have given way to parties or state organisations whose core has been the modern educated middle strata. Yet the role and performance of political parties has not been dramatically changed as a result of economic development and an associated growth of social diversity in Middle Eastern states. In the two most developed states (Egypt and Iran) the evolution of political parties has been very different: in the former a period of limited party competition developed, whereas in Iran a Muslim fundamentalist party gained control of the political system. The Ba'th succeeded in seizing power in Iraq and Syria, but took on the form of a state-organised party. The evolution of party in the contemporary Middle East is linked to the way in which the monarchs and landlords were overthrown and with party–army relations. The Ba'th in Iraq and Syria and the single-party organisations in Egypt will be highlighted to illustrate this evolution.

The bureaucratic organisation and the clandestine cell party

In Egypt, the political parties were not directly involved in the overthrow of the monarchy, and as a result the Free Officers sought to establish a supportive constituency by using the state which they had seized for these ends. Between 1953 and 1956 British, French and Israeli attacks on Egypt facilitated the mobilisation of national support for the regime, although the instrument to do that was rather crude. The Liberation Rally was a bureaucratic mechanism for organising demonstrations and rallies, even though it did draw on popular sentiment. In 1958 the National Union was formed. This organisation was more than an organisation for channelling national support against the former colonial power and a range of internal enemies; it was a more sophisticated bureaucratic machine, with an ideological justification supportive of its anti-party position: parties divided the nation and spoiled national mobilisation for economic and social development. Such a rationale was hardly credible when the National Union was organised along the administrative lines of the Ministry of the Interior and, though centrally controlled, government passed a circumscribed power to those local élites who had not been affected by the land reform: the established middle peasantry. Because the regime established the National Union and the ideology of the regime was inchoate, everybody and anybody was recruited into the membership. When Nasser dissolved it, this moribund organisation died without a whimper even though it had a membership of 6 million. It was hardly surprising, since membership meant 'the redress of grievance, protection of existing rights, the retention of social prestige, and attainment of minimal qualifications for co-optation into higher political echelons'.[29]

A more serious attempt at forming a political party occurred in 1961–2. The approach was more overtly corporatist. The Arab Socialist Union (ASU) was to represent the 'national alliance of working forces'. In so doing, it fell between two stools. On the one hand it aimed at national recruitment for regime support, and on the other required the mobilisation of militants committed to a regime which had formulated something like an ideology and at least a clear programme: the socialist transformation of Egypt. As John Waterbury has pointed out: the ASU was to do everything: 'pre-empt all other political forces, contain the citizenry, and through the vanguard, turn it into a mobilisational instrument with a cutting edge'.[30] Waterbury neatly condenses the contradiction in these goals with his account of the trial of Ahmad Kamil, former officer, security official and ASU apparatchik: 'organising Socialist Youth [a part of the ASU] or tapping phones . . . were routine activities that in Kamil's laconic rendering apparently had no qualitative difference between them'.[31] Indicative of the caution of the regime in recruiting those who were ideologically committed to transforming Egypt, the recruitment of those at the top of the ASU was based on loyalty to President Nasser. The Vanguard could not survive because it was organised by those who had no sense of what a vanguard meant. Clement Henry Moore supplies the information: of 131 ministers, only 2 held party position before becoming ministers, whereas 83 held party positions after it. He pithily describes the ASU as 'hardly a vanguard for recruiting the top political leadership, the party was a rearguard for retiring it'.[32]

The greater penetration of Egyptian society by the ASU was facilitated by the expansion of the state's control of the economy during the early 1960s. By the mid-1960s, one-third of the Egyptian work force was employed by the state and in the villages the state controlled the all important Co-operative Boards. In the Middle East, it was not only republics which developed such organisations. In Iran, the Shah established the Rastakhiz party and used the state's bureaucratic and economic power to drum people into it.

The development of the Ba'th party (which originated in Syria and spread to Iraq) is rather different.[33] It emerged as a party independent of the state and attracted the new generation of young educated nationalists. In Syria, the entrenched power of landlords and the consequent electoral failure of the Ba'th caused it to seek alliance with nationalist officers and send young adherents to the military academy. Ideological and factional conflict within the party subsequently led to civilian party leaders seeking military support and Ba'thist officers seeking alliances with civilian party leaders. This tendency increased after the 1963 coup, when the Military Committee intervened to establish a Ba'thist government. This Committee was wholly military and had been organised separately from the civilian party. As civil party leaders amalgamated with military Ba'thists an intense power struggle developed, and party structure and membership radically changed. The party had been based on a cell system with tiers of local, provincial and national congresses. Since the congresses did have a say in defining party principles and electing the leadership, and since representation at congress was based on the number of full members, top political leaders recruited relatives and friends, thereby evading the internal party regulations which laid down strict guidelines for party membership. Those who were committed to the party and party principles were swamped by the new members. Not only did the party come under the control of the military but it shifted away from its original structure of a cadre party based on democratic centralism. Ironically, non-ideological members were recruited to resolve divisions within the party which had ideological overtones: the significance of class analysis, the relative weight to be given to socialism and nationalism and to Syrian and Arab nationalism.

One further result of this internal party struggle was the advancement of the rural minorities (particularly the Alawites) within the party. Because of its secularism the party had appealed to the minorities rather than to the Sunni Muslim majority, as it had appealed to those of rural and provincial origin rather than to those of urban big town origin because of its emphasis on peasant rights and land reform. Reinforcing this process was the fact that key members of the Military Committee were Alawites. The party became increasingly identified with the provinces and the rural minorities, and as the party became more influenced by Marxism and secularism, Ba'thist rule generated large-scale opposition from the towns, the merchants and Sunni Muslim fundamentalism. Party and state became increasingly one after 1970, when Hafiz al-Asad in a coup removed radical elements and attempted to use the state to conciliate urban Sunni Muslim Syria and attract back urban capitalists who had fled to Lebanon. The failure of a more pragmatic and conciliatory policy to woo the opposition was undertaken at the cost of a party life independent of the state, the military and the internal security forces. The change in party structure and the process of recruitment (and, above all, the military connection) has subverted the independence of the party from the state. Having sought a clientele in the officer corps, the Ba'th in Syria became a relatively passive client of the military.

In Iraq, a somewhat similar development of the party took place although there was not such a clear subordination of party to army.[34] As in Syria, it appealed to young, educated Pan-Arabists. The party was small and weak in 1958 when the military overthrew the monarchy, but it did come to power in 1963 for nine months after conspiring with a group of non-Ba'thist officers. One factor in the overthrow of this Ba'thist regime was its attempt to establish a National Guard as a counterweight to the army, and this alienated the officer corps. The Ba'th again came to power in 1968 (again through a military coup) and although Ba'thist officers were involved the civilian wing of the party had a far greater degree of control. The first President after the 1968 coup was a retired Ba'thist officer, Ahmad Hasan al-Bakr, but power lay with Saddam Husayn, a civilian and provisional regional secretary since 1963. Saddam Husayn controlled the army by organising the promotion of officers who were from his home town of Tikrit, and by establishing party control over the army in which only the Ba'th party could organise. Although the party has only around 40 000 full-time members and party and state structures remain separate except at the upper echelons, the Ba'th does place members in key positions or attempts to recruit sympathisers who are technically and administratively able. Party committees have a role in formulating policy and government that of implementation. The Ba'th in Iraq (even when in power) is clandestine and conspiratorial and its relatively privileged members act as the eyes and ears of the regime. In more recent years the dynamism of the party has been eroded by the more personalistic leadership role of Saddam Husayn, leader of the party and head of state.

Conclusion

Participation by parties in the political system, and participation in the parties that have been able to secure power, has been relatively limited. One of the main factors limiting the role of parties in the Middle East has been the power of individual leaders like Nasser, Anwar Sadat and Saddam Husayn. The way in which regimes have used the party as an arm of the bureaucratic apparatus for regime support and political control has been a further factor. The prevalence of military regimes and the results of parties seeking political alliances with the officer corps have acted as yet another constraint on the performance of parties. Yet the bleak performance of modern parties must be placed in the historical context of a structure of society and power where parties could make no breakthrough against the landowners and tribal chiefs.

Nor have other forms of participation been widely available in the Middle East. Trade and professional unions have been subordinated to regime-organised parties (as in Egypt), or the leadership has been closely vetted (as in Iraq and Syria). In the Gulf states and Saudi Arabia, trade union activity is banned. In Lebanon, where there has been a greater freedom to organise, a substantial section of the working-class has been Syrian or Palestinian, and come under the supervision of the security and immigration services.

In conclusion, the Middle East has proved a harsh environment for party politics. Parties have more frequently been an instrument of control and a means by which regimes could involve key sectors of the population in a passive way. The ASU incorporated large numbers of the Egyptian citizenry but particularly targeted the skilled working class, middle-class intelligentsia and professionals and the middle and rich peasantry. After the Iraqi Ba'th came to power in 1968 it has played a supervisory role through a party membership recruited on a selective basis. When parties like the Ba'th have taken over they have generally suppressed or subordinated other political parties. In Iran the brief period of party politics following the fall of the Shah saw a concerted drive by the clergy to establish total political control. The absence of participation through organised party structures has hardly been remedied by other forms of institutional participation. Where assemblies have been established or re-established (as in Jordan, Kuwait and Iraq) they have had very limited powers when compared to those of the monarchs and presidents. In the case of the first two states, those elected tended to be from notable families, and in the case of the latter from the Ba'th party. What participation there is, then, tends to be limited to supporters of the system or regime. In most Middle Eastern states there are informal mechanisms for consultation through personal ties and connections, but Lebanon has dramatically illustrated the problems of a system wholly based on a personalistic patron-clientelism.

5. Conclusion

Parties in the Third World tend to be weak because they lack autonomy, authority and prestige. Where independence has been recent and opportunities for political organisation prior to independence have been limited, it is clear why this should be so. Under colonial rule parties have either been élitist groupings closely associated with the colonial regime, and hence lacking a popular base, or oppositionist movements denied the political space to develop on a broad basis. In the former case, adaptation after independence is made difficult by the need to conduct a hasty mobilisation among hitherto neglected groups. In the latter, the passage to independence may bring with it both popularity and power, but the party itself tends to be weakened (paradoxically in some ways) by its close and immediate association with power.

In the transition from opposition to power, the resources of the movement are frequently stretched to the limit; while the leadership swiftly becomes remote, the party lacks the substantial core of middle-level activists and workers which enable it to establish itself soundly among the mass of a population eager for results. Party activists have to be moved into administrative and governmental positions, and the tasks of political mobilisation and organisation tend to be carried out (if at all) by newly-appointed state functionaries rather than by autonomous citizens. Power corrupts: it is inevitable that state resources will be used politically to shore up the regime, and almost inevitable that the party will become above all a channel for patronage and the purchase of political support. It is no accident, therefore, that parties in the Third World tend to be agencies of the state rather than vehicles for the autonomous political mobilisation of the citizenry behind clearly-defined political programmes with strong ideological underpinnings. Whether the party has been a loose coalition of notables favoured by the colonial regime, or an oppositional force active in the pursuit and winning of independence, it is thus likely to face real problems after independence. A further factor causes problems for political parties in newly-independent states. In a context of recent independence, opposition may appear (and be depicted) as verging on treason. The themes around which ruling parties are likely to mobilise are those of nationalism, independence, dignity and sovereignty. Calls for unity – stressing the danger of fratricidal conflict – are likely to predominate. In such a context, the problems of opposition (already made difficult by the close links between the ruling party and the state) are exacerbated.

It is not surprising, in the light of these problems, that parties in Africa and the Middle East have tended either to be swallowed up in the machinery of state (as in Egypt and Kenya), or to be swept aside. The Ba'ath parties of Syria and Iraq have survived and prospered by tying themselves to the state in the form of the military; those of an increasing number of African states (typified in different ways by Zambia, Tanzania and the Ivory Coast) have succeeded by becoming unequivocally parties of government, rather than contestants among others of equal status in a competitive system.

What is perhaps surprising, at first sight, is that parties in Latin

America should appear so similar to those in the other two areas examined, despite the absence of a recent past of colonial rule, and despite the ethnic, religious and linguistic divisions which have made political mobilisation problematic in those regions. We have argued, however, that in some ways the history of élite-controlled export-led development (and its crisis after 1930) can be seen as a functional equivalent to colonial rule and its demise. The rapid development of mass-based parties in Latin America after 1930, the tendency for mobilisation to take place primarily from within the state rather than outside it, and the frequency with which a movement organised from within the state was successful in mobilising such a proportion of the population that peaceful competition within the electoral system seemed fruitless are all factors which offer immediate parallels with African and Middle Eastern experience. In the case of Mexico, in particular (where the revolution offers a closer parallel with the process of decolonisation and independence, at least in so far as the political consequences for the victorious movement are concerned) we have a successful single party which bears direct comparison with those of Africa.

All three areas have in common a close identification of successful parties with the state. Success in such conditions goes along with both a lack of autonomy, and a weakening of the conditions for successful competition for power; it is therefore the closeness of party and state which accounts most satisfactorily for the failure of competitive liberal democracy in the Third World. It also accounts for the fact that change tends to come (if at all) in violent (or at least unconstitutional) ways.

However, recent developments in Latin America (where the process has run longest) suggest that this may not be so for all time. Single parties can establish themselves solidly, as they have done in Mexico and Cuba; but elsewhere it seems that the cycle of instability can exhaust itself if élites become persuaded that the use of state resources to perpetuate party dominance is counter-productive, and if leaders can win acceptance for moderation in policy and tolerance in political partisanship. If this is so, stable single parties and stable competitive systems may both be features of Third World politics in the future.

4

The Military

1. Introduction

The military has played a central role in Third World politics since independence. There have been many attempts to explain military intervention but (in the main) they have proved inadequate to account for the great range of interventions. Some (like S. E. Finer) have pointed to the sociocultural environment as the key factor. Finer has argued that a low level of political culture is likely to result in military intervention. He gives limited independent criteria of a 'low' political culture, and cause and consequence are quite similar: military intervention itself seems to indicate a low level of political culture. In any case, there is little reason to think that either Zambia or Colombia have a political culture distinct from their neighbours, and every reason to doubt that Lebanon has a higher political culture than Egypt. Morris Janowitz (1972) focuses wholly on the characteristics of the military: the superior quality of its organisation and the shared values of the officer corps. Yet the military has frequently been fragmented and has produced a wide range of political ideologies: nationalist, populist, monetarist, socialist, conservative and radical. The frequency of purges also sheds doubt on such unity of organisation or values. Other explanations have focussed *inter alia* on personal ambition, corporate motives and class interests. Yet none of these theories has satisfactorily explained why the military has intervened in some states, and not in others. In the following section we try to indicate the range of variables which have contributed to the military's involvement in politics.

Military interventions frequently establish military regimes or result in a group of officers appointing a civilian government and

115

acting as arbiters of policy and politics. The officers justify military rule on the grounds that the army represents the national interest, or that only military rule can secure and maintain a stable political order for economic development. Indeed, in the 1960s, leading American political scientists regarded the military as the only institution which could modernise their societies. Military governments, however, have frequently been viewed by the citizenry as illegitimate, and a widespread civilian protest rather than a stable political framework for development has been the result.

In many cases, military regimes hand power over to civilian governments as a result of failed policies, civil protest and, at times, because the officers have viewed their role as temporary. In other cases, generals and colonels gradually civilianise themselves as they loosen their connections to the military establishment.

Whatever the nature of military rule, there is a general tendency for the soldiers to establish a veneer of civil legitimacy, either through presidential plebiscites, the incorporation of sympathetic individuals or civilian parties or through establishing new political organisations. Although the military has intervened decisively in politics in the Third World, military withdrawal and varying patterns of civilianisation suggest a limited belief in the legitimacy of their own rule.

2. The military in politics in Africa

Since independence in (or about) 1960, the military has supplanted civilian governments in nearly half of Africa's states, while in many of these states (especially in Anglophone Africa), one wing of the military has subsequently been displaced by another – as in Nigeria in July 1966, 1975, and 1985 and Ghana in 1978 and 1979. Several other states (as noted below) have experienced serious coup attempts. However, there are also a sizable number of states which have retained their civilian governments over a long period, often under the nationalist leaders who brought their countries to independence. The list sub-divides into a smallish group of states, including Botswana, the Ivory Coast, Senegal (since Mamadou Dia's attempted coup failed in 1962), Swaziland and Tunisia, which have experienced neither coups nor serious attempts at a coup, and a second group of states which have kept their civilian leadership but where there have been significant coup attempts. Among the latter group, with the date of the attempted coup in brackets, are Gabon (1964), Angola (1977), the Gambia (1981), Kenya (1982), and Cameroon (1984). Though the civilian leadership has survived in states such as these, it is not because the military has not tried to remove them or because they have a higher level of political culture than the countries where the armed forces have successfully intervened. It is indeed difficult to validate the argument relating to political culture by comparing one African state with another. The significant fact is that, by comparison with the developed states, virtually all African countries are weak in terms of political culture and are, therefore, susceptible to military intervention; to this extent, Finer's argument is valid.[1] Which regimes survive and which are toppled by military coups appears in part to be a matter of chance.

However, the element of chance must not be exaggerated since it is possible to explain on rational grounds the survival of civilian regimes; two explanations stand out. The first is the external dimension, which is especially important for French-speaking states. All the latter maintain military technical assistance agreements with France and several of them (including Cameroon, Gabon, the Ivory Coast and Senegal) have entered into defence agreements also. Though France has retained a few military bases in Africa, she has reduced her direct military presence in the continent in favour of expanding an airborne rapid deployment force (RDF) stationed in the metropolis. In the past decade, the RDF has intervened in Chad, Djibouti, Shaba (Zaire), Mauritania, the Central African Republic, and (covertly) in Angòla. Such intervention has not been needed in the core Francophone states, which have developed tight security arrangements of their own and in which (to quote Luckham) 'France's military weight has been cast firmly behind the ruling class, a good indicator being its role as their major weapons supplier'.[2] Most of the Francophone states still obtain the bulk of their military equipment from France and also look to her for training and other support. However, a caveat should be entered at this point: Guinea under Ahmed Sékou Touré (1958–84) affords an example of a French-speaking state whose internal security services and links with a neighbouring state (Sierra Leone) were adequate, without French underpinning, to survive a serious coup attempt in 1970 and to maintain a civilian regime over a 26-year period.

There is another aspect of the external dimension which merits attention – that is, the use of African armies (as distinct from French or other European forces) as an instrument of foreign policy in relations between African states. Arnold Hughes and Roy May have examined 29 instances of (mostly bilateral) trans-national military intervention in Black Africa between 1960 and 1984: they identified 18 cases as regime-supportive and six as regime-opposing interventions. Their other five examples fall into the *state* supportive category, where the object of external inter-vention was to ensure the survival of the state itself in the face of internal disintegration and external aggression, rather than to maintain (or undermine) a particular regime (Chad is a case in point, except that Libya acted until recently to support Goukouni Oueddei both in government and opposition, and always to promote its own interests). Guinea and Tanzania especially have provided military assistance to threatened regimes; by contrast, Nigeria has not deployed its substantial military power externally to any great extent. Firm evidence of regime-opposing military intervention is difficult to obtain, though the Tanzanian army's overthrow of Idi Amin, the Ugandan dictator, in 1979 is a clear-cut case. More work needs to be done in this field, but among the tentative conclusions that emerge from the work of these authors are, first, that short-term bilateral interventions (such as the dispatch of Senegalese troops to the Gambia in 1981) have been very successful, and secondly, that civilian regimes (often radical and frequently poor) have been more likely than military regimes to use their national armies on external military missions.[3] Zimbabwe's intervention in Mozambique in 1985 on behalf of Samora Machel's beleaguered government in its fight against rebels belonging to the Mozambique National Resistance (MNR), suggests a further (somewhat obvious) general conclusion, namely that the motives for external intervention may be mixed. The stationing of more than 10 000 Zimbabwean troops in Mozam-bique is in part a good neighbourly gesture, but it is also a costly one and underlines the importance that Zimbabwe attaches to keeping open the vital supply line between the key port of Beira and Harare, the Zimbabwean capital.

A second explanation for the survival of civilian regimes is the political skill shown by leaders such as Habib Bourguiba of Tunisia, Felix Houphouet-Boigny of the Ivory Coast, Hastings Kamuzu Banda of Malawi, Julius Nyerere of Tanzania, and Kenneth Kaunda of Zambia. The converse would also appear to be true: the lack of political skill may precipitate a coup or encourage a counter-coup. Cases in point in Nigeria were the handling by the federal government and the Western regional government of the crisis in the Western Region in 1964–5, which necessitated bringing in the army to help restore order, and Major-General Aguiyi Ironsi's unification decree of early 1966 abolishing regional civil services. Again, the 1967 military take-over in Sierra Leone represented a failure of leadership on the part of Sir Albert Margai, the prime minister, and his advisers.[4]

We have examined in detail elsewhere the case of Nigeria, where the military (led by a predominantly Ibo group of majors and captains) intervened in January 1966, and where a counter-coup was staged six months later by mainly Northern junior army officers and 'other ranks' drawn from all parts of the north.[5] That case study is instructive for a number of reasons. It shows first that the interaction of political and organisational variables differed over time: an army which had been predominantly non-political before the coup of January 1966 became politicised after it, as army discipline broke down and civil–military boundaries fragmented. Secondly, the coup leaders in January 1966 (as distinct from the army officers as a whole) were radically inclined and had clear political objectives: they sought to sweep away the old, conservative political order which rested on Northern dominance. Thirdly, the case study shows that ethnicity and regionalism became more important as vehicles of political expression after the January coup than they had been before it, and that the flashpoint occurred when these vertical cleavages in society became intertwined with organisational tensions within the army. Finally, it suggests that personal motives (such as the fear that their promotion would be blocked) might have influenced both the conspirators in January 1966 and those who staged the counter-coup the following July.

Further lessons can be learned from other states where coups occurred, including Ghana, Uganda and Dahomey (now Benin). In Ghana in 1966, the military explained that it had intervened to get rid of an autocratic and corrupt regime which had bankrupted the economy, forged links with the Eastern bloc despite its official policy of non-alignment, interfered with the army and police, and established a private army – the President's Own Guard Regiment (POGR) – 'as a counterpoise to the Ghana armed forces'. The latter claimed to have no political ambitions but promised to hand over power to a properly elected civilian government once constitutional integrity had been restored and Ghana's economy had been revived. In the main, the stated reasons were the real reasons for the military takeover: the pro-Western coup-makers did have a profound contempt for Nkrumah and the CPP, though the main spur to their intervention was probably the army's deep-seated grievances against the government. Above all, there was resentment at the expansion (with the help of Soviet security advisers) of the POGR and a fear in some quarters that this well-armed and equipped force would eventually replace the regular army. There was resentment, too, at the invidious position in which the army had been placed during the 1961 Congo operation by the regime's political machinations and at the dismissal in August 1965 of Major-General S.J.A. Otu, Chief of the Defence Staff, and his deputy, Major-General J. A. Ankrah.[6]

In Uganda, in 1971, Major-General Amin was strongly motivated by personal fears and ambitions, though corporate reasons were present on this occasion too – the military resented the preferential treatment given to the Special Forces (an élite unit equivalent to Ghana's POGR) and to a rapidly growing para-military police organisation called the General Service Unit. To what extent was the military also motivated by economic interests? Objectively, military privilege was probably not threatened by President Obote's 'Move to the Left' since his government seemed incapable of enacting its socialist proposals. However, elements within the army may have *believed* that a socialist state would eventually be established in Uganda to the detriment of their own economic and social positions, and that a less well-off army would be made to undertake self-help projects, including the building of roads, bridges and schools, on Tanzanian lines.[7] In Dahomey, which experienced six military coups and counter-coups in nine years (1963–72), the backdrop to intervention was deep regional and ethnic animosities, a three-cornered struggle for political supremacy, a weak economy, a high level of unemployment, trade union resistance to austerity cuts, and a politicised military hierarchy presiding over a cleavage-ridden army.[8]

These and other cases suggest that the factors to be taken into account in explaining military intervention in Africa are frequently multiple and complex. These factors may include the level of political culture and the economic conditions prevailing in a particular state; the political motivation and ideological persuasion of the coup-makers; factional rivalries and class interest; the personal ambition of military officers and NCOs and the protection of the corporate interests of a military which, as Clapham has noted, is in most cases 'the armed wing of the bureaucratic bourgeoisie';[9] the political skill (or lack of it) shown by the incumbent leadership; the demonstration effect of other coups; and external alignments. On rare occasions another factor may be the manipulation by foreign powers and interests, though there are usually sufficient internal causes of military intervention as to render the conspiracy argument suspect. The 'mix' between these variables will differ from one state to another: thus, the corporate interests of the army seemed to count for less in Nigeria in January 1966 than they did in Ghana the following month, while the political leanings of the Nigerian coup-makers evidently counted for more. To construct a typology of military interventions is not easy – Huntington's three categories of breakthrough, guardian and veto coups are only partially relevant to Africa.[10] While certain generalisations about military intervention in Africa can usefully be made, each case is ultimately *sui generis,* to be understood only by studying the military organisation of the state concerned and the political and socioeconomic context in which that organisation operated.

Military rule

In Uganda in 1985, the military regime headed by Lieut-General Tito Okello appointed as ministers a number of former members of Milton Obote's ousted administration; among them was Mr Paulo Muwanga (the ex-vice president) who became prime minister for a short period. This action was entirely atypical. Normally, on assuming power the military suspends the constitution, dissolves the civilian government and parliament, disbands the existing political party (or parties), and detains the political leaders of the former regime. The military also establishes a new structure of control, with ultimate authority vested in a military council, thus providing (at least initially) a form of collective leadership; this council (possibly representative of the country's main regional-linguistic groups) will rule by decree, but will tend still to rely heavily (especially in economic matters) on the former bureaucracy, whose middle-class attitudes and values its members are likely to share. (Populist radical regimes such as those of Libya under Colonel Muamar al-Qaddafi, Ghana under Flight-Lieut Jerry Rawlings, and Burkina Faso under Captain Thomas Sankara have varied this structure by introducing people's defence committees.)

The policies pursued by the military, once established in power, will depend on its character and aims. In Martin Dent's classification, a 'caretaker' regime is pledged to restore constitutional integrity and clean up the mess left behind by the politicians; a 'corrective' regime seeks to correct certain profound deficiencies in the old civilian order (such as the four-state basis of the federal constitution and the regional nature of the political parties in pre-1966 Nigeria); and the revolutionary regime aims to transform the structure of society and to end the prevailing pattern of élite rule.[11] In practice, the first two categories shade into each other (both being a type of guardian regime), while the performance in office of several military governments (including those of Jamal Abd al-Nasser in Egypt and Ja'far Numeiri in the Sudan) have fallen short of their initial revolutionary promise, and are more correctly designated as reformist rather than revolutionary. In this section, we focus on the non-revolutionary regimes – whether classified as reformist, corrective or caretaker – though much of the discussion is relevant to the revolutionary type of regime also.

Certain observations (which command wide acceptance) can be made about military regimes. First, the military's hierarchical command structure and the habits of discipline and obedience of its members may lead a military government to believe that merely to issue a command is to have it obeyed. Military rulers may also fail to appreciate that sensitive issues – like those of the census and revenue allocation in Nigeria – cannot be depoliticised. A second (and related) point is that the military lack an organised popular base and easy means of communicating with the people. An alliance with the police (who work among the people) may go some way towards repairing this deficiency – it did so in Ghana during the first period of military rule (1966–9), but not in Nigeria under Major-General Ironsi, the head of that country's first military government (January–July 1966).

In the third place, military regimes seek to compensate for their relative isolation and lack of experience in government by gaining the support of groups not too closely identified with the previous regime. The extent to which they do so may, of course, vary from one regime to another. In Ghana, the National Liberation Council (1966–9) courted civil servants, chiefs and members of the legal profession and the universities, as well as leading politicians who had opposed Nkrumah. Ghana's second military regime (1972–8), on the other hand, looked for allies less to the lawyers and other professional and propertied classes than to the ordinary people. In Nigeria, General Ironsi deliberately distanced himself from the old politicians and turned for advice about the North to the Sultan of Sokoto. Lieut-Colonel (later General) Yakabu Gowon, his successor, worked closely with former politicians – especially during the civil war – though most of them had belonged to opposition parties. Brigadier Murtala Mohammed (1975) appointed professional and technical experts rather than politicians to civil commissioner posts at both federal and state levels, and incorporated chiefs within the reformed local government structure.

A fourth observation that can be made about military regimes is that they may acquire civilian trappings in order to increase their legitimacy and reduce the stigma of illegality which attaches to their assumption of power by force. For example, a military government may hold presidential elections and seek to build up a national party linked to (and controlled by) itself, as has occurred in Egypt, Mali, Somalia, Togo and Zaire. This was never attempted in Nigeria, but in Ghana General I. K. Acheampong sought, through the power-sharing device of 'Union government', to perpetuate military rule by establishing it in civilian guise.

Fifthly, however, 'civilianisation' may merely serve to increase the difficulty, which all military governments face, of maintaining organisational cohesion. The danger is that army officers involved in government will become divorced from the army command structure, giving rise to conflict over policies. This occurred in Nigeria in Gowon's later years in office when the Supreme

Military Council deferred the return to civilian rule beyond the scheduled date (1976), while the army command favoured early withdrawal. On another level, internal jealousies may be created if (for example) the head of the military government should be less senior in rank than serving officers, thereby disrupting the army's hierarchical organisation. However, conflict on this score is not inevitable as the case of Mali (where Lieutenant Moussa Traoré assumed power following the 1968 coup) clearly shows; indeed, tension may be more likely to occur when there is an intergenerational gap between senior officers ruling the state and younger, better educated and more radically-minded junior officers serving in the armed forces.

In the sixth place, the military, despite its image of moral integrity and puritanical spirit, may not in fact provide cleaner and more honest government than its civilian predecessor. In Ghana, the later Acheampong years (1975–8) were marked by massive corruption, while in military-ruled Nigeria the name of state governor had, by 1975, become a by-word for corruption. Again, the human rights record of most military regimes is no better (or worse) than the civilian governments which they supplanted; true, the record in Amin's Uganda and Jean-Bedel Bokassa's Central African Republic was appalling, but so it was also in Equatorial Guinea under Macias Nguema, a civilian ruler, while conditions in Sékou Touré's Guinea were not much better.

Finally, even a military regime which had no obvious political motive for intervention may be sucked into politics as the boundaries between the military establishment and its sociopolitical environment become blurred. Thus in Ghana, the NLC (1966–9) became subject to ethnic (as well as personal) divisions, and was accused (probably unfairly) of promoting Ewe political interests. In Nigeria, as we suggested above, the majors who staged the January 1966 coup had political motives, but the army as a whole was not politicised; however, politicisation increased following the coup and led to moves to regionalise the army and eventually to Biafra's attempted secession.

The question of whether a military government is better equipped than a civilian government to play a developmental role is more controversial. We focus on Nigeria. During the first period of military rule in Nigeria (1966–79), sectoral performance was impressive in the building, construction, manufacturing and oil sectors, while the country's infrastructure (including transport and energy) benefited from heavy investment. On the other hand, performance in the agricultural sector was poor and, as the oil boom ended in the late 1970s, the government had to resort to large-scale borrowing. There was evidence of substantial mal-administration and (despite Murtala Mohammed's efforts to check it in 1975) of corruption. Overall, the military record was dis-appointing and was certainly no better than might have been expected of a civilian government, similarly blessed with an oil bonanza. Though, on the political front, the military had created a stable political order since the civil war ended in 1970 and had strengthened the position of the centre in relation to the constitu-ent states of the federation, its legacy to the successor civilian government in 1979 was a sluggish economy, a worrying level of inflation, a serious balance of payments deficit, and mounting problems in the social sphere.

In Ghana, the first military regime (1966–9) had a better politi-cal and economic record than the second regime under General Acheampong (1972–8), partly because its rule was shorter and its aims – essentially to revive the economy and restore constitutional integrity – were more modest. In most respects the Acheampong government proved very disappointing: on the economic front the level of both cocoa and gold production fell and export earnings declined at a time of high world market prices and of in-creasing demand for imported goods; and while agricultural out-put (particularly of rice and maize) did expand (if at the cost of increased social inequality) in the early years, local food pro-duction subsequently dropped sharply. The poor overall per-formance of Ghana's second military regime, as well as the indif-ferent record of the Nigerian military, reinforces the conclusion that military regimes do not have any marked capacity to promote economic development. Other conclusions can be drawn. Because of the restrictions which they place on political party activity and representative institutions, military regimes curtail rather than promote political development. Again, while non-revolutionary military regimes may (like their civilian counterparts) undertake some redistribution of political and economic power among élites, they will maintain the socioeconomic *status quo* and the links (in the economic and defence spheres) with the international capi-talist system. As Ruth First observed, 'the coup as a method of change that changes little has become endemic to Africa's politics'. Empirical evidence certainly suggests that the military in Africa does not possess any exceptional political skills which render it more capable of effecting social change, whether in a progressive or conservative direction, than a civilian government.[12] There is therefore a sense in which Milton's words 'New Presbyter is but old Priest writ large' aptly describe the change from civilian to military rule.

Military withdrawal

In Anglophone Africa, military withdrawal has tended to lead to the resurrection of multipartyism following a handover process not dissimilar to that by which the British colonial administration transferred power to newly-independent governments. In both Ghana in 1968–9 and again in 1979, and in Nigeria in 1978–9, the military government supervised the drawing up of new democratic constitutions, under which strongly contested multiparty elections were held. Following the declaration of the results, the armed forces handed over power to the newly-elected civilian governments. In Francophone Africa, on the other hand, the tendency has been for the incumbent military regimes to form single parties and then hold 'plebiscitary' presidential and parliamentary elections in which the president and national assembly members are returned with overwhelming majorities,[13] thus legitimising their stay in office. A military ruler determined to cling to power may also develop a clientelist political base among civilian leaders and interest groups; this is what President Mobuto Sese Seko has succeeded in doing in Zaire, but what General Acheampong failed to achieve in Ghana.[14]

Of course, the institutionalisation of military rule (or complete military withdrawal) are not the only alternatives open to the military; the latter may withdraw partially and then exert a dominant influence on the civilian government which it has itself put in office. We must ask whether complete military withdrawal, following an extended period of military rule, is desirable or sensible in view of the continuing importance of the military as a major interest group. A related question is whether the prospect of stable civilian government would improve if the military was accommodated in the various organs of government, including the legislature and executive. The predominant response to such questions in Anglophone Africa – alike among politicians, professional groups, the academic community and trade unionists – has been to insist on complete withdrawal. In Francophone Africa, these sort of questions are ignored by military rulers bent on staying in power. Though these rulers may dress their governments in civilian clothing and embellish them with representative institutions, the essential character of their rule remains military and authoritarian.

3. The military in politics in Latin America

Patterns of military intervention in politics in Latin America are best understood against the background of early independence, export-led development, crisis in the 1930s, and the search for renewed growth thereafter, as outlined in Chapters 1–3. Despite improving levels of economic and political development, and steadily increasing professionalisation of the armed forces, there seems to be no tendency for the propensity of the military to intervene to decline over time. Indeed, the contrary appears to be the case. Not only has military intervention and prolonged military rule been a marked feature of politics in Latin America over recent years, but it seems to have been most pronounced in the most highly developed states of the region.

Despite the constant militarisation of politics in the region in the nineteenth century (particularly in the wake of independence as rival armies struggled for control from country to country), it would be misleading to see any major continuity between military intervention in the nineteenth century and today. Recourse to arms on the part of groups contending for power in the decades after independence was a virtually continent-wide phenomenon, and armies were raised and dispersed as the rhythm of conflict rose and fell. But the 'men on horseback' who dominated much of the early politics of states such as Venezuela, Colombia, Bolivia, Peru and Mexico (where the legacy of fighting over independence was most marked) were rarely leaders of a professionalised army clearly set apart from civil society. Rather they were the acknowledged leaders of regional forces (frequently closely associated with one or another set of economic or social interests) who took up arms to challenge other contending groups for power. The dividing line between military and civil callings was blurred to the point of virtual obliteration. As Walter Little argues:

> The military were ill-equipped, ill-disciplined, and largely untrained. Staffed by adventurers and manned by the criminal and the luckless, they were in no sense institutionalised forces. Moreover, civilians were as ready to use force as the military, and just as successful commanders turned to politics so did leading politicians take to the field of battle. In an age when the private army flourished the military–civilian distinction is of uncertain relevance.[15]

Such conflicts and forms of rule had their drawbacks when the primary necessity once order had been achieved was to guarantee it for the future, and establish stable conditions for the development of the export economy. Successive armed raids on the state could only threaten this stability, and the civilian élites associated with the export sectors generally frowned upon military adventures, and sought peaceful compromise rather than the exclusive acquisition of power by force. As export sectors strengthened and new élites established themselves, there was a widespread tendency for the military to be pushed into the background.

Between 1880 and 1930, then, when the export economy was in its heyday, élitist civilian rule rather than military intervention was the commonest pattern. By and large, the civilian élites associated with the dynamic export interests were able to take a share of power and to hold it by consent. Such exceptions as there were reflected either the continuation of conflicts arising out of post-independence territorial settlements, as in Peru after the War of the Pacific (1879–82), or the hold of an apparently unbreakable syndrome of factional conflict, as in Colombia, where a series of bloody confrontations led to violent civil war in the 1890s, or in Venezuela, where the 'peace and prosperity' brought by oil was secured through the dictatorship of Gomez until 1935. The armed forces of the different states were largely domesticated in this period, and played the role of willing allies of 'modernising' élites, acting as they did (most notoriously in Central America) as shock troops to force the peasantry off the land as commercial agriculture advanced.[16] Only rarely did the military themselves seize power on behalf of modernising interests, but where they did (in Uruguay under Latorre and in Brazil at the outset of the Republic in 1889) the beginnings could be discerned of what was to be the twentieth-century tradition of intervention where civilian élites were proving incapable of handling the structural changes dictated by the evolution of the international economy, and the place of Latin America within it.

This largely new role in the twentieth century was made possible by a process most strongly in evidence over the first three decades, the professionalisation of the armed forces of Latin America. This was achieved, once the armed forces had been generally subjected to civilian control, by the hiring of military missions from such sources as Prussia, France, and Britain, and was reinforced (particularly from the 1920s on) by the practice of sending officers abroad for specialised training.[17] This development did not in itself prompt military intervention, but the new standards of professional training and changed patterns of recruitment and promotion created an institution which frequently acquired an identity self-consciously different from that of its civilian masters, and at times resentful of their amateurism and élitism. Early evidence of this new mentality was seen in Brazil in the 1920s, where junior officers mounted successive rebellions through the decade, or in Chile in the same period, where the military intervened in 1925 (albeit briefly) on behalf of reformist civilian currents in the country.

Although the increased visibility of the armed forces reflected changes which had taken place in the military institution, it also reflected a growing air of political crisis in the civilian regimes under which the export economy had flourished. In Brazil, the narrowly-based alliances of regional oligarchies had been unable to respond with anything but repression, which the army was frequently called upon to administer, as new social forces (in part spawned by the booming Brazilian economy) clamoured for a voice. In Chile, significantly, the collapse of the nitrate sector in the wake of the development of synthetic substitutes in Germany had brought about early in that country what was to be a generalised phenomenon within the next decade, the collapse of the export base of the economy. In country after country, the old élites lost control of the political situation after 1930. The result was a prolonged political crisis which invariably brought the armed forces closer to power. It is worth noting that in the one country where the social tensions created by the rapid development of an export-based economy led to revolution and civil war before the crash occurred (Mexico), the consolidation in power of a capable new bourgeoisie led to the marginalisation of the armed forces from power, a situation that remains unchanged today.[18]

The contemporary pattern of military intervention has its roots, then, in the weakness of ruling civilian élites, rather than in factors wholly internal to the military themselves, or in historical traditions. Wherever economically dominant civilian élites have lost the ability to rule by consent the military has intervened, sometimes simply to guarantee the continued hold of those élites on power, but as frequently to force radical changes in the content of policy and in the nature of political authority. This radicalism, however, has generally had a single end, and as a result clear limits. It has invariably been aimed at reorienting national development in order to take account of changed circumstances in the international economy and in national and international politics, while preserving private property, promoting capitalist accumulation, and curbing the independent power of the working-classes. On occasions, this has meant bitter conflict with traditional élites. As regards the strategies adopted towards the urban and rural working-classes, they have generally varied in accordance with the nature of the economic programmes taken up by the military and the social bases cultivated, and have ranged from authoritarian incorporation to the most violent repression and exclusion.

One can easily identify interventions in the wake of the collapse of the export economies which were intended to defend (or restore) traditional élites: Uriburu's coup in Argentina in 1930, or the intervention of the high command in Brazil in the same year before power was reluctantly handed to Vargas may serve as examples. The more common pattern, in 1930 or after conservative options had run their course, was for factions strongly opposed to ruling élites to force their way to power. This was true of Sanchez Cerro in Peru in 1930, of the younger officers who surrounded Vargas in Brazil, of the Argentine officers who seized power in 1943, and gave way to Perón in 1946, and of the 'military socialists' who took over in Bolivia from a civilian élite discredited by a failing economy and the catastrophe of the failed 'Chaco

War' (1932–5) against Paraguay – launched, Malvinas-style, to distract attention from problems at home.[19]

The Bolivian officers, like practically all those mentioned here, drew their inspiration largely from European fascism, interpreting it as anti-imperialist, nationalist, statist and authoritarian, and fundamentally opposed in temper to the liberal democracy they associated with élite rule and foreign influence. They saw in it also a solution to the problem of supplanting failed élites without letting power fall into the hands of dangerous radicals. This was, after all, a period in which the Communist party was influential in Latin America, along with the rival doctrines of socialism and anarcho-syndicalism, and to many observers it seemed that the belligerent and alienated urban masses in particular were threatening to seize power and launch a revolution. Military intervention in the period, therefore, tended to be simultaneously consciously radical and consciously counter-revolutionary, and in this respect some parallels may be drawn with the present.

In the 1930s and 1940s, then, the most characteristic military interventions were nationalist, developmentalist, anti-élite and authoritarian. They generally sought to break with the *laissez-faire* patterns of economic growth experienced in the past and checked by the depression. In addition, they generally moved fairly rapidly away from institutional control of government by the military itself, either through the emergence of a single prominent individual building a personal political base (as with Perón in Argentina), or through the forging of links with reform-minded political parties (as with the military society RADEPA in Bolivia in 1943). Only where the continuing tradition of politics was heavily authoritarian was the 'democratic' content of military intervention likely to be high, as in Venezuela in 1945, where young officers brought AD (*Acción Democrática*, Democratic Action) to power.

In Venezuela, however, the intervention of 1945 came as a response to ten years of military rule in the wake of the death of the dictator Gomez, sometimes mildly reformist but subject to periodic impositions of a highly authoritarian nature. This pattern of conflict and competition for political power within the military has been common, and it means that the military cannot be treated as a united and homogeneous whole. In the case of Venezuela, democratic government was short-lived, brought to an abrupt halt with a counter-coup in 1948.[20] One of the leading figures of that counter-coup (Major Marcos Perez Jimenez) was eventually able to establish himself as a dictator, but a further democratic military movement in 1958 (in association with united civilian élites) led to the successful consolidation of democracy. Since that time, the two leading parties of the period, *Acción Democrática* and COPEI (the Social Christian party) have alternated peacefully in power and avoided military intervention. Elsewhere, competition for power between the military and civilians has gone on alongside competition for power within the military itself. Perón's nine-year period as President of Argentina between 1946 and 1955, during which he was elected and re-elected, saw the armed forces emerge as a strong base of anti-Perónism, but divide into factions urging different solutions to the Perónist menace.[21] Within the civilian–military conflict that has marked Argentina ever since there has been an active struggle for supremacy within the military itself. This has meant that successive military regimes have sponsored very different 'projects', most notoriously between 1966 and 1973, when the successive regimes of Ongania, Levingston and Lanusse attempted authoritarian reconstruction, populist mobilisation, and finally conciliation leading to the return of Perón. Factions have not always been so finely balanced. In El Salvador, for example, where the grip of the armed forces on government has been virtually continuous since the ousting of the dictator Hernandez Martinez in 1944, reformist alternatives (emerging at intervals of fifteen to twenty years) have never survived for more than a matter of months. Military factions pressing for moderate reform have held power briefly in 1944, briefly again in late 1960 and early 1961, and most recently in the junta installed in October 1979 and toppled in January 1980.

It should now be clear that although something of a very general regional pattern can be discerned, the dynamic and form of military intervention have varied quite substantially from country to country. Secondly, episodes of military intervention should not be examined in isolation, but in the context of sequences of political involvement *vis-à-vis* civilian politicians and within the military itself. This does not make generalisation impossible, but it recommends caution, and due regard for the particular circumstances of individual cases of intervention.

Despite some strong general trends which have deservedly captured much scholarly attention, the pattern over the last two decades has also been one of considerable variety. Since 1960 Colombia and Venezuela have established themselves as secure democracies, while Peru has experienced a strongly reformist military regime between 1968 and 1975, and (after an internal coup) a more orthodox conservative administration largely concerned with handing power back to civilians, which it did in 1980. Brazil, meanwhile, a fragile multiparty democracy between 1945 and 1964, experienced a military intervention in that year which led to 21 years of military rule, ending in 1985 when the armed forces finally lost control of the complex electoral system which they had manipulated to maintain themselves in power throughout the period. Similarly lengthy periods of military rule, in highly developed countries with a long and virtually unbroken tradition of civilian rule, commenced in Chile and Uruguay in 1973, ending in Uruguay in 1985 and continuing in Chile today.

Patterns of civil–military relations and the significance of intervention may vary from case to case. But even so there are a number of common characteristics that distinguish recent military regimes from their predecessors and suggest that they represent a new departure in some ways. First of all, it has generally been the armed forces as an institution (through its high command) that has seized control, rather than individual rebel or relatively junior officers. Secondly, they have generally done so not with a view to a speedy return to civilian rule, but with the intention of ruling for the foreseeable future. In Argentina, Peru, Brazil, and Chile, between 1930 and 1964, sixteen military interventions gave rise to periods of rule of just over eight months on average; five interventions since have so far accumulated sixty years of military rule, an average of twelve years for each period.[22] Thirdly, these regimes have generally created a repressive apparatus far more thoroughgoing and sophisticated than commonly organised in the past, seeking to eliminate physically perceived threats to their continuation in power.[23] The use of repression and torture is not new, but its highly institutionalised and public application is, as is the range of targets (embracing political activists, trade unionists, and the radical sons and daughters of urban élites). This is linked to a fourth characteristic, born out of the 'cold war' and the spread of cold war doctrines through United States training programmes: a pervasive concern with national security rather than external defence as the primary focus of military activity.[24] These common characteristics arise from a common syndrome: the establishment of these regimes in response to a process of social mobilisation and polarisation too acute to be resolved by élite co-operation and compromise, and threatening to spill over into radicalism or socialism.

On other dimensions the degree of innovation is as marked, but less uniform. As regards economic policy, for example, the regimes of Chile, Uruguay and Argentina after 1976 embarked upon different but comparable ultra-liberal 'monetarist' policies aimed at eliminating the 'artificiality' of previous industrial development and restoring the authority of the market, while Brazil in particular has continued to promote a model of state-led industrialisation far closer in nature to the Mexican pattern of development.[25] As regards political orientation, the Peruvian regime in the period 1968–75, while authoritarian in nature, was fundamentally reformist rather than reactionary, and sought (though without conspicuous success) to develop a broad social base.

The most successful (and influential) attempt to capture the novelty and the common characteristics of these recent, long-lived regimes was O'Donnell's model of the 'bureaucratic authoritarian' regime, which saw their origins in the crisis of import-substituting industrialisation and stressed their technocratic and anti-popular orientation. Despite the criticisms to which it has been subjected, it remains a stimulating and innovative analysis.[26]

Finally, we might ask whether the current crop of military regimes in Latin America have been at all successful, on their own terms, either in the economic or the political field. On the economic front, they have not generally claimed an advanced degree of understanding. But whether reformist (as in Peru) or reactionary (as in Chile, for example) they have claimed the ability to push through programmes where civilians have lacked the authority (or tenacity) to do so. They have depicted themselves (and at times have been depicted) as unconstrained by partisan political loyalties, able to take a long-term view, and willing to provide the space for technocrats to apply the policies necessary to secure economic progress without bowing to undue political pressure. This perspective is naive, and has generally led to disillusionment. The military have invariably found themselves as deeply committed to specific political options and as deeply embroiled in 'politics' as their civilian counterparts, but generally lacking in the political awareness and skills to manage the situation.

In general, military regimes which have set themselves up to rule for the longer term in recent years in Latin America have adopted economic programmes already formulated before they came to power, or produced programmes in retrospect to justify what they have done. The experience of recent regimes in Argentina, Uruguay and Chile suggests that the appeal of 'monetarism' lies not so much in its economic logic as in its promise to remove economic management from the political arena. Secondly, some of its appeal derives from the attractiveness of an explanation for economic decline and political crisis which blames two of the traditional whipping boys of the military everywhere – civilian politicians and the working-class. Thirdly, the military have a tendency to interpret economic policy (and their role with regard to it) in military rather than in economic terms. They are more swayed by notions of 'mission', 'discipline' and 'sacrifice' than by the logic of economic argument; they see their task as 'seeing through' a necessary but unpopular policy, and are therefore reluctant to abandon it in the face of manifest failure. Fourthly, this latter characteristic combines with the curtailing of debate and democratic control to make changes of course difficult: if opposition to existing policy is defined as treason, and if it is argued that the honour of the armed services is at stake, it is unlikely that policy alternatives will be freely canvassed and developed. Loyalty and respect for hierarchy may make it institutionally difficult to question prevailing orientations from within, while criticism and comment from outside is likely to be dismissed. Fifthly (for similar reasons) the military are likely to make use of power for their own corporate advantage. Spending on defence, military salaries, and the acquisition of fancy hardware are likely to work against any attempts to reduce spending, and to create a privileged group reluctant to abandon power. Finally, the combination of newly-privileged groups reluctant to abandon the political arena, and dogmatic commitment to particular economic policies for reasons which have little to do directly with their economic content, is likely to produce unpredictable results when a consensus is finally reached that those policies have failed. The consequence may be aimless drifting at the mercy of events, or reckless adventure (as in the Malvinas). Once the original 'mission' has failed, military governments are likely to prove more than usually ineffective, lacking in authority, and hard to shift.[27]

Equally hard lessons have been learned in Latin America with regard to the ability of the military to bring about political change. It is clear that military intervention over a lengthy period has the effect of freezing the political situation, rather than allowing for a renewal of political leadership among civilians. It is not coincidental, in this regard, that the military tend to be replaced, once they eventually withdraw from power, by the very political forces (and often the very individuals) they initially removed. This was the case in Peru in 1980 with the return of Belaunde, in Bolivia in 1982 with the return of Siles Zuazo (president in the 1950s), in Brazil in 1985, with the election of Tancredo Neves (a former prime minister from the Goulart period), and in Uruguay, where Sanguinetti represents the anti-military wing of the old *Colorado* party. Not only do the military fail to 'renew' civilian politics, they set up a dynamic which works to block their own early exit from power. First, they politicise the armed forces themselves, so that leading officers come to consider themselves natural contenders for power; secondly, they create particular bodies (primarily the expanded intelligence services or political police) which gain sufficient autonomy to work for (and prolong) military incumbency; and thirdly (as a result of the material advantages of power on the one hand, and the fear of reprisals for crimes committed while in office on the other), they breed powerful practical reasons for clinging to power for its own sake. In the circumstances, it is not surprising that military handover to civilian rule has generally been marked by a profound crisis made up of three separate strands. The first is a desperate economic crisis, made worse by policy drift and the protracted process of withdrawal; the second is a crisis of political succession, brought about by the persecution of civilian politicians, the suppression of popular alternatives, and the attempt to secure a degree of continuing influence; and the third is a crisis of civil–military relations, arising out of the need to investigate crime and corruption within the military institution itself in the face of hostility to such investigation.

The recent experience of military intervention in Latin America is of major significance for two reasons. It has provided a number of cases of long-term military rule in which the military have enjoyed considerable autonomy from civilian control, and thus provided a test of the ability of the military to rule in circumstances of their own making. And it suggests (because for the most part these regimes have governed the socially and economically most advanced countries of the region) that it would be optimistic to assume that as development continues the prospects for military intervention recede. On the first score, the lesson is that the negative features of military rule are not avoidable extras, but reflections of the intrinsic nature of the military institution. On the second, it is that there is no simple correlation between level of socioeconomic development and propensity for military intervention.

4. The military in politics in the Middle East

In the contemporary politics of the Middle East the military has played a decisive political role. It was officers who brought down the monarchies of Iraq (1958), Egypt (1952) and Libya (1969) and ushered in an era of radical republicanism. In Syria, from independence onward, there have been successive coups, and the main arbiter of political change has been factions within the officer corps. Although there have been degrees of civilianisation in Iraq and Egypt, the officers have been incorporated in various ways in the highest institutions of state. The biggest domestic threat to the Jordanian and Moroccan monarchies has come from attempted military interventions. Only Tunisia, Lebanon, Saudi Arabia and the small Gulf states have remained immune from a politicised military. All of these have either very weak military establishments (like Lebanon), or a pattern of recruitment favourable to the ruling families. In Saudi Arabia, the army is an amalgam of tribal recruits from the interior, historically loyal to the ruling Saud family, and a regular army with a number of princes in command positions. In Jordan, recruitment has been from bedouin tribes traditionally loyal to the king.

The 1950s and 1960s were the decades of intervention. Although the military has remained politically important in the 1970s, in contrast to this earlier period the officer corps has been relatively quiescent. The intensity of military involvement in the affairs of state has historical precedent. In the Arab and Ottoman Empires, imperial rulers and local governors frequently became the prisoners of the local garrisons. Mamluk slave armies controlled most of the Fertile Crescent between the thirteenth and fifteenth centuries. It was the decomposition of the Janisaries (an Ottoman force) and their resultant control over many regions of the Empire that heralded Ottoman decline. Both Mamluk and Janissaries were very different from the contemporary military: they were purposely recruited from slave outsiders in order that they would remain aloof from the wider society and wholly loyal to the Sultan. Only in the late nineteenth century did a formally-organised army, paid for out of state revenue, come into existence. The collapse of the Empire during the First World War brought with it the establishment of new armies in the successor states of Iraq, Syria, Lebanon and Jordan. These new Fertile Crescent armies were part and parcel of a new state apparatus which had the task of forging control over societies which had become increasingly autonomous from any central control during the preceding century.

Although there has been a history of military involvement in the Middle East, it was only after independence in the Fertile Crescent (Iraq, 1932; Syria, Lebanon and Jordan, 1946), the establishment of a unified Iran in 1925 and a fully independent Egypt after the Second World War that professional armies independent of external control with a trained officer corps came into existence. It was not long after independence that the Arab officers moved into the political arena. The Iraqi army staged a coup in 1936, four years after independence, and three years after Syria became independent there were three coups within one year. One common feature of these first coups was that the officers (with some justice) viewed the civilian government as corrupt and incapable of handling the affairs of state. The Bakr Sidqi coup of 1936 came after the Iraqi army had been called in to quell Kurdish and Assyrian rebellions in northern Iraq and a widespread tribal uprising in the south brought about by the machinations of civilian politicans in Baghdad. Although the first Syrian coup involved the personal ambitions of various officers, reflected divisions over a pro-Iraq or pro-Saudi foreign policy and was encouraged by the CIA to contain domestic unrest, of greater importance was the defeat of the Syrian army in the 1948 war with Israel and the disgust over the chicanery involved in the provision of supplies to the front line. The Free Officers who removed the Egyptian monarchy in 1952 were also influenced by the 1948 defeat and associated governmental scandals. Only the Jordanian army acquitted itself well in 1948, and it remained aloof from politics.

A second type of intervention that has been common in the Middle East has been the reformist coup organised by politicised officer corps, most marked in Iraq and Syria in the 1960s. There, officers intervened as members (or supporters) of political parties and movements. Various shades of nationalist groupings recruited from the officers, or encouraged party members to enter the military academy. Such a pattern was set early in Syria when Akram Hourani encouraged young political supporters to join the officer corps. When his Arab Socialist party united with the Ba'th party, even though the latter endorsed civilian government the Ba'th found itself inextricably linked to a group of political officers. As the army became more and more the pivot of Syrian politics during the 1960s, change of government through coup became the regularised mechanism of succession as officers of differing socialist and nationalist orientations led their tanks on the presidential palace. The only way in which civilians could wield influence was through allies in the officer corps, but rather than controlling their supporters and sympathisers in the army, the party politicians became their clients. A very similar pattern of military involvement emerged in Iraq during the 1960s. The Libyan coup of 1969 was led by Muamar al-Qaddafi who purposely joined the army with the aim of organising a group of 'free officers' on the Egyptian model to overthrow the monarchy.

One result of the politicised military was the greater weight given to ideological issues. Even where the motivation for a coup was one of political ambition, officers felt it necessary to dress their intervention with a heavy programmatic element rather than the usual clichéd attack on corrupt and venal politicians. The model was set by Egypt in 1952, although it was to take a decade for that regime to move from pragmatism to an ideological programme.

Interventions in the Middle East have followed different patterns. With two exceptions they have been led by relatively junior officers, and in many cases as a result of a crisis (or crises) which civilian regimes have been unable to manage. Personal ambition has certainly played a part, and ideology has also impelled officers to intervene. The 1969 coup in Libya resulted from a fusion of these two latter factors.

The two exceptions to the general pattern of coups by junior officers have been Iran and Sudan. In the case of the former a military government under the commander of the Imperial Guard was appointed by the Shah desperate to control the massive civilian protests which were bringing desertions from the army and air force and resulting in the sapping of the military government's resolve. In Sudan, the army high command took over to resolve intra-élite conflict in 1958 and again in 1984 to forestall a more radical movement against a decadent regime which had brought the country to bankruptcy.

Military regimes

It is not possible to describe all the governments established by military interventions as military regimes. In many cases, the resultant governments were not wholly military. Officers have co-opted civilians, the proportions of officers have frequently been low, civil institutions have been established and coup leaders like Nasser and Qadaffi have created high degrees of personal power. Rarely has the high command ruled as a junta. In Iraq and Syria, where the army has been persistently interventionist, only under Syria's Shishakli (1949–54)[28] and Iraq's Qasim (1958–63)[29] has the military been the major instrument of rule. In Iraq and Syria regimes have (at different times) been led by military 'strong men', but in Syria between 1963 and 1970 there was a symbiotic relationship between the Ba'th party and the army, as there was in Iraq after 1968. Even after 1970 when the civilian wing of the Syrian Ba'th was eclipsed, it was a faction within the military which came to power and their ties were based on common kinship and sectarian group membership as much as military position. It is more accurate to describe Syria as being ruled by the clan of the president through special military forces than as a military regime.

Egypt comes the closest to a military regime in the period between 1952 and 1970.[30] The Free Officers established the new

Egyptian Republic although over time the military component has varied. Nevertheless, a very high proportion of top political positions in central and local government were held by officers and former officers. Between 1952 and 1969 33 per cent of political leaders were officers. Members of the Revolutionary Command Council held the key ministries after 1953 and in the 1960s as vice-presidents or deputy prime ministers supervised blocs of subordinate ministries. At the upper echelons of the Nasser regime, the Presidential Council (the main advisory body to Nasser), military representation reached 83 per cent. To over-emphasise military representation, however, is to distort the supremacy of Nasser. Officers who did hold key positions were in them at the President's behest. After the 1969 coup in Libya (as in Egypt) the military has remained exceptionally privileged but power is concentrated in the president who relies on revolutionary committees and the popular militia as a counterweight to the army.

Given the range of military and quasi-military regimes in the Middle East it is not easy to identify any particular pattern of military rule. It is possible, however, to indicate some linkage between the nature of the coup organisers and certain ensuing political processes. Where the traditional regime of landlords increasingly came to rely on a strong army but where junior and middle ranking officers came from different social strata or from deprived sects distinct from the ruling group, military rule has been reformist. This has been the case in Iraq (1958), Egypt (1952), Syria (1963) and Libya (1969). Where the military has intervened in the context of domestic disturbance, military government alone (or in conjunction with civilians) has strengthened the power of the centre. This has taken place in Iraq (1936) and Syria (1949).

The case of Syria is instructive since there have been military regimes of both patterns, and it is illustrative of the way in which class and sectarianism have influenced military rule. French colonial rule created distinct administrative districts based on Syria's heterogeneous, geographically compact sects, enhancing the power of local tribal and religious leaders. When Syria became independent in 1946, it was left to the army to quell a messianic uprising in the poor Alawite mountains and a Druze revolt led by the tribal leadership in the south. The centrality of the army as a national and nationalist institution was badly tarnished by its defeat in the 1948 war although the three coups of 1949 (led respectively by Colonels Zaim, Hinnawi and Shishakli) restored it to the centre of politics. These military-dominated governments had no distinctive economic policies, but they did expand the power of the state: sectarian representation was abolished, a new civil law code was introduced and the role of religious leaders reduced. Under Shishakli, sectarian and tribal privileges vested in the tribal and religious leaders were abolished and the basis of a new statewide education system was founded.[31] One effect of the strengthened centre was that although the autonomies of the peripheral regions were undermined, the power of the landlords was enhanced and a nascent peasant movement was crushed.

A second type of military rule emerged in the 1960s.[32] It was partly the result of a changing pattern of recruitment into the army and resulted in a more rural and small town background representation in the officer corps and a clear distinction between it and the grand landowning families controlling parliament. By the early 1960s there was also a disproportionate representation of the Druze, Alawite and Ismaili minority sects in the army because they were based in the rural areas and a military career provided a channel of social mobility. Between 1963 and 1970, officers largely from the minorities thus ruled in harness with various factions of the civilian Ba'th party and (under the slogans of popular democracy and scientific socialism) introduced measures which favoured the rural hinterland of the big towns. In the rural areas, land was distributed to the peasantry and some state farms were established. Foreign trade, banking and commerce, almost wholly located in the big towns, were nationalised. The proportion of Sunni Muslims (the overwhelming majority) represented in cabinets declined from 82–94 per cent between 1942 and 1961 to just above 70 per cent in the 1962–70 period.[35] Of greater importance (certainly in the eyes of many Syrians) was the increasing number of Alawites in the officer corps, and particularly their tenure of key command positions. This has remained the same in the 1970s and 1980s and despite the conciliatory economic liberalism of Hafiz al-Asad's post-1970 policies the urban commercial classes (consisting largely of Sunni Muslims) have opposed the regime as narrow, sectarian and clannish. Such sectarian complications have been less apparent in Iraq, Libya and Egypt, although the bulk of the officers who took power were socially distinct from the ruling families, landlords and tribal chieftains.

Other than the measures aimed at greater equity, the performance of the military in economic development has not been markedly successful, save where oil has allowed governments to make mistakes without any significant economic penalty – as has been the case in Libya and Iraq. Even the reformist regimes which have emphasised a more equal distribution of wealth have tended to benefit the middle and wealthy peasantry and the urban middle-classes to the disadvantage of the big landlords and the poor and landless peasantry. What has been common to the reformist military regimes has been the growth of the state through nationalisation and bureaucratic employment. For the Egyptian Free Officers it has been argued that such growth has been a function of the need to create a constituency for their illegitimate accession to power. Whether there was such a conscious motivation behind the policies pursued, it is certainly a pattern common to Iraq after 1958 and Syria in the 1960s. It is also likely that other factors are at work. Even though there was no evident decrease in the military component of the Syrian regime after 1970, government encouraged the private sector, and while there was a significant decline in the military component of Egyptian government during the Sadat era there was also a strong shift to encourage private business. Military government or not, both the Syrian and Egyptian governments (both lacking an oil export economy) moved in the same economic direction.

Military withdrawal

Military withdrawal from politics is again not so distinct a phenomenon in the Middle East since military and quasi-military regimes have tended to be linked to political parties, or to have a more or less indirect connection to sectarian groups, as we have indicated for Syria. In Egypt, there has been a 'demilitarisation' of cabinets and the establishment of a controlled multiparty system but it has been exceedingly gradual extending over a twenty-year period. Nasser established a state party system and Sadat extended it, albeit within strict limits. Yet Egyptian leaders since 1952 have been military men: Nasser organised the Free Officers, Sadat was a member and Husni Mubarak (who succeeded him) was a former career air force officer. In Iraq and Syria, the military is central to politics, but cannot be said to rule directly. The relationship between party and army (and between particular clans in both army and regime) is more important than the officer corps *per se*. In the case of Syria, since 1970 the core military support for the regime lies with specially-organised forces loyal to the president outside of the regular army. One might say that the army has withdrawn from politics but the political leadership has created its own military arm to secure the regime. Iraq has not gone to such extremes, but since the accession of Saddam Husayn as president the party has atrophied, the army has increasingly been involved in a full-scale war with Iran and the president presents himself as the hero, ideologue and saviour of the nation. In fact, both Presidents al-Asad and al-Husayn, despite some degree of domestic popularity, use an efficient and ruthless set of security networks within party, army and Interior Ministry based on a handful of relatives and individuals wholly dependent on them for their positions. Military appointments and positions are vetted and (as a result) top military commanders do not have an independent power base even in the army.

The only sense in which there has been a military withdrawal from politics in Iraq and Syria is that power has accumulated to the presidents who (through the control of appointments in army, party and government) have become more pivotal in policy formation than factions within the officer corps. Despite the great power of the Iraqi president, the party does have more of a role than in Syria. Saddam Husayn (unlike Hafiz al-Asad) was a civilian and his path to power was through the party. Even though military commanders sit on party policy committees there is little reason to think that they have any more weight in policy formulation than top civilian party members. The extent of civilianisation in post-coup politics in the Middle East is a consequence of increased presidential autonomy from the officer corps, and the imperative to incorporate technocrats and create a social base of support. This kind of civilianisation has, however, not generally decreased the role of the security services, most of which tend to be run by former officers or presidential relatives.

5. Conclusion

In all three regions, the military has extensively intervened in politics to overthrow civilian regimes, although there are many states which have remained free from the disease. In the introduction we pointed out the inadequacy of general explanations of military intervention, and it is clear from the specific cases that both the causes of intervention (and the reasons for the survival) of civilian regimes are multiple. There is no correlation between level of development and intervention. Indeed, Latin America (the most highly developed of the three regions) has produced the longer-lasting military regimes. Nor is there necessarily any clear political programme which military regimes have followed. It might be expected that government by officers would be conservative, and it has frequently been reactionary and highly repressive. Yet many Middle Eastern governments, which have been formed from or by coup-makers, have been radical. In Egypt, Syria, Libya and Iraq the officers removed the kings and landlords, established republics, redistributed land and nationalised industry and commerce. From Latin America, only Peru has produced a reformist military, and from Africa, Ethiopia has produced a *soi-disant* Communist regime. Notwithstanding the radical tendencies of the junior officers in some Middle Eastern states, there have been many coups which have left the structure of society unaltered but established the officer corps as the pivot of politics and introduced an inflammatory spiral of coup after coup. Despite the radical pretensions of certain African regimes, such as those of Burkina Faso and Ghana under Jerry Rawlings, the maintenance of a social *status quo* is much more an African pattern.

If there is any broadly similar framework for interventions in the three regions, it is the inability of civilian regimes to manage political problems or social and economic crises. The different political crises resulting from the collapse of the export economies brought the Latin American military to the centre of politics, suppressing the social discontent expressed by the working-class or acting as the mediator between the working-class and the industrialists. In the Middle East and a number of African states, tribal, ethnic and sectarian conflict has influenced intervention and had an impact on the nature of military rule. Nigeria and

Syria are perhaps the two most notable examples of a military reflecting broader societal divisions, while the Ugandan and Iraqi militaries are among those which have also rested to some extent on particular tribal or religious communities.

There is little evidence for the argument that the military provides the order to spur economic development. The extent to which the economy performs well would seem to be a function of non-military factors. Nor is it necessarily the case that the military can even produce order: the 1966 intervention in Nigeria led to civil war. In Latin America any 'order' that has been established has been at very high human cost.

Despite the extensive involvement of the military in politics, and their obvious ability to use force against opposition, in all three regions there have been pressures to civilianise in one form or another. At times the pressures have come from civilian political groupings and at times from the military itself. In many cases, the military constructs civilian front organisations or staffs cabinets with apolitical technocrats. Even when the military retires from politics, it remains a force behind the scenes, and at minimum a powerful pressure group whose interests and views must be taken into account.

5

Revolution

1. Introduction

Revolutions are momentous events, involving deep and fundamental social, economic and political change. Because so much is
at stake, they are usually violent and bloody affairs. The analysis
of revolution is also contentious. Some of the revolutions we
consider here would not be considered revolutionary by many
who participated on the revolutionary side in the overthrow of
the *ancien régime*. This is certainly the case for the Ethiopian and
Iranian revolutions, in which groups with very different visions of
the future combined and then slaughtered each other. Because
revolutions are so contestable and have a strong ideological
component to them, we introduce our chapter on Third World
revolution by raising some broader considerations of the topic.

Much of contemporary thinking about revolution is drawn
from the historical experiences of the 'great' revolutions of
France, Russia and China and the specificity of these revolutions
is frequently incorporated into general conceptions of what
constitutes a revolution, and what differentiates revolutions from
other kinds of change. Such historically-based criteria can lead to
a certain rigidity in the analysis of revolutions, even though some
Third World societies have borne a certain resemblance to the
social and economic context from which the 'great' revolutions
have sprung: the emergence of capitalist relations of production,
limited industrialisation, a small working-class, a population
heavily engaged in agriculture and large-scale inequalities.

Analysis of revolution has been undertaken not solely in the
light of past revolutions, but also in terms of a continuing ideological tradition of revolutionary theorists and practitioners. The

theory and practice of revolution is so closely entwined because the theorists and practitioners have been one and the same. Marx, Lenin, Trotsky and Mao Tse Tung immediately spring to mind; not only did they write about revolution, they struggled to bring it about. Their intellectual and political roles and their involvements in and accounts of revolution have created a chain linking Marx's nineteenth-century class analysis to twentieth-century revolutions. Indeed, individuals like Amilcar Cabral, Franz Fanon, Che Guevara and Regis Debray (who have been revered as authentic writers on Third World revolution) have also been involved in actual revolutions. And yet all of the movements with which they have been associated were not based on Marx's revolutionary proletariat but peasant guerrilla movements, and although this revolutionary tradition of people's war was popularised by Mao Tse Tung none of these writers was Maoist. Although the chain linking revolutionaries is not a clear-cut one, because it originated with Marx the authenticity of a revolution is usually assessed by the extent to which class elements are involved in the revolutionary process and – the extent to which a revolutionary regime implements socialism.

The nature of the link between the revolutionary process and the regime which emerges from it draws attention to the utility of the distinction between revolution from above and revolution from below. Theda Skocpol conceives revolution from below as an inherent part of 'social revolution'; for her revolutions are 'rapid, basic transformations of a society's state and class structures; and they are accompanied and in part carried through by class-based revolts from below'.[1] In our examination of the experience of revolution in the Third World we consider how particular paths to revolution influence the outcome.

We have also taken into account the significance of external factors. Third World revolutions have been accompanied by high levels of external intervention, both in support of and in opposition to revolutionary movements. Since the Second World War, the United States has, at various times, advocated reforms by Third World regimes to head off revolution, condoned savage repression and directly intervened in the domestic politics of states undergoing upheaval. The Soviet Union and China have offered assistance to movements and helped consolidate regimes which appear to them as revolutionary, even though such assistance has often been linked to a strategic interest.

2. Revolutionary regimes in Africa

Of the many possible candidates for the designation 'revolutionary regime', very few states qualify. None of what Rosberg and Callaghy described as the 'first wave' of socialist states (those which became independent in or about 1960)[2] was revolutionary in the sense in which we have defined revolution at the outset of this chapter. Take Guinea and Tanzania. Sékou Touré ruled Guinea tyrannically for 26 years (1958–84), but never converted it into a fully-fledged socialist state;[3] indeed, in the final years of his rule, the socialist option was in practice de-emphasised as the country was opened up to the West and foreign mining companies were allowed to play a dominant role in its economy. In Tanzania's case, the socialism which had emerged as a result of the Arusha Declaration of January 1967 was of a non-doctrinaire, pragmatic kind; it entailed interesting political and socioeconomic experimentation but not social transformation. This is not surprising: Tanzania is not, and has never claimed to be a Marxist–Leninist state, but belongs to that category of states which (like Algeria under Ahmed Ben Bella, Egypt under Nasser, and Ghana under Nkrumah) can be more aptly described as 'populist socialist'.

We had to wait until the 1970s before regimes emerged in Africa which can, with any confidence, be described as revolutionary in intent. Of the 'second wave' of socialist states, some – notably the ex-Portuguese ruled states of Angola, Mozambique and Guinea-Bissau – emerged in each case *from below* following a protracted liberation struggle under a leadership guided by a Marxist–Leninist ideology, while in others – above all in Ethiopia and to an extent in Somalia – 'revolutions' were imposed *from above* by military regimes. It needs to be stressed that the successful waging of a liberation struggle does not in itself guarantee that the consequent regime will necessarily be revolutionary. The ideological commitment of the national leadership is important, though Amilcar Cabral of Guinea-Bissau put ideology into perspective when he stated that

National liberation, the struggle against colonialism, the

construction of peace, progress and independence are hollow
words devoid of any significance unless they can be translated
into a real improvement of living conditions.[4]

The historical experience of the peasantry (and the nature of its
links with the leadership) may count for more. The context in
which power is transferred, and the determination of the leadership to take firm control of the state apparatus, may also be
important in shaping the kind of policies which are subsequently
pursued. In Rhodesia – Zimbabwe – the liberation struggle was
followed by a general election and independence was achieved
(in 1980) as a result of a negotiated settlement; this may have
served to reduce the revolutionary zeal of Robert Mugabe's
government.[5] Certainly the record to date suggests a programme
of moderate reform attuned to the reality of Zimbabwe's geo-
political situation rather than a fundamental restructuring of the
economy and a transformation of the social relations of production.
This may change but for the present (as Mr Mugabe admitted on
the eve of the ruling party's second congress in 1984) 'there are
very few people of Marxist–Leninist orientation even in the
leadership'.[6] Zimbabwe is therefore excluded from consideration.
Our case studies are limited to Mozambique and Angola (as
representative of revolutionary regimes which emerged from
below), and Ethiopia (as representative of a revolution imposed
from above).

Mozambique[7]

After achieving independence on 25 June 1975, the political
leaders of Mozambique had to convert FRELIMO, the nationalist
movement which had spearheaded the struggle against Portuguese
colonialism, into a political party capable of establishing a new
political and socioeconomic order; at its third congress in February
1977, FRELIMO was formally transformed from a front into a
vanguard party. The leadership had also to extend the high level
of political consciousness achieved in the liberated areas to the
rest of the country, and in 1975 established *grupos dinamizadores*
(dynamising groups) for this purpose. These groups afforded
FRELIMO a means to spread its message but they achieved only

limited success and, lacking management and other technical skills, they also failed to step up production.

The constraints within which the government had to operate were formidable. The predominantly agricultural economy was in a parlous condition, having been crippled by the long years of war and hit by rising oil prices. Economically, the country remained intensely dependent on the regional sub-system (centring on South Africa) which it supplied with electricity and labour. The administrative structure was weak and the exodus of white managers, technicians, shopkeepers and traders in 1975–6 meant that trained manpower (which was desperately short at all levels) was not available to sustain the extensive measures of nationalisation that were undertaken, to revive flagging industrial output, and to underpin bold experiments in the state farming sector. The transportation, marketing and distribution systems were in a state of collapse. A National Planning Commission was established with East European help at the end of 1977, but the system was overcentralised and compartmentalised and led to the setting of unrealistic targets.

At its congress in 1977, FRELIMO decided that agriculture should become 'the base and industry the dynamizing factor for development'. However, in practical terms little was achieved and three years later production in all sectors still fell below pre-independence levels. Though sugar had once again become the major export crop, food had still to be imported. Imports generally had risen sharply, and the result was a growing foreign exchange crisis. Distribution problems, and the influx of peasants to the urban areas, led to food shortages and food rationing in the towns; speculation and black marketeering grew alarmingly; and unemployment increased rapidly as the South African mines reduced their recruitment of Mozambican workers. The difficulties facing the government were made worse by a prolonged drought in parts of central Mozambique and by acts of sabotage perpetrated by opposition groups, notably the Mozambique Resistance Movement (subsequently designated the Mozambique National Resistance, MNR), which was strongly backed by South Africa. The government had therefore to spend more on defence and security than the country could afford; this fact, and substantial expenditure in the spheres of health and education (in which the record was impressive) meant that the level of state consumption was high. Beset with mounting problems, President Samora Machel's government introduced in 1980 a series of domestic reform measures which made farm and factory managers responsible for looking after workers' interests, authorised the sale of state shops to private traders, invited Western business interests to invest in Mozambique, and gave the army (which had earlier been converted from a guerrilla army into a regular army with ranks, insignia and medals) a more conventional military role than previously. In the external sphere, the president put pressure on the Patriotic Front (which was directing the Rhodesian liberation struggle) to accept the Lancaster House agreement negotiated with the British government and thus bring to an end a war that was very damaging to the Mozambican economy.

Sadly, on the home front the result was the abuse of power rather than increased economic efficiency. Steps had therefore to be taken to counteract the bureaucratisation and overcentralisation of the party and state structures. Managers were allowed to continue to run the factories, but were required to consult their workforce. Workers' committees were revived, made popularly elective, and given a major say in formulating the 1982 state plan. Ministries were reorganised, state firms were given a shakeup, and the army (though allowed to retain its new command structure) was made to renew its links with the people and help again in producing food. As a result of decisions taken at the fourth FRELIMO Congress in April 1983, the emphasis was shifted away from the big state farms (which had a poor production record) and in favour of private peasant production – peasants, for example, were paid higher prices for their produce. To help overcome the distribution problems, private trading was still permitted, though made subject to more stringent controls; the inefficient people's shops were abolished and consumer cooperatives were encouraged to handle the sale of food in urban areas.

Steps were taken to reorganise and revitalise FRELIMO so that it could effectively represent again the interests of the workers and peasants, and assert control over the state apparatus which, in the hands of the technocratic élite, was felt to be endangering the revolution. At the fourth party Congress in 1983 the central committee was more than doubled in size (from 54 to 128), and a majority of its members are now workers and peasants not directly linked to the central state apparatus. However, FRELIMO became subject to internal division, thereby adding to the existing problems of winning popular support; the task of asserting military control over the whole country was a daunting one. Mozambique's economy was critically weak, and many of her people were starving. It was in these circumstances that in March 1984 Mozambique signed a non-aggression pact with South Africa – the Nkomati Accord – on terms dictated by the white-ruled Republic: the South African government undertook to withdraw its support from the MNR and the Mozambican government to stop backing the African National Congress (ANC), the leading South African nationalist movement; the two governments also agreed to promote closer economic relations between their two countries. South Africa has cynically flouted this agreement and has continued to provide enormous quantities of supplies to the MNR, both directly and (according to Mozambican government sources) via neighbouring Malawi and Swaziland. The result has been to create a critical military situation in Mozambique, to play havoc with the Mozambican economy and to cause massive social dislocation as peasants, caught up in the fighting, have been forced to abandon their homes. Given this record of continuing hostility towards Mozambique, it is understandable that most Mozambicans are not convinced by South Africa's plea of innocence over the death (in October 1986) of Samora Machel in a plane crash just inside the South African border. The new president, Joaquim Chissano, is committed to continuing his predecessor's policies. Close relations with Zimbabwe have been retained and more Zimbabwean soldiers have been sent to Mozambique, though those already there are reported to be disenchanted with the poor performance of the 30 000-strong Mozambican army.[8] A contingent of troops from Tanzania has also joined the struggle against the MNR.

Angola[9]

The Angolan case study shows that there are differences between revolutionary regimes, even when they originate in the same way: Angola, like Mozambique, achieved independence from Portugal in the mid-1970s following a prolonged liberation struggle. We take the similarities first and then the differences, though neither is a discrete category.

Like Mozambique, Angola entered independence under a government committed to Marxist–Leninist principles; the ideology was, however, somewhat eclectic, and was interpreted pragmatically to fit the Angolan context. The ruling *Movimento Popular de Libertação de Angola* (MPLA) announced in December 1977 that the movement would be transformed into a party; FRELIMO had already made this change, though for different reasons. In Angola, the object was to rid the MPLA of President Agostino Neto's opponents rather than (as in Mozambique) to institute orthodox Marxism–Leninism. Thereafter, power became increasingly centralised in the hands of the president (José Eduardo dos Santos following Dr Neto's death in September 1979) and the prospects of establishing 'people's power' through neighbourhood committees and workers' discussion groups receded. By 1980, however, the MPLA could afford to relax its centralised control and created predominantly elected bodies dominated by workers and peasants; these were a 223-member national assembly and assemblies in each of the provinces.

The Angolan regime, again like that of Mozambique, inherited a shattered economy and a poor communications network, and was desperately short of skilled manpower – there was a wholesale exodus of Portuguese citizens in 1975, while indigenous trained personnel were very scarce (the government launched an ambitious educational programme). Sweeping nationalisation measures were similarly introduced, bringing some 80 per cent of Angola's enterprises under the state, thereby reinforcing the need for foreign technical assistance and equipment to run them.

But there were differences from Mozambique also. One of these stemmed from the fact that three nationalist movements had fought for independence. This basic 'communal tripolarity', as John Marcum has called it, had persisted throughout the liberation struggle and had been reflected in the 1975 constitutional arrangements that paved the way to independence. A government of national unity had been established, but quickly collapsed. The power struggle had been internationalised, the decisive factor proving to be the massive Soviet and Cuban intervention on the side of the MPLA, which was strongly entrenched in the major urban centres. However, the southern-based *União*

Nacional para a Independência Total de Angola (UNITA), led by Dr Jonas Savimbi, never relented in its bitter opposition to the ruling MPLA, and civil war has plagued central and southern Angola throughout the post-independence period. (In recent years, too, the Mozambican regime has faced a virtual civil war situation as a result of the increased activities of the MNR.) UNITA is backed by South Africa, whose troops have made innumerable incursions across the Angolan border, allegedly in pursuit of guerrillas belonging to the South West Africa People's Organisation (SWAPO), and by the United States which (early in 1986) undertook publicly to provide it with military aid (sophisticated Stinger anti-aircraft missiles were reported to have been supplied soon afterwards). Only when a Namibian settlement has been achieved is the government likely to reduce the present high and costly level of Cuban and Soviet military aid, and to be able to cut its spending on armaments.

Heavy defence expenditure places a heavy burden on the economy and, as in the many other African states where it occurs, reinforces external dependency.[10] The economy is in a mess, with continuing difficulties in production, marketing and distribution, despite the fact that Angola's revolutionary rulers (unlike those of Mozambique) sit astride a potentially very rich country, with vast mineral deposits and fertile land and a relatively low population (under a tenth of that of Nigeria but inhabiting a larger geographical area). This potential is far from being realised. Agricultural output is low: cash-crop production has not reached the levels achieved before independence, when Angola had a thriving commercial agricultural sector and was the world's fourth largest producer of coffee. UNITA guerrilla attacks in the Central Highlands region – the country's maize-producing and cattle-rearing area – are part of the reason why the government has failed to achieve self-sufficiency in food production, resulting in substantial food imports; these attacks also seriously disrupt the country's transport and distribution system. Poor distribution results periodically in acute food shortages in Luanda, the capital, and other urban centres. There is also widespread absenteeism and low productivity in industry.

Angola's revolutionary regime inherited important extractive industries and this, too, sets her apart from poorly-endowed Mozambique; in other respects, however, she has (like Mozambique) a weak industrial base. The regime's policy has been to tolerate foreign-owned enterprises so long as Angolan interests are respected. In the vital mining sector, the government has re-negotiated contracts with America's Gulf Oil Corporation to work the extensive oilfields in the Cabinda enclave (oil provides over 60 per cent of Angola's foreign exchange) and with Diamang (the Angolan Diamond Company) to mine the country's diamonds. Though the state has acquired majority shareholding in both these undertakings, effective control (including day-to-day operations) remains with the foreign companies. If we add that Angola's trade is still overwhelmingly with the West, we can underline a further point of importance which emerges from the Angolan case study, namely that a revolutionary regime, no less than a capitalist-oriented one, can exercise some autonomy and pursue policies which are antithetical to the interests of its foreign backers – in this case, the Soviet Union and her allies. Moreover, the Angolan government (despite its agreement with Gulf Oil) has continued to espouse (and substantially to base its internal policies on) Marxist–Leninist doctrine. It has also resisted American pressure to order the withdrawal of Soviet and Cuban military personnel; but, equally, it has not allowed the Soviet Union to establish a military base in Angola. Pressure from South Africa, Angola's near neighbour, has been harder to withstand and under the Lusaka Agreement of February 1984, Angola had to undertake not to harbour SWAPO guerrillas fighting to free Namibia in return for a pledge that South Africa would withdraw all her troops from Angolan territory. A joint monitoring commission was set up to supervise the implementation of this agreement, which has been flouted by South Africa.

Ethiopia[11]

The military did not so much instigate the revolution in Ethiopia as act against the background of student and trade union protests. Possibly, it turned to socialism (first moderate and then revolutionary) for pragmatic as well as ideological reasons: socialism offered it a way both of stemming urban protest and of meeting peasant demands for land reform, and thus of putting maximum distance between itself and the old discredited order.[12] Following its direct assumption of power in September 1974, the military (ruling through a co-ordinating committee or 'Derg') imposed tight control – censorship was reintroduced, strikes were banned and trade union leaders arrested, the university was closed, and a literacy campaign (*zemacha*), designed also to mobilise peasant support for the revolution, was launched in the rural areas. In 1975 the Derg extended state control of the economy by national-ising the banks, and insurance, industrial and commercial com-panies. It also nationalised urban and agricultural land (a signifi-cant proportion of which had been granted by Emperor Haile Selassie to the nobility), and sought to assert rural control through peasant associations. Some 30 000 associations were eventually established and made responsible for implementing the rural land reforms, but most were ineffective; peasants generally were reluctant to supply the cities with foodstuff. All urban land and all rentable houses and flats were nationalised and urban associ-ations (*kebeles*) were set up to administer the properties and improve roads, schools and other amenities in their neighbour-hoods. Urban workers gained less from the revolution than the peasants, and resented the loss of their right to take strike action; students and professional groups in the urban areas were also alienated. Many students especially belonged to the Ethiopian People's Revolutionary Party (EPRP), a Peking-oriented Marxist group which adopted the tactics of urban guerrilla warfare and was brutally crushed by the military during the 'Red Terror' of 1977–8.

Rural disaffection was much harder to deal with. While the rural land reforms won grass-roots support for the regime in certain parts of the country, they were bitterly opposed by local and provincial leaders. Outside secessionist Eritrea, against which the Derg fatefully despatched troops in November 1974, the main centres of opposition to the government were in the northern provinces of Tigré, Begemder and Wollo, in the south among the Afar and Oromo groups, and among the ethnic Somalis. New movements seeking autonomy or even secession emerged, prominent among them being the Tigré People's Liberation Front (TPLF) and the Oromo Liberation Front (OLF). Not only did the land reforms remain unpopular in the northern provinces, but the government policy of forcing many Amharic and Tigrean people to settle in the agriculturally vital southern provinces offended the Oromos, who constitute by far the largest linguistic–ethnic group in Ethiopia, and resulted both in a growing number of them joining the flow of ethnic Somali refugees to Somalia and increased support for the OLF. The Derg, under its leader Lieut-Colonel Mengistu Haile-Mariam, survived precariously with the help of Soviet military advisers and more than 17 000 Cuban troops. By 1979, following successful offensives in both the Ogaden and Eritrea the previous year, Ethiopia achieved (and has subsequently maintained) a semblance of political stability. However, the cost in human suffering of the regime's survival has been very high; this suffering has been enormously compounded in recent years by severe drought, which has spread to areas in the south of the country not previously affected. Colonel Mengistu himself became chairman of a National Natural Disaster Rehabilitation Committee whose formation was announced in October 1984. The previous month, in his speech on the tenth anniversary of the revolution, Mengistu had launched a ten-year Development Plan under which priority was to go to agriculture, with the intention of achieving self-sufficiency in grain by the end of the Plan period (1994). The area given over to state farms, despite their poor production record, was to be doubled and the number of peasant households organised into producer co-operatives was to be increased from under 2 per cent in 1984 to over 50 per cent by 1994. The Plan envisaged that the economy would be fully 'socialised' by the latter date.

The final shape of the revolution in Ethiopia has not yet been determined and a People's Democratic Republic has still to be created. The ruling Provisional Military Administration Council (PMAC) is now underpinned by a Workers' Party of Ethiopia (WPE) which (after a long delay caused by the military's fear of restricting its own freedom of action) was formally established in September 1984. The party organisation follows closely Soviet and Eastern European models, and is in the hands of party cadres trained in the Soviet Union and Eastern Europe. The WPE is a vanguard party dedicated to the building of 'scientific socialism', but virtually the same military clique dominates the party's top organs – both the politburo and the central committee have a strong military representation. The 14 regional party organisations and mass organisations such as the peasants' associations and trade unions are subject to tight central control. The party membership is heavily military, bureaucratic and intellectual in composition and peasants and workers are, as yet, only thinly represented.[13] On present evidence, it is unlikely that the WPE will enable the military regime to generate political support for the measures which it has taken; the effect of the latter has been to stimulate the nationalist claims of the country's non-Amharic communities, thereby hampering the regime's ability to build upon its early reforms. The problem of communalism remains extremely serious; the new constitution (now being drafted) is expected to confer some form of limited autonomy on Ethiopia's major linguistic–ethnic groups ('nationalities'), as was promised by the Derg in 1976. Present policies tend to benefit the Amharic people and are reminiscent of those pursued by Haile Selassie; so, too, is the PMAC's response to the challenges which face it – forcible (indeed brutal) repression is preferred to negotiation and compromise. (A quarter of the 1984–5 budget is allocated to defence, compared with 10 per cent for agriculture.) Perhaps the root of the regime's difficulties lies in its imposition from above of socioeconomic policies which do not correspond with the realities of Ethiopian life.

Conclusion

We have distinguished between revolutionary regimes which emerged from below, and those which were imposed from above. While the guerrilla activity associated with the former was rooted in the countryside, the latter were faced with the problem of asserting control over the rural areas – peasant associations were set up for this purpose in Ethiopia. Each type of regime felt the need to create institutions through which political and socio-economic order could be established and maintained, but whereas – in the case of Mozambique and Angola – this involved transforming the former liberation movement into a political party, in Ethiopia a political party to underpin the regime had to be created *de novo*.

The similarities between the two categories of regime are as striking as the differences. All the three regimes which are the subject of our case studies base their policies on considerations of *realpolitik* as much as on Marxist–Leninist ideology; this is a matter of necessity rather than (or at least as much as) of choice – even Angola (potentially by far the richest of the three countries examined) has to rely on the mining activities of multinational mining corporations to keep its economy afloat. In no case does attachment to revolutionary principle reduce external dependence, which is acute in the case of Ethiopia and hardly less so in the case of Angola, though instances do occur where a regime asserts some autonomy. Despite a commitment to mass political participation (especially on the part of Angola and Mozambique) each state remains subject to centralised, bureaucratic and (above all in the case of Ethiopia) repressive control; this accounts, in part, for the challenge posed by powerful linguistic–ethnic minorities and other opposition groups. Each of our three regimes has made good progress in the literacy, educational and health spheres. However, expenditure on social welfare, coupled with heavy spending on defence and security, has made for a high level of state consumption, with serious consequences for the balance of payments. The latter, in each case, has been made worse by the need to import food on a large scale – a reflection of low agricultural output, drought conditions, and poor distribution.

Africa's revolutionary regimes are 'progressive' in the sense that each is committed to creating a new pattern of socioeconomic organisation. Though aspects of Islamic fundamentalism came to the fore under Numeiri in the Sudan, none of the 'second wave' of African socialist states is likely to experience a backward-looking Iranian-type revolution. In most respects, however, the designation 'progressive' is misleading: while some revolutionary measures (such as land reform in Ethiopia) have been undertaken, the living conditions of the people have not been improved. Natural calamities – in the form of drought on the one hand and flooding on the other – are partly to blame. Other explanations may be that (in the absence over most of the continent of a proletariat class) the objective conditions for revolution in Africa do not yet exist, and that the Afro-Marxist states operate within an international capitalist environment that is inimical to their attempts to effect a socioeconomic revolution. Certainly, the support given by South Africa and the United States to UNITA in Angola and by South Africa to the MNR in Mozambique has had very damaging consequences. Finally, some responsibility for poor performance must lie with the revolutionaries themselves, in so far as they introduced sweeping measures of reform but lacked the state capacity to sustain them.

3. Revolutionary regimes in Latin America

Despite its turbulent history, Latin America has produced very few regimes which could be described as revolutionary. In Mexico (1910–17) and Bolivia (1952) old élites were overthrown by popular uprisings attended by considerable violence, and radical policies were subsequently instituted. In both cases, however (as we shall see) the initially radical impetus was lost, as mobilising peasants and workers found themselves outmanoeuvred; they lost out to middle-class coalitions more or less firmly in control of the state. More recently both Cuba (1958–9) and Nicaragua (1979) have seen dictators overthrown by widely-backed popular uprisings, and both have embarked on socialist paths – Cuba through adherence to an increasingly orthodox Marxist–Leninist model, Nicaragua in a context of pluralism. We might add to these four cases that of Guyana, a state claiming to be socialist but with little justification for doing so. There is a second revolutionary current in the region: the succession of guerrilla movements (mostly failures) which sprang up in the wake of the Cuban revolution. In the absence of a clearly identifiable colonial enemy of the kind found in Portuguese Africa, it is difficult for such movements to gain ground or to develop into genuine struggles for national liberation, but the success of the FSLN in Nicaragua, the survival of the guerrilla groups in El Salvador, and the surprising development of *Sendero Luminoso* (Shining Path) in Peru suggest that this tradition may not yet be exhausted.[14]

The Mexican and Bolivian revolutions

In Mexico and in Bolivia, a popular uprising overthrew a narrowly-based old regime; in both, workers and peasants played significant roles in the period of revolutionary upheaval, and in both they seemed to make early and very substantial gains. But (again in both cases) they lost out before too long to a middle-class-dominated coalition which had succeeded in seizing hold of the state. In the end, a party broadly representing these bourgeois or middle-class sectors (the PRI in Mexico, the National Revolutionary Movement (MNR) in Bolivia) was able to establish its ascendancy over mobilised workers and peasants, largely as a result of an ability to divide them against themselves, and to subordinate their demands to its own. In each case, the successful party developed an ideology that was both nationalistic and anti-imperialistic, but which displayed little that was remotely socialist in character.

The Mexican revolution was a long, complex, untidy and bloody phenomenon, stretching over more than two decades, and can be touched on only briefly here.[15] The major protagonists were the social forces produced by the country's rapid export-led development and incipient industrialisation under the dictatorship of Porfirio Diaz (1876–1911): entrepreneurs and urban professionals demanding genuine liberal democracy, and led by Francisco Madero; peasants pushed off communal land by the encroachment of commercial farming, the best known being those of Morelos led by Emiliano Zapata; and workers in Mexico City and other major centres throughout the country. The names of the losers – Madero, Zapata, Francisco 'Pancho' Villa – are far better known than those of the winners – Carranza (assassinated in 1919), Obregon (assassinated in 1928) and Calles. In the wake of the failure of Zapata and Villa in 1915 to cement an alliance that would enable them to govern the country, it was Carranza, Obregon and Calles, over more than a decade, who gradually imposed the ascendancy of a modern and commercially oriented northern bourgeoisie, paving the way for the reforms made by Cardenas (1934–40) to incorporate workers and peasants in a subordinate role into the revolutionary settlement.[16] This 'triumph of the bourgeoisie' in Mexico, which has given rise to a long-drawn out process of capitalist development under the unbroken rule of the PRI, owed much to the rift between peasants and urban workers, the latter embracing liberalism rather than socialism, and suspicious of the Catholicism and backward-looking communalism of the former. Where urban workers participated in the revolution they did so on the whole alongside the bourgeoisie, most notably in the 'Red Brigades' raised by Obregon from among the organised workers of Mexico City to fight against the forces of Villa and Zapata.[17]

A number of characteristics of the Mexican revolution find parallels in the case of Bolivia.[18] The Bolivian revolution began with the dramatic overthrow of the old regime between 9 and 11 April 1952, largely as a result of the defeat of the army at the hands of a militia dominated by the radical tin miners. It brought to power the MNR, a movement-based nationalist party tainted in the 1940s with suspicions of fascist leanings. In the immediate aftermath of its taking power it could not stem the demands of workers and newly-mobilised peasants for far-reaching reforms. In the months following the uprising the peasants threw land-owners off the land and took possession of it for themselves, and this situation was recognised and formalised in a substantial reform programme launched in 1953. Meanwhile the workers (led by the militant miners' union, the FSTMB) had gained a dominant position: in the mining industry itself they were able to win the nationalisation of (Bolivian-owned) tin mines, and the introduction of a limited form of workers' control. It seemed, then, that the workers and peasants were calling the tune. How-ever, within four years Siles Zuazo (successor to the first presi-dent of the revolution, Victor Paz Estenssoro) had imposed an IMF-backed stabilisation programme, cut miners' wages, and broken a strike called in protest. In later years the army was rebuilt, the MNR moved further to the right, and the radical impulse was entirely exhausted in a cycle which ended with the authoritarian dictatorship of General Hugo Banzer (1971–8).[19]

One reason for this was that the land reform programme of 1953 gave the land to the peasants in individual plots. This had the double effect of creating an impregnable electoral majority in the countryside (loyal to the president and successive presidents, and willing to side with the government against all comers so long as their new title to the land was honoured) and of breeding among the peasants a degree of conservatism which led them to oppose the more radical initiatives subsequently essayed by miners and other workers. As in Mexico, workers and peasants were divided, though in this case it was the peasants who first sided with the government. The second reason for the failure of the radical initiatives taken at the outset was that many miners under FSTMB leader Juan Lechín rejected the Trotskyist Workers' Revolutionary Party (POR) and joined the MNR with the inten-tion of forcing it to the left. This 'entryist' tactic failed, largely because the methods used to impose MNR control alienated many miners, and forced Lechín to rely heavily on the coercive power of government. Siles Zuazo was later able to make use of rival pro-Moscow Communist groups historically at odds with the Trotskyist POR to divide the workers further, and find new allies for his own cause. The upshot was that the petty-bourgeois nationalism of the MNR proved triumphant, and the radical impetus of the immediate post-revolutionary period was lost.

Cuba and Nicaragua

By 1958 the Mexican revolution had long lost its radical impulse, and the Bolivian revolution had rapidly followed suit. Additionally, United States intervention in Guatemala had cut short an incipient process of radicalisation there. In no Latin American state was there evidence of anything which could be described as socialistic, let alone revolutionary. This makes all the more astounding the establishment and consolidation of a socialist state closely tied to the Soviet bloc in the small island of Cuba, 90 miles from Miami, and once described as 'almost a state of the union'. The success of the revolution is all the more surprising if we consider that Fidel Castro launched his bid to overthrow the dictator Fulgencio Batista as a radical democrat rather than a Marxist revolutionary, and that the organised working-class of Cuba played a relatively small part in the revolution.[21]

During the first six decades of the twentieth century Cuba was shaped by the development of sugar for export on a massive scale, and the close involvement of the United States in its economy and its politics.[22]

It was the rural workers in the sugar industry (employed seasonally in cutting and processing cane and forced to scratch a living from their own inadequate plots of land during the rest of the year) who formed the bulk of the guerrilla army which came together in the two years after the landing of the *Granma* and the departure of its twelve surviving occupants into the Sierra Maestre. The urban working-class, either enrolled in the pro-Batista 'yellow' unions or loyal to the pro-Moscow Communist party (known as the Popular Socialist Party, PSP), rallied late to the revolutionary cause.

A second feature of substantial importance was that the dictatorship collapsed relatively early, before the struggle to overthrow it had turned into a nationwide civil war. Thirdly, Castro led the campaign as a radical democrat, rather than as a publicly-avowed Marxist, and there is no reason to believe that this was a calculated act of deception on his part. Fourthly (and almost

uniquely) the revolution radicalised after the entry of the victorious guerrilla army into Havana on 1 January 1959, moving rapidly
towards an explicit commitment to socialism and a far-reaching
programme of collectivist agrarian reform and nationalisation
once its leaders realised that substantial social reform would
prove impossible otherwise. The fifth feature of the Cuban revolution (and the source of much of the interest it has attracted
worldwide) was its lack of Marxist–Leninist orthodoxy, even after
its declaration of adherence to Marxist–Leninist principles. This
lack of orthodoxy was most clearly reflected in an international-
ism based not upon the organisation of vanguard parties aimed at
winning the proletariats of other nations to the revolutionary
cause, but upon what was christened the '*foco*' theory: the idea
that a group of committed revolutionaries could launch a guerrilla
war from an isolated and defensible area away from major cities,
and create a revolutionary situation by their heroic example.[23]
On the whole, this strategy (by no means necessarily a straight-
forward distillate of the Cuban experience itself) proved a failure,
generating or inspiring failed guerrillas in Guatemala, Colombia,
Venezuela, and (most notoriously) Bolivia, where Ernesto 'Che'
Guevara lost his life in 1967. On the other hand, it played its part
in rescuing the idea of armed struggle from years of Stalinist
neglect, and matured into a more sophisticated appraisal of the
need for more organic links with the masses; in a modified form
its influence may be seen in the Nicaraguan revolution, and to
some extent in the wars of national liberation in Southern Africa.[24]

Before the revolution, United States investment in Cuba was
higher (on a proportional basis) than anywhere else in Latin
America. Historically it had been most significant in the sugar
sector, but the process of diversification had brought United States
domination in most modern industrial sectors of the economy
too. This (along with the virtual stagnation of the Cuban economy
since levels of sugar production and export reached their peak in
the 1920s) enabled Castro to give his campaign against Batista a
nationalist and anti-imperialist character. In a different way,
Nicaragua falls into the same category. United States economic
interest in Nicaragua was low – lower in fact than anywhere else
in Central America. This was however no more than a facet of
the close political involvement of the United States, and the consequence of their opting to control the country, since the 1930s,

through the proxy of the Somoza family. Somoza senior made his career as commander of the National Guard set up by the Americans in preparation for the departure of the Marines from the country in 1933; by 1979 his son Anastasio (the second of his sons to inherit the presidency) was the head of a multimillion dollar business empire which accounted for more than half Nicaragua's total GDP.[25]

At the heart of the Nicaraguan economy was the agricultural export sector, based initially on coffee and after the Second World War on cotton and cattle as well. The expansion of the latter two commodities pushed formerly self-sufficient peasants off the land into precarious seasonal employment, and created the radicalised semi-proletariat which (as in Cuba) formed the backbone of the liberation struggle. From inauspicious beginnings along *'foco'* lines in 1961 the FSLN (Sandinista National Liberation Front) – named after the nationalist hero of struggle against United States occupation between 1929 and 1933, Augusto Sandino – developed in the 1970s into a mass movement. Divided into three currents which proved complementary rather than conflicting – endorsing respectively strategies of insurrection, prolonged popular war in the countryside, and proletarian organisation and revolution – it eventually won a position of unchallenged supremacy in the struggle against the Somoza dictatorship.[26] Determined to cling to power at all costs, Somoza pursued a policy of outright refusal to accept any compromise, marked by the assassination of Conservative opposition leader Pedro Chamorro in 1978. It was in part the perception on the part of the leaders of the FSLN that Somoza would not accept any compromise, and their insistence on the need to take up an armed struggle against the dictatorship, which enabled them to take the lead in opposition to the regime. The second factor which won them widespread backing was their orientation of their programme toward the needs and aspirations of the majority of impoverished workers and peasants in the country, and their insistence on the need for radical reforms.

Despite the tendency of the more myopic North American critics to see the Nicaraguan revolution as an exact replica of the Cuban revolution, there are several significant differences between the two. On the one hand, the Nicaraguan revolution may appear more radical: the Sandinistas were clearly committed to socialism before they took power, and won popular support on that basis. Secondly, the process of political mobilisation went far further before the Sandinistas came to power (as a result of the far greater impact of the civil war) than the parallel process in Cuba. Thirdly, however, the Sandinistas were insistent (and have remained insistent) that they drew their inspiration from a variety of sources, of which their own reading of Marxist theory was only one. They saw themselves as nationalists, and gave far greater prominence to national symbols of opposition to imperialism (the taking of the name of Sandino, obviously, being the major example) than to foreign models of any kind. This was also true to a certain extent, of course, of Cuba. Where the Sandinistas differ considerably is in their receptiveness to radical Catholicism and to liberation theology, as witnessed by the presence of priests in the Sandinista movement and in the government.[27] The Sandinista leadership has consistently resisted the definition of the revolution as purely Marxist in inspiration and purpose. Fourthly (and most significantly), the post-revolutionary policies applied by the Sandinistas have differed substantially from those applied in Cuba. They have resisted the temptation to turn their backs on Nicaragua's orientation towards agricultural exports, whereas the Cubans initially launched an all-out drive to diversify and industrialise, before settling back in the end to the realisation that for the foreseeable future sugar would remain the engine of growth in the economy. Furthermore, they have refrained from moving against the commercial export farmers, setting up state monopolies to export their produce but offering remunerative prices and guaranteeing that productive land farmed efficiently will be left in the hands of its owners. This represents a combined political and economic strategy, made possible by the massive authority of the Sandinistas (and the head start gained as a result of the forced takeover of the properties of the Somoza clan, and of unused or underutilised land). Perhaps most significantly, they have opted not to break with Western democratic practices (they can hardly be described as practices current at any stage in the past history of Nicaragua itself), but rather to allow opposition parties to organise and participate in conventional elections. The fruits of these policies were seen in 1984, when Daniel Ortega was elected to the presidency with some two-thirds of the total number of votes cast.

These policies are entirely consistent with the past commitments of the Sandinistas, reflecting a desire (perhaps utopian) to institute in Nicaragua a democratic brand of socialism subordinated neither to the West nor to the Soviet bloc. It is clear, however, that for Nicaragua (as for Cuba) the most pressing reality is the hostile international environment in which the newly-established socialist regime finds itself. Cuba moved early and definitely into the Soviet bloc. The same option is not open to Nicaragua, and it remains to be seen whether the revolution can survive at all in the face of unrelenting external pressure.

Latin American revolutions

The four revolutions considered here have in common the fact that their leaders were drawn overwhelmingly from the petty-bourgeoisie or the bourgeoisie, and that the working-class – and particularly the urban industrial working-class – played minor roles in them. In itself this is no more than a reflection of the historically-shaped social structure of Third World countries, in which export sectors take the place occupied by advanced industry in the developed world. In fact the leading protagonists in the revolution (in social terms) came from the most advanced sectors of the export economy, or were created by it: the displaced peasants of Morelos State, and the mixed working population of the north of Mexico, along with the new bourgeoisie spawned by development; the tin miners of Bolivia; and the semi-proletariat of the countryside in Cuba and in Nicaragua.

The prominence of petty-bourgeois leaders recalls Amilcar Cabral's dictum that this class will necessarily take the lead in colonial revolutions, and suggests that even these revolutions in the politically independent states of Latin America may be approached in these terms. The different outcomes in Mexico and Bolivia on the one hand, and Cuba and Nicaragua on the other, confirm the precision of Cabral's argument that only where such leaders explicitly adopt a socialist programme conceived in the interests of the worker and the peasant majority ('commit suicide as a class') will the movement they lead turn in a revolutionary direction. It is instructive that this pattern did develop in the two countries most directly affected, well into the twentieth century, by North American economic and political imperialism: Cuba and Nicaragua.

A final feature worth noting, too, is that in the four cases of Third World revolution considered here, the *ancien régime* that fell was particularly weak, with a narrow social base and an isolated and corrupt leadership. With the exception of Bolivia, the form taken by this leadership was a personal dictatorship. The presence of corrupt and isolated personal dictatorships in Mexico, Cuba and Nicaragua (reminiscent of similar regimes in Ethiopia and in Iran) suggests that personal rule may be as likely as colonial rule to give way to social revolution. The collapse in the mid-1980s of the Duvalier and Marcos dictatorships in Haiti and the Philippines respectively confirms the fragility of personal rule of this kind, whether 'traditional' or 'modernising' in intent. It also suggests (as does Cabral) that socialism is by no means the automatic outcome.

4. Revolutionary regimes in the Middle East

There is a wide gap between most Western analyses of radical political and social change in the Middle East and those of indigenous writers. For most outsiders, change has been less than revolutionary because it has not fitted with the general constellation of factors commonly associated with the three major aspects of revolution: the causes of revolution, the revolutionary process and post-revolutionary social, economic and political transformation. First, despite continuing political upheavals in the region since independence, political change has been caused as much by national issues as by social or economic ones. Secondly, in the Arab states, the revolutionary process has been initiated by conspiratorial officer groups without widespread popular participation. Thirdly, sustained social and economic change has not resulted in any fundamental change in class structure, political participation, ideological innovation or institutional creativity. The overthrow of the Shah of Iran in 1979 was a result of long-term structural causes and the revolutionary process was violent and bloody and involved massive popular participation. Yet for most Western writers the events in Iran lacked one other ingredient commonly associated with the outcome of revolutions: some progressive content. The regime which emerged from the revolutionary process was dominated by religious fundamentalists whose political goals were to establish theocratic rule.

One of the major problems of analysing revolution in the Middle East, then, is the absence of clear revolutionary achievements. Although the changes which have taken place do not fit with any theory of revolution (most of which encompass a comprehensive set of social, economic, political, institutional and ideological indices), some deep changes have taken place and do form something of a political pattern. In the first place, many of the monarchies which were established during the nineteenth and twentieth centuries have been destroyed and republics have replaced them. Big landlords have been displaced and their large landholdings have been redistributed. Key sectors of the economy – heavy industry, banking, insurance and oil – have been nationalised. All of these changes have gone along with some structural reforms, and have been affected by external circumstances.

During the twentieth century, the role and functions of the state increased, and with it the expansion of education. While this change was taking place, political institutions became increasingly controlled by landlords and economic policy generally favoured the landed interest, industry and industrialisation were given limited attention, and for the most part trade was in the hands of foreign companies. Furthermore, after the Second World War, the British maintained a military presence in many states of the area and during the 1950s the United States began to replace the European states as the defender of the West and pivot of anti-Communism, policies which necessarily involved support for friendly regimes. Internal problems of social and economic reform became intertwined with varying degrees of foreign control. One additional factor affecting domestic politics in the Arab states was the establishment of Israel in 1948 and the defeat of the Arab armies, which discredited the governments which had sent them to Palestine purportedly for the Arab national cause. In the aftermath of defeat, scandals about front line supplies linked the Egyptian monarchy and Syrian regime to corrupt contractors. The defeat emphasised the impotence, corruption and inefficiency of civilian government and heightened the reform movement among a younger generation of nationalists.

Jamal Abd al-Nasser, the organiser of the 1952 coup in Egypt, expressed the voice of the new generation when he wrote:

> We were fighting in Palestine, but all our thoughts were concentrated on Egypt. Our bullets were directed at the enemy trenches, but our hearts were hovering over the distant motherland, left an easy prey for hungry wolves to ravage.[28]

The ideas and movements which sprang up in the 1940s and 1950s were nationalist and reformist. It was in the process of consolidating power that more radical ideas were introduced.

Reform and revolution in the Arab world

The first upheaval took place in Egypt in 1952. It was nationalist in orientation and aimed at creating 'a strong liberated Egypt'. In the process, powerful ruling groups were attacked: the big landowners, the old politicians and high bureaucrats. Nasser explained the attack on these groups by reference to corruption, to maldistribution of land and overspending on salaries. They were not considered revolutionary measures but 'steps necessary to redress and efface the traces of wrongs done in the past'.[29] As one authority on the Egyptian economy has written, the land reform was

> seen as a serious aspect of the more fundamental problem of growing poverty and . . . overpopulation in the countryside, and it was conceived as an element of a 'development' package including industrialisation and land reclamation . . . The broad purposes were clear – to provide a solution to Egypt's economic problems, aggravated by a population explosion in a restricted area.[30]

The redistribution of land, the establishment of co-operatives, the provision of credit and services through government agencies were aimed at solving Egypt's imbalance between population, resources and domestic capital rather than establishing a revolution. Although there was a concern for social justice embodied in the land reform, the large numbers of landless did not benefit from increasing government regulation of the rural economy.

Again, industrialisation was aimed at strengthening a diversity of Egypt's national economy rather than at establishing socialism or even state control of the economy. It was ten years after the overthrow of the monarchy that more radical economic measures were implemented. The National Charter of 1962 rewrote the history of Egypt's last decade and promulgated the principles of the 1952 revolution in very different terms: 'the ending of feudalism', 'the ending of monopoly and the domination of capital over government, the elimination of imperialism and traitorous Egyptian collaborators' were three of the six principles. Despite the radical tone of these principles, national unity was emphasised as against class struggle: 'The Egyptian people refused the dictatorship of any class and decided that the dissolution of differences among classes should be the means to real democracy for the entire working forces of the people'.[31]

The regime, of course, was speaking in the name of 'the Egyptian people', and the changes which took place during the 1950s and early 1960s were imposed from above. Regional conflicts with Saudi Arabia, the opposition of the United States and the West, the alignment with the USSR and the failure of Egypt to consolidate the United Arab Republic with Syria because of Syrian domestic class and political forces were the major factors which brought about greater public ownership. The actual process of nationalisation was ethnically discriminatory as much as directed against a particular class. There was some correlation between big landowners and the monarchy and the Turco-Egyptian élite which was of varied Ottoman background on the one hand, and the merchants and manufacturers and traders who were of Lebanese, Syrian, Greek and Armenian stock on the other. There were factors other than an 'internal revolutionary' dynamic that affected the processes of change after 1952, even if social and economic policy derived from the particular developmental imperatives of Egypt's demographic and resource problem.

One feature of post-1952 Egyptian politics on which many writers have focused is the problem of participation, and this broader issue has been dealt with in chapter 3. It is relevant to point out here that the post-1952 regime was locked in a contradiction which made the development of a revolutionary cadre extremely difficult. Ideology developed on a pragmatic and *ad hoc* basis. Ideological changes were announced by Nasser after consultation with his closest advisers. In such circumstances, members of the state political organisations simply shifted with the prevailing political wind. Only in the mid-1960s was an institute established for cadres of the Arab Socialist Union (ASU), and although the graduates from there played a radical role within the Union they were not able to transform the ASU, but became ensnared in factional conflicts and identified as factional supporters of Ali Sabri, a leading political figure.[32] Indeed, the attempt to build a committed ideological cadre foundered on the absence of participation in formulating that ideology, with the result that such organisations lacked any autonomy from the central and local government structures and were part of the bureaucratic machinery.

That the 1952 overthrow had failed to put down any deep roots became increasingly apparent on Nasser's death. The ideology which had cohered during the 1960s became generally known as 'Nasserism' and the nomenclature reflected the personalistic basis which the Egyptian system had taken. Sadat's accession brought the dismantling of a whole range of state controls, the return of foreign capital and the resurgence of a new wealthy class, a consequence of the return to a market economy. One result of these changes was the re-emergence of certain elements of the old landed class among the new wealthy after the '*infitah*' (Arabic for opening).

In summary, a new political system emerged after 1952. The monarchy and a small number of large landowners were removed. Army officers, relying on the support of the upper and middle peasantry, shaped a new authoritarian system which relied heavily on the military, the security forces and the bureaucracy. Nasser was the pivot of the system, shifting powerful former members of the Revolutionary Command Council between key institutions. There was limited ideological clarity, which made it difficult to establish a core of committed cadres who could deepen the socialist tendency within Egypt. There was a concern for social justice and egalitarianism, but it did not extend to the poorest in the rural areas, nor to the growing urban poor. These problems were to be tackled through industrialisation engendered by the twin pillars of foreign capital and extracting surplus from the agricultural sector. The goals and methods were reformist and developmental rather than revolutionary. And although sections of the peasantry were beneficiaries, they were also rather passive accomplices in a development process which was centralised and bureaucratically controlled. Development from above followed a political revolution from above. It should also be mentioned that although the new rulers lacked both revolutionary credentials and ideology and were gradualist, external pressures were a constraining factor on the new Egyptian regime, as the 1956 Suez invasion was to indicate.

Much emphasis has so far been placed on Egypt and the consequences of 1952 because the other self-styled revolutions in the Arab states followed a similar pattern and indeed were influenced by 'Nasserism'. The Iraqi monarchy was overthrown in 1958 by a group of officers after a prolonged period of nationalist agitation. The landlords were dispossessed and land redistributed. Although the regime which emerged was beset by conflicts between communists, Ba'thists and nationalists, by factions within the officer corps and by the spasmodic outbreak of fighting by the Kurdish national movement, the Hashimite monarchy and the landlord–tribal shaykh dominated political system was destroyed. In Syria, a more protracted political struggle took place between 1958 and 1966, removing the big landowning families from their positions.

All of these changes can be categorised as political revolutions which fundamentally changed the political system and established a much stronger role for the state over the economy. They have reflected a shift in the social basis of power away from the large private property-owners to salaried state-employed modern educated nationalists. The political revolutions which overthrew the old landed class did not lead to a permanently-established state capitalism. In the 1970s Egypt and (to a lesser extent) Syria opened their economies to private foreign investment, reflecting the unresolved problem of whether industrialisation should take place under the aegis of the state or of private control.

Of all the Middle Eastern Arab states, the only one with some claim to revolutionary status is South Yemen – or, as it is more correctly called, the People's Democratic Republic of Yemen (PDRY). Here, socialism of an Arab nationalist or Islamic variety is eschewed in favour of a commitment to a more Third World internationalist socialism. The Yemeni Socialist party is the ruling body, and grew from the National Liberation Front which fought the successful liberation struggle against the British, culminating in independence in 1967. Although the state has established full control of the rather underdeveloped economy and the party is committed to economic and social transformation, the achievements of the PDRY have been limited by two factors. First, British colonialism largely ignored the countryside (where the majority of the population lived) and developed the service sector associated with Aden port which went into decline with the departure of the British and the closure of the Suez canal in 1967. Secondly, underdeveloped productive forces with the majority of the population involved in subsistence farming and a lack of human resources have placed severe constraints on revolutionary socialist change.[33]

The Iranian revolution

Iran has followed a very different pattern from the political revolutions in the Arab states.[34] There is a superficial similarity in that the regime changed from a monarchy to a republic. The overthrow of the Shah in 1979 was one of the most spectacular political upheavals in the Third World. The Shah's regime was not a shaky monarchy but a powerful centralised autocratic state possessing a strong and feared security service in Savak and an apparently loyal and cohesive officer corps. Unlike Egypt, Iraq, Syria and Libya, it was not a revolution from above but one which had massive popular participation. Yet the outcome of the revolutionary process was a clerical, authoritarian regime. The forces which overthrew the Shah came from all urban social classes, the different nationalities and ideologically varying political parties and movements, but an Islamic Republican was eventually declared. Although Islam has been a salient part of Libyan ideology after the 1969 revolution, in Iran Islam was a major mobiliser and it was the clergy organised in the Islamic Republic Party which came to power, established an Islamic constitution and dominated the post-revolutionary institutions.

The outcome of the Iranian revolution illustrates the paradox of a revolution from below in which there was mass participation but which resulted in one narrow and traditional sector predominating. Iran provides the paradox of a revolution which was theocratic and reactionary, in the true sense of a return to the past.

The causes of the revolution were the socioeconomic changes which occurred during the 1960s and 1970s, the alienation and politicisation of the different strata because of the Shah's autocracy and the recrudescence of an Iranian nationalism triggered by the Shah's close relationship to the United States.

The development of a capitalist agriculture along with a weakly implemented land reform programme, industrialisation and the expansion of education, employment and services in the urban centres led to large-scale migration from the countryside of the rural poor who became the main component of the urban demonstrations when the economic crisis struck in the late 1970s. The urban middle-class and intelligentsia were affected by the inflation, food shortages resultant from decreasing agricultural productivity and (perhaps more importantly) by the level of repression. James Bill describes the thorough penetration of Iranian society by the security system.[35] He tells how eight middle-class Iranians who were old and trusted friends used to meet regularly to discuss sociopolitical issues. They drew up a confidential one-page statement of their concern about corruption, injustice and oppression. Each member took a copy and the rest were locked away. Five months later the head of Savak called one of the men in and produced one of the original eight copies. The circle of friends never met again. Needless to say, there was also strict censorship and supervision of higher educational institutions.

Students were a particular target of the state, and in the movement to depose the Shah they played an important role reflecting the dramatic expansion of education. Between 1963 and 1977 enrolment in secondary schools increased from 369 069 to 741 000, in technical, vocational and teacher training from 14 240 to 227 497 and in universities and colleges from 24 885 to 154 215.[36]

The demands of this middle sector were for liberalisation and a more secular rather than Islamic brand of nationalism. The recent migrants from the countryside demanded better social and economic conditions and, along with the bazaar, a mixture of merchants and traditionally organised craftsmen, supported the fundamentalist clergy's call for an Islamic state. The merchants had also been affected by the increased power of the state. The growth of large industry controlled by the royal family, through its Pahlavi Foundation, and a handful of families and the attempt by the state to take control of bazaar organisations alienated the conservative, religious merchant class in Iran. Their historic connection to the clergy presented a dual threat to the regime since their financial support made possible the clergy's independence of state control even under the centralising Shah Mohammad Reza Pahlavi.

The social and economic changes which took place were fuelled by oil revenues which increased from $555 million to $20 billion between 1963 and 1976. Although much of government spending found its way into the pockets of a few aristocratic and upper-class families and high state officials, large sums were spent on industrialisation and infrastructural development. The construction industry (in particular) boomed. Such large-scale development increased the numbers in education and salaried occupations, and also the working-class. One scholar of Iranian history has estimated that the latter increased fivefold between 1963 and 1977. Excluding the unskilled labourers who flooded into the town the total size of the working-class has been put at about 1¼ million.[37] Another 1 million or more formed an urban sub-proletariat. This new working-class was controlled by state-organised trade unions.

For Iranian Islamic and secular nationalists the Shah's economic and foreign policies were symbolic of Iran's subjugation to foreign powers. In the economic sphere, foreign interests predominated. By the mid-1960s not one Iranian held a key managerial post in the oil industry. Foreign investment (particularly American) played a large role in economic development from the middle of the 1960s. American companies were involved in joint ventures with state and private companies in petrochemicals, steel, rubber, pharmaceuticals, construction and agribusiness. Increasing oil revenues did not alter Iran's dependence on the United States for arms; in the 1950s, the United States gave aid for building up the Iranian armed forces and by the 1970s Iran was able to purchase large stocks of military hardware and became the major pillar of the Nixon doctrine whereby regional states undertook to guarantee Western security. Oil wealth and the strategic concerns of the United States led to massive expenditure. Between 1972 and 1976 Iran spent $10 billion on armaments. At the time of the Shah's overthrow there was a further $12 billion in the pipeline. Most were bought from the United States and by 1976, there were about 20 000 American military advisers in Iran. Many Iranians believed that such dependence on the United States went against the Iranian national interest, that the military expenditure was a gross waste of national resources and that the armed forces could not absorb such levels of armaments. Co-operation with Israel (particularly the supply of oil) went against the grain of Islamic and the general Third World nationalism of many Iranians, particularly the young.

At the apex of the system was Mohammad Reza Pahlavi. He formulated policy in all key areas. The wealth accruing to his relatives took place under his protection. The squandering of oil wealth, the vicious role of Savak, the privileged position of the armed forces, the corruption of officials and the alliance with Israel and the United States were all placed at the door of the Imperial Palace. Symbolic of the Shah–United States connection was the fact that it was the CIA which returned the Shah to power in 1953 after he had left the country following nationalist pressures.

There was, then, a combination of social classes adhering to varying ideologies of which an intertwined Islam and Iranian nationalism proved the most effective mobiliser. The most-often shouted slogans in mass demonstrations were 'death to the Shah', 'hang the American puppet', 'independence, freedom and Islam', and 'God is great'.

It was the urban unskilled migrants from the countryside and fundamentalist students who formed the backbone of support for Ayatollah Khomeini, a puritanical fundamentalist who had never compromised with the Shah's regime and was uncorrupted and incorruptible. He had attacked the Shah's reforms of 1962–3 for dictatorship and selling the country to foreigners. It was his followers among the clergy who established hegemony after 1979 in part as a consequence of his mass following and in part because of their position as a semi-organised network of religious teachers and students throughout the country. The decentralised *komitehs* (committees) in Teheran and the provinces were controlled by Khomeini's clerical followers who organised the urban poor into *pasdaran* (revolutionary guards). In the period between the departure of the Shah and the establishment of the Islamic republic, the *komitehs* took over the running of the towns. Since the security police and military services had been utterly discredited through their support for the regime the *pasdaran* were the major force for order, and played a key role in removing any political challenge to the fundamentalist group. Khomeini had swept to power with broad political support, but his followers were able either to neutralise or pick off one by one the political organisations and groupings of liberal constitutionalists among the clergy, the Marxist Fidayin, the radical Islamic Mujahidin, the liberal National Front and the communist Tudeh.

The revolution took place with amazing popular support and removed what had seemed one of the most impregnable Third World regimes backed by the power of the United States. The determination of Khomeini and the bravery of tens of thousands of individuals demonstrating against armed security forces mobilised by the personality of Khomeini, Islam, nationalism, liberation and Marxism ultimately brought to power a brutal and fanatical section of the clergy. What happened was revolutionary, but paradoxically the outcome was reactionary. In this case, revolution from below did not produce a social revolution.

5. Conclusion

In the Third World rebellions, popular uprisings and mass demonstrations have been frequent occurrences. Rarely have they been converted into revolutions. In our examination of the three regions emphasis has been placed on why political revolutions have produced reformist regimes rather than social or socialist revolutions, and on the severe problems of consolidating revolutions. The reason for such a focus is the limited number of full-blooded revolutions which have transformed both state and society and the obstacles (both internal and external) to implementing revolutionary programmes.

Nationalism has been a salient feature of Third World revolutions. Economic domination or political subjugation by a colonial or foreign power was a factor in the Cuban, Nicaraguan, Mozambican, Angolan and Iranian revolutions. In the case of Ethiopia and Iran, nationalism played an important part in mobilising support for the post-revolutionary regime. The greater stress on nationalism rather than on restructuring class relations in Egypt, Iraq and Libya is an important factor in placing them in the reformist rather than revolutionary camp. Personal dictatorship has also been a common element. Iran, Ethiopia, Mexico, Cuba and Nicaragua all had either corrupt or authoritarian emperors or presidents. Even Mozambique, Angola and Guinea-Bissau were ruled from the metropole by the Portuguese dictator, Salazar.

One problem in studying revolutions is that even after a revolutionary process has ended, it can still be unclear whether the outcome is revolutionary. After more than ten years it is not obvious what direction the Ethiopian regime will take. Avowedly communist, the Workers' Party of Ethiopia, the revolutionary vanguard party, was organised long after the revolution and owes its existence and ideological persuasion to Colonel Mengistu. Despite dramatic changes in the nature of authority and land-ownership, there is also a decidedly 'Nasserist' tinge to the Ethiopian regime.

Ethiopia highlights two further questions about revolutionary regimes in poor and multiethnic societies. First, without significant economic growth, what benefits can accrue to a society where millions live on the brink of starvation? Secondly, is economic growth possible in a poor society where one component of revolutionary consolidation is to generate support through a nationalist appeal against a variety of independence movements calling for self-determination. Ethiopia brings to the fore problems peculiar to revolutions: the issues of democracy, self-determination and revolutionary state power and of human immiseration and revolutionary progress.

If Ethiopia starkly raises anew some issues of revolution in the Third World, so too do the contemporary revolutions in Iran and Nicaragua. In Iran, a massive popular uprising translated into a revolutionary process wherein all sections of the population (workers, the middle-classes, traditional merchants, students and different nationalities) were mobilised under the banner of Islam and nationalism. Yet a very narrow sector of the clergy (based on a vengeful and punitive brand of Islam) was able to consolidate through external problems: a threat from the United States and a war with neighbouring Iraq. A revolution from below (sparked by demands for democratic rights and freedom from oppression) resulted in rule by a clergy whose position and status had long been in decline. Nicaragua highlights the problems of a popular revolution from below, classically trapped between a commitment to a democratic process and the requirements of consolidating a revolution under external economic and political siege.

These issues of democracy, self-determination and external threat are not new issues in revolutions, but are linked to their success or failure, and in underdeveloped peasant societies – like Russia or China of the past, and Ethiopia and Nicaragua of the present – can have a tragic human dimension.

6

Women in Third World Politics

1. Introduction

In previous chapters, we have covered broad historical issues, or focussed on topics drawn from the traditional repertoire of comparative politics. In this chapter we complement the account given so far by examining aspects of social, economic and political change in the Third World from the perspective of gender. Beyond their differences, political parties and military regimes in the Third World have one thing in common: they are predominantly or wholly male-dominated institutions. And, as our conclusion to this chapter will show, Third World revolutions have only been partially successful in challenging this pattern of male domination. Too often, too, historians of social and economic change in the Third World have been blind to the part played in it by the subordination of women to the authority and designs of men.

Our decision to concentrate this material in a single chapter rather than to disperse it through the book piecemeal should not be taken as signifying adherence to the idea that the topic lacks connections with the other themes pursued, or is to be treated as an optional extra. On the contrary, it reflects our belief that a perspective focussed on gender illuminates (and materially advances) our understanding of the issues considered thus far, and that the coherence, the theoretical importance and the critical power of such a perspective is best appreciated through a unified and extended treatment of the kind we attempt here. The topic is one of such evident significance that no further justification for its inclusion is required. Even so, it is worth stressing the point that a direct focus upon gender relations is indispensable for a full understanding of the mechanisms by which the political and economic penetration and reshaping of the Third World has been carried through. In many ways, men have been the agents and the beneficiaries of 'modernisation', and women its victims.

A focus on gender is illuminating in four ways. The focus on gender relations is valuable in itself; secondly, because it is a perspective which focusses upon personal relations and the lives of the majority of the population, it approaches the issues considered from the underside of the state- or government-centred, macropolitical point of view adopted thus far; thirdly, it is a *critical* perspective, and as such subjects approaches which leave its concerns out of account to a vital and fruitful scrutiny; and finally, it generates a framework within which the political and economic issues we have thus far considered to some extent separately for reasons of analytical convenience can be seen 'in action' together in specific historical circumstances. The isolation of 'politics' as a separate aspect of social reality is at best a necessary evil, and we have been at pains throughout to stress the range of internal and external social, economic *and* political factors shaping the Third World. We are able to draw here on a valuable and rapidly-growing literature which has begun to remedy a missing dimension to our proper understanding of the dynamics of that process.

Given the considerable and rapidly expanding literature, and the wide range of issues involved, an attempt to cover the topic of women in Third World politics in a single chapter must necessarily be selective. We have chosen to focus on illustrative issues within each of the three areas upon which we concentrate, rather than to cover a single set of topics in less detail for all three areas. In relation to Africa (where the impact of colonial rule has been greatest and most recent) we concentrate upon colonialism and modernisation; for Latin America (where the process of industrialisation has proceeded furthest) we look at resulting patterns of employment and political participation; and for the Middle East (where long-established cultural patterns remain influential) we look at the impact and continuing significance of Islam. In conclusion, we consider the relationship between separatism, socialism in the Third World, and women's liberation.

2. Africa: colonisation and modernisation

In pre-colonial African societies, great variations existed in the
social and economic positions of women, and little generalisation
is possible. The impact of colonialism, however, was broadly
uniform. Such status and independence as women enjoyed were
diminished, and such rights as they possessed were undermined.
The colonial rulers who came out to Africa from Europe carried
with them 'Western' conceptions of gender relations and responsibilities, and came at a time when these allowed only the most
restricted public roles to women. What is more, the governing
classes in the colonies were exclusively male, and disposed to
assume that men in the societies they governed exerted authority
over women, or to grant it to them where they did not. The
combination of the imposition of 'Western' conceptions of the
proper role of women and the organisation of family life and the
creation of colonial economies tied into the international capitalist
economy substantially worsened the situation of women.

This is not to say that women were particularly favoured in
pre-colonial Africa. The development of African societies – partly
under external stimuli but largely as a result of internal dynamics
over centuries – led to a process of stratification which tended to
undermine their status well before the colonial period. Etienne
and Leacock identify a development from egalitarian through
'ranking' or transitional to hierarchical or stratified societies,
largely as a result of the development of trade. Initially 'women's
and men's rights and responsibilities were conceived and institutionalised as parallel rather than hierarchical, and the activities
and organisations of each sex spanned both public and private
life'.[1] The transition to hierarchical social organisation was well
advanced by the colonial period, and the subordination of women
was an integral part of it. A parallel analysis is provided by Sacks,
who discusses the shift from communal to kin corporate and
eventually to class society, and sees as central to it the decline in
the status of women from 'sister' – 'one who is an owner, a
decision maker among others . . . , a person who controls her
own sexuality' – to 'wife' – 'a subordinate in much the way Engels
asserted for the family based on private property'.[2] In some cases
(as among the Baganda), the process of subordination and the
destruction of horizontal solidary associations among women

was virtually complete before the colonial period proper began. Elsewhere (as among the Ibo of southern Nigeria), it was greatly accelerated in the colonial period. Roberts is right, therefore, to point out that by the modern period 'in many (if not most) societies in Africa, few women had either individual or collective rights in land to maintain except access conditional upon becoming and remaining wives', and to argue that the development of capitalism in Africa deepens already existing gender divisions and women's subordination.[3] The autonomy and independence that women enjoyed in substantial parts of early pre-colonial Africa had already been largely eroded before the colonial period began.

Colonial rule, however, accelerated and deepened the subordination of women. Disregarding differing family structures and roles, colonial authorities recognised and strengthened men as heads of families; women who had access to land under customary law or usage found their role and their entitlement were not recognised by colonial authorities; as export crops were developed, land, credit and technology were given to men; where education was provided, boys were favoured over girls, and girls were often trained only in suitable 'domestic' skills; and where Africans began to win access to jobs in colonial bureaucracies, positions with status became an exclusively male preserve.

The advent of colonial bureaucracies and the development of export-oriented colonial economies led, therefore, to a marked deterioration in the role and status of women in non-Muslim African societies; and to the extent that the new leaders of Africa after independence inherited the bureaucratic and economic structures of the colonial period, the position of women continued to deteriorate. To illustrate this, we examine four areas where the position of women was once favourable, but has deteriorated in the colonial and independence periods.

First, women had often enjoyed considerable autonomy in terms of family organisation and residential arrangements. They often lived in all-female residential compounds, extended families, or (in polygamous societies) in relatively independent and virtually female-headed households. In all of these circumstances women were more likely to enjoy a degree of autonomy or derive support from other women in the residential group. The former arrangement in particular made for co-operation and mutual solidarity among women. As Robertson points out, too, in her study of the Ga women traders of Accra in Ghana, it facilitated co-operative trading and production ventures.[4] In addition, where isolated nuclear families were not the norm, kinship ties between women provided support networks independent of individual husbands and men collectively. One should not over-look the relatively weak position of women in patrilocal societies, who move to the husband's village and kin on marriage, or ignore the fact that the primary motive of polygyny was that it enabled a single man to marry (and thus secure the unpaid labour of) a number of women, and hence increase his wealth. Nevertheless, such family and residential arrangements contained advantages for women which could easily be lost with the introduction of the nuclear family as a norm.

Secondly, women in pre-colonial Africa often had effective control of economic resources, in money or land. The extent to which agriculture was a female preserve has been well docu-mented by Boserup, who describes Africa as 'the region of female farming par excellence'.[5] In many rural societies where women cultivated the fields, they would dispose independently, and on their own account, of any surplus remaining once house-hold subsistence needs had been met. Out of these activities sub-stantial trading networks controlled by women emerged, as sur-plus grain would be traded for sheep, goats or cattle, or vice-versa. Similar trade networks extended to urban areas. Again, Ga women traders were not accountable to their husbands for their business transactions, and would even charge interest (at rates of up to 30 per cent per month) for lending money to them. The heavy involvement of women in cultivation and trade had its drawbacks. It meant that women generally were subjected to a 'double shift', as they were still responsible for domestic tasks. Among the Nandi of Kenya, for example, the working day of the average woman was four hours longer than that of the man, and male work (here as elsewhere revolving around cattle) was less physically demanding.[6] But direct involvement in production and control over the product gave women a degree of autonomy which was of considerable consequence.

As incorporation into a cash economy proceeded, one of two things happened. Either women were excluded from areas of production in which they had previously been involved, and relegated to the 'domestic' sphere, or the productive activities in which they continued to engage were deformed and devalued in a new context. For example, in her field work among the Kaonde community of Mukunashi in north western Zambia (an area scarcely penetrated by the cash economy until very recently), Crehan found that it had been common practice for men to prepare fields for their wives and other dependants, and for the women who cultivated the crops to have exclusive rights over the distribution of food from their granaries. As over a third of households in the area were female-headed, women enjoyed considerable autonomy in their daily lives, although they were still subject to the authority of male kin, and burdened with heavy tasks, the worst being their responsibility for fetching and carrying water and firewood. The situation of relative autonomy was transformed as the government-created agricultural board introduced ploughs and hybrid seeds, and promoted the cultivation of maize as a cash crop, by men, on cleared, ploughed, and demarcated fields, with guaranteed purchase of the crop. All agricultural extension workers were men, and parallel government schemes taught domestic skills in local schools for girls. The consequence of this development was a devaluation of the productive role of women, who were left farming irregular plots with hoes and local seed, and found themselves increasingly relegated to a purely 'domestic' role as their production was no longer vital to the survival and reproduction of the family group.[7] Similarly, among the Baule of the Ivory Coast, Etienne found that in the pre-colonial economy men had controlled the distribution of yams, while women had controlled that of cloth, intercropping cotton in the yam fields, spinning and dyeing thread for the men to weave, and engaging in or directing long-range trade of the resulting product. In the colonial era, the importing (and subsequent manufacture) of thread relieved male weavers of their dependence upon female spinners, and eventually the introduction of cotton as a cash crop with new seed and technology controlled by men broke the interdependent relationship between women and men entirely. In the wake of these developments, women lost land rights and control over production, and became labourers on fields owned by individual men. These trends were reinforced by the growing availability of manufactured cloth, purchased with the proceeds from cash crops such as cotton, cocoa and coffee controlled by men.[8]

Thirdly, women might play a key role in certain traditional societies. Thus, among the Akan in central and southern Ghana, the importance of 'queen mothers' derived from the system of matrilineal descent and the supposition that 'blood alone can be transmitted by and through a female'.[9] The queen mother was something of a 'king-maker' in that she put forward the name of her chosen candidate for chief to the Stool elders who made the election. In exceptional circumstances, she might assume a more active leadership role: this occurred in Ashanti in 1900 when, in the absence of the Asantehene (who had been removed and deported by the British four years earlier), it fell to Yaa Asantewa, the Asantehemaa, to call the nation to arms against the imperialist usurper; the war that followed is named after her. Moreover, in certain traditional societies (as in that of the Mende in Sierra Leone), a woman might even become chief in her own right. The decline of chiefly power, which occurred under colonialism (above all in French Africa) and was accelerated after independence, thus undermined the position of those women who had occupied positions of authority in traditional society.

Fourthly, even where men were clearly dominant in most spheres of public life, it was common for associations of women to control areas of interest to them, and to provide alternative structures of power, representation, solidarity and control. Such institutions have been described in some detail for the Ibo of southern Nigeria, and are of particular interest because of the decentralised political system under which they lived, and their relevance to the 'women's war' of 1929. Ibo communities west of the Niger were governed by a male *obi* and a female *omu*. The latter had her own council of elders parallel to that of the *obi*, and oversaw affairs of particular interest to women. Significantly, these were not confined to the 'private sphere', but centred upon the management and running of local markets, and the resolution of other public issues in which women were involved. The *omu* consulted and worked through a representative body of women from the community, the *ikporo ani*. In addition, women came together in associations which linked those born in a particular village (*umuada*), and those resident in a particular village (*inyemedi*). The institutionalised assembly of the latter, the *mikiri*, was a significant force in community life.[10]

As recent scholarship has led to greater understanding of the role of women in pre-colonial society in Africa, episodes of conflict and resistance in the past have been reinterpreted, or examined in a light very different to that in which they were seen by the colonial authorities of the time. The 'women's war' of 1929 in southern Nigeria is a case in point, and it provides valuable evidence of women's roles in production, and of the resistance they offered to attempts to reduce their status. In the 1920s (as the British in Nigeria promoted the policy of indirect rule), previously autonomous villages were being grouped together under the command of newly designated 'Warrant Chiefs'. Unusually, women had benefited from the introduction of cash crops, as they controlled significant aspects of palm oil production, and had a virtual monopoly over cassava, too. The power men derived from their control over land was increased by the system of male authorities imposed by the colonial rulers, and the economic interests of female producers were threatened by attempts to subject them to regulations and control. The resentment felt by women was brought to a head in late 1929, when successive incidents in Owerri province persuaded them that taxation established for men in 1928 was to be extended to their activities. As a result, women's solidary organisations were activated in widespread protests, demanding among other things the appointment of women as district officers and warrant chiefs. In the ensuing uprising tens of thousands of women mobilised over an area of 6000 square miles of Calabar and Owerri provinces; native courts were attacked, and warrant chiefs ridiculed, as women drew upon networks and ritual traditions that had maintained their status in pre-colonial society.[11] The movement was put down by force of arms, leaving over fifty dead. Remembered in colonial records by the dismissive term of the 'Aba riots', it is recalled among the Ibo themselves as *ogu umunwanyi* – the women's war.[12]

To say that the role and status of women deteriorated in the colonial period and continued to decline following the achievement of independence is undoubtedly valid as a general statement. However, not only was this decline more marked in some spheres of economic activity than in others, it was also not universal. As Hill's studies of rural capitalism in West Africa (based on research carried out mainly in the early 1960s) showed, women might still play a key role in certain industries and even possess considerable entrepreneurial skills. Thus, in addition to the 111 men who owned kraals within, or nearly within, the Ashaiman–Dodowa area of the Accra plains, there were five women kraal owners, responsible between them for 482 cattle. One of these women, writes Hill,

> had once been a cocoa carrier at Aburi. Later she was a pig-trader and then a cattle trader with the assistance of a Fulani, on whose death she turned to cattle-rearing. There are 222 animals in her kraals, about 50 of which are owned by her daughter; if it is true, as she insisted, that only 6 relatives have 17 animals in her herds and that she has given up caring for animals for private owners, it may be that she herself owns over 100 cattle.[13]

Another of Hill's case studies pointed to the important contribution made to the local fishing industry by 'the wives' of the Ewe seine fishermen in south eastern Ghana. They cooked and provided for the men, but also bought the catch on preferential terms from the net-owner's 'company', preserved the fish (usually by smoking) and resold it, retaining any profit. A few women themselves owned nets, which were large and costly, while others – more than the men cared to admit – financed the purchase of nets out of the large profits which, in a good season, they made out of reselling the fish.[14]

Further evidence of women's activity in non-settler West Africa is to be found in the works of Arhin and Garlick. In his study of West African traders in Ghana, Arhin points out that modern markets were mostly operated by women, both because the apparatus of the modern state had brought peace to the market place and also because modern markets were for sedentary rather than itinerant traders.[15] Garlick, who also concentrated on Ghana, found that while most market women in Accra made very little from their trading activities, some of those who dealt in imported textiles in the mid-1950s 'had incomes of several hundred pounds a year and some had incomes running into four figures'.[16] In Kumasi, too, several women trading in imported cloth prospered throughout the 1950s: they made wholesale bulk purchases from the United Africa Company and other European companies and found retail sales outlets through market 'mammies' to whom they themselves resold the cloth on a wholesale basis. However, adverse political conditions in the late 1950s began to work against them, and in the 1960s the rising price of imported textiles and import restrictions made necessary by the shortage of foreign exchange, coupled with a decline in the cocoa trade, knocked the bottom out of a once flourishing business. This affords an example of how women suffered from exposure to modernisation, understood as increased integration into the international capitalist economy.

In the colonial and post-independence periods, then, women retained a foothold in certain spheres of economic activity, including aspects of the cattle and fishing industries, while losing it in others. Their management of what were mostly small-scale enterprises might make a vital contribution to the survival of the household, and provide a basis for some degree of power and prestige. Nevertheless, their position tended to be undermined as new and better opportunities were made available to men, and the significance and the standing of their production declined. The superior access of men to education, capital, and the employment of wage labour provided them with new opportunities and devalued women's work.[17] A case in point is provided by the deterioration in the material circumstances and the standing of the Ga women traders of Accra mentioned above as they met competition from men with access to imported goods, capital, and extended trading networks. The women were pushed into less profitable areas of trade, found their margins reduced and the competition among themselves increased, and were transformed over time from relatively prosperous independent traders into precarious, poor and marginal street sellers typical of urban economies throughout the Third World today.[18]

As we have seen, colonial policy in Africa played a significant part in furthering these developments. In Africa, colonisation and 'modernisation' went by and large hand in hand. However, as our example of the Kumasi textile traders shows, the process of 'modernisation' itself may have negative consequences for women, regardless of whether it occurs under colonial rule or not. This is important for two reasons. First, it brings into our discussion areas of the Third World (such as Latin America) not recently under colonial rule; and secondly, it explains how it is that the situation of women can continue to deteriorate after independence and the departure of colonial rulers, as the process of male-dominated development continues. We have already seen how women can be either excluded from production or reduced to inferior status as the nature of the economy changes and men move into new areas of activity. Chaney and Schmink have argued that it is a general feature of the development process that new technology and opportunities are channelled overwhelmingly towards men, thus increasing their productivity relative to women. In combination with an ideology which preaches that woman's place is in the home, this leads to a reduction of opportunities and a lowering of status for women.[19] Other research suggests that the process is strongly reinforced (even in the absence of direct colonial involvement) by the attitudes and practices of development agencies in the Third World. Male planners and 'experts' tend to ignore (or devalue) the direct contribution made by women to production; resources are channelled towards men; women are the targets of programmes on 'home economics' rather than agricultural production techniques; overall, women are driven back into the domestic arena, and hence 'domesticated'.[20] Evidence from independent Zimbabwe suggests that this pattern of development is strongly entrenched. Under the Land Resettlement Programme land was being made over to individual males, while programmes for women were developed not by the Ministry of Agriculture, but by the Ministry for Community Development and Women's Affairs, and concentrated on home economics and small-scale craft and related projects. Jacobs comments as follows:

> The problems of peasant agriculture and resettlement in Zimbabwe have sometimes been construed as ones of unused peasant lands or of motivating women to participate in the economy. Neither contention corresponds to their situation in rural areas: any under-utilised land is white-owned, and women already participate economically on a massive scale. Rather, the 'problems' are their continued lack of rights over land and over the means of production, and definitions of development which implicitly exclude women.[21]

Women in Africa, then, generally played an important part in production in pre-colonial societies, usually (though not always) in connection primarily with the growing of subsistence crops. In addition, in colonial West Africa in particular, they played an important part in trade, often on an entirely independent footing.

Where settler agriculture developed in east, central and southern Africa, the undermining of African peasant production and the spread of wage labour for which men were favoured tended to destroy the role of women in production, and weaken the trade networks upon which they depended. In economies which became primarily labour reserves, the departure of the men (often for protracted periods of time) increased the burden on women as they sought to combine subsistence agriculture and cash-cropping with heavy household duties. And in general, European settlers, traders and entrepreneurs – either ignorant of the role of women in African societies or hostile to it – conducted their business through men rather than through women. Even after independence, men continued to be the favoured targets and the major beneficiaries of national and international development programmes, and the status of women continued to decline.

3. Latin America: paid work and political participation

Parallels can be found in Latin America for many of the issues discussed already in relation to Africa. The status of women on the eve of conquest varied. In Mexico, a class society was beginning to emerge under Aztec rule, and the dominance of the predatory 'war economy' over production for subsistence and exchange had weakened women's productive role and status.[22] In the Andean area, in contrast, the Incas had exploited (but not destroyed) a system in which women enjoyed considerable control over resources and the products of their labour, and were able to pursue their collective interests and maintain a degree of autonomy through religious cults and associated social and political networks.[23] In Mexico, the imposition of colonial rule accelerated the process of stratification and hastened the process of women's subordination; in Peru (where women enjoyed greater autonomy), male *curacas* were recognised as leaders, and women became legal minors, lost the land which supported the activities of their cults, and became liable to incarceration and subjection to forced labour in *obrajes* (textile workshops) run by Spanish bureaucrats and entrepreneurs. Overall, the impact of colonial rule seems to have been similar to that in Africa. Even today the process of incorporation into 'Western' society continues. The account by

Brown and Buenaventura-Posso of the integration of the Amazon-dwelling Bari into Colombian society since the 1960s provides a graphic description of the rapid undermining of sexual and social egalitarianism, and the imposition of hierarchy and male supremacy along with the destruction of self-sufficient subsistence farming in which women played a central productive role.[24]

The process of modernisation, too (occurring in this case outside the context of colonial rule) has had a marked effect on the role and status of women. A good example is provided by Young's reconstruction of the changes taking place in the Zapotec highlands of Oaxaca in Mexico over the last century. Although women do not appear to have ever had appreciable political power, they had some autonomy in the last century as a consequence of their usufruct rights in community land, reciprocal labour arrangements, and their position as skilled weavers producing cotton lengths and wicks for lamps and candles. Trade in these provided the range of goods required from outside this relatively self-contained and self-sufficient community. After 1870, however, cotton cloth production declined as it met competition from factory production within Mexico, and coffee was introduced as a cash crop through local *caciques*. Rapid changes came after 1930, when the pace of monetisation of the economy quickened, an active market in land developed, and differentiation began to occur. With the shift from cotton cloth production to coffee, women had lost a skilled activity which they could combine effectively with household duties, and control over a vital input to household budgets. In addition, competition between households had eradicated reciprocal labour practices, and increased the burden of work which women faced.[25] 'Modernisation' here (as in Africa) had adverse consequences for the relative standing of women.

However, we wish to extend our focus here by turning our attention to the emergence of wage labour, and assessing the balance of costs and opportunities as far as women are concerned. We shall then be able to assess the political consequences which follow from the ability of women to earn a wage. Young's study of Oaxaca makes an excellent starting-point. As a result of the process of differentiation in the area a complex 'three-class' society has emerged: employers of labour (*ricos*) and sellers of labour (*pobres*), and peasant households dependent on family labour but not obliged to seek paid employment outside. The situation of women varies from case to case. The wives of the rich farmers are able to lead lives of leisure or run shops or small businesses. Those on the family farms contribute increasingly heavy amounts of unpaid labour in coffee production, particularly at harvest time. And the wives of the poor (without sufficient land to secure their subsistence) are forced to seek work as agricultural labourers, where they can find it, or as domestic servants. For all but the wives of the wealthy, a clear deterioration in status and increase in the burden of work has taken place. Two points emerge from this analysis. First, deterioration in status is associated with the emergence of cash-cropping on peasant land, and with the proletarianisation of a substantial proportion of the population. Among the poor, men and women share the burden of proletarian status. Secondly, however, women bear the greater burden. They are subjected (either seasonally or permanently) to a double shift of work, and excluded from the leisure activities and consumption habits (cafe society, tobacco and alcohol) enjoyed by men. Here, at least, wage-earning by women indicates poverty and a desperate struggle to survive, rather than a widening of opportunity. Similar evidence from Colombia and Peru suggests that in the countryside women turn to wage labour only as the family becomes unable to secure its survival otherwise, generally as it approaches landlessness. The work available is generally low in status, in domestic service or in labouring tasks, poorly paid, and additional to the burden of work already borne.[26]

Increased entry of women to the labour market does not necessarily mean enhanced status, either in terms of work or in terms of standing within the family and the community. This is the more so because women's participation in productive labour – particularly in the countryside – has consistently been under-reported in census data. What appears to be entry to the labour market may in fact be a shift from productive labour on one's own land to poorly-paid work outside.

As regards the involvement of women in wage labour in the urban economy, the picture is a little more complex. Where labour-intensive industrialisation has occurred, employers have often preferred women for monotonous and repetitive work, particularly where the task has involved activities or skills easily associated with 'women's work' in the home. The most significant example in this respect has been the textile sector; at the turn of the present century 45 per cent of workers in textile factories in Brazil were women. There is a clear parallel here with other experiences of early industrialisation. In general, as industrial production has become more diversified, capital intensive and technologically complex, women have tended to be replaced by men, and the percentage of women in the labour force has fallen. Thus in Brazil again, by 1970 the proportion of women employed in the textile sector had fallen to 35 per cent, and only 17 per cent of workers in manufacturing industry were women.

The relative decline in opportunities for female employment in manufacturing industry and the formal sector in general, along with the increased flow of women to the cities, has forced women into the 'informal sector', in which work tends to be precarious, poorly-rewarded, low in status, and outside any legislative protection in terms of minimum wages, conditions of employment, or workers' rights. One aspect of Latin American migration which contrasts sharply with the case of Africa is that a majority of migrants have tended to be women, and for the most part young single women. A major source of employment for such women in the cities of Latin America has been domestic service. For example, of the adult women who migrated to Lima (the Peruvian capital) between 1956 and 1965, 30 per cent entered work as domestic servants; this accounted for over 62 per cent of those who entered the labour market. In 1970, there may have been as many as 90 000 servant women in the city.[27] The majority were single, aged between 15 and 24, lacking education beyond primary level, and without children. They were generally recent migrants from small towns or rural areas within relatively easy reach of Lima itself, and from lower-class families. For these women, domestic service provided a bridge between life in the provinces and life in the city; but for the great majority, their 'career' ended in their mid-20s and they married and became full-time housewives. All aspired to continue working (preferably on their own account as seamstresses or in similar occupations), but few were able to acquire the necessary capital or education. As entry into domestic service does often coincide with migration to the city, it can provide a basis for getting to know the ways of the city, and in a minority of cases can be combined with education or other forms of self-improvement. But it is generally an interlude between childhood and marriage. This is confirmed by similar statistics from Brazil, Argentina, and Chile: most domestic servants are recent migrants to the city, and most fail to proceed to better jobs in the formal sector. Indeed, it has been argued that their time in well-appointed middle-class homes gives them aspirations which cannot subsequently be satisfied, while their isolation from working-class networks of support prevents their establishing contacts which might open other avenues. Domestic service may thus well be a bridge that leads nowhere.[28]

Most Latin American women who enter the workforce do so from necessity rather than from choice. And for the great majority (particularly those married and with children) opportunities in the formal sector are scarce. Hence the significance of the 'informal sector'. In the struggle to survive women seek to turn to account their 'domestic' skills, often engaging in a wide range of time-consuming and poorly-rewarded activities, generally carried on along with child care, food preparation and other household responsibilities. Lobo's excellent study of Ciudadela Chalaca, a shanty town in Callao, within the metropolitan district of Lima, provides a case in point. She describes the activities through which Julio and Helsomina and their six children seek to survive and better their situation. Julio, a full-time worker in a belt factory, works as a tailor from home at evenings and weekends, and sells as scrap tin cans and other metal collected by his children. Helsomina has variously raised small animals such as guinea pigs, sold vegetables in the market, rewound into balls for subsequent sale scraps of wool gathered by her cousin in the textile factory where she works, brewed chicha for sale, bought food and other supplies in bulk for resale, and rented out space in her newly-acquired refrigerator. Taken together, such activities add enough to the income of the family to pay for materials to construct a solid house, and to educate a daughter as a secretary and a son as an electrician.[29] A study of the informal sector in Mexico confirms the view that for most women, entry to it is a matter of desperation rather than choice.[30]

Many activities in the 'informal' sector consist of highly exploitative work which significantly reduces the cost of labour to entrepreneurs. In much of Latin America, capitalists seek to compete with foreign and domestic competition by going back to the practice of 'putting-out' – shifting their activities from purpose-built factories to the homes of (mostly female) workers, and transferring to them the responsibility for acquiring and maintaining the necessary machines. A notorious example is provided by the garment industry. In Nezahualcoyotl, a suburb of Mexico City, an estimated 3000 unregistered domestic seamstresses sew up garments on machines that they themselves rent or purchase, picking up the cut material from downtown Mexico City and returning the finished garments. The pay is low, the business clandestine, and workers are subject to the impositions of inspectors who have to be bribed into silence, and uncovered by protective legislation of any kind.[31] It is difficult to see in work such as this any element of 'emancipation' for the women who do it. It is better seen as a subsidy to capital from a vulnerable and highly exploited segment of the labour force.

It is not surprising then, that until recently there has been considerable pessimism as to the job prospects for women in developing industrial society in the Third World, and in Latin America in particular. It is commonly argued that women tend to be pushed out into the highly exploitative informal sector as industry becomes increasingly capital-intensive and skill-oriented.[32] Some recent developments make these assumptions questionable, but (as we shall see) they do not in the end suggest that access to the labour market alone promises to change the status of women in the Third World. Particularly where industrial development has advanced considerably in Latin America, the trend of falling female participation in manufacturing industry is being reversed. This is largely a consequence of the organisation of large-scale modern industry in the garment and electronics industries, and therefore largely concerns the employment practices of major transnational corporations. In statistical terms, the consequences can be striking. In Brazil, for example, after falling steadily throughout the century, the rate of female participation in manufacturing industry rose sharply in the 1970s. By the end of the decade, practically a third of workers in manufacturing in the leading industrial state of Sao Paulo were women.[33] Such industries have concentrated, however, in the free-trade zones set up especially to attract multinational assembly operations (on patterns previously associated with the Far East), and here the proportion of women employed is far higher. In the free trade zone set up on the Mexico–United States border as many as 85 per cent of employees are women.[34]

In such industries as these, wages may be good by local standards, though many times below those multinationals would pay in the developed world. It would seem necessary, therefore, to revise our assumptions regarding the prospects for the incorporation of women into the modern manufacturing sector. On closer inspection, however, it is not possible to be so optimistic. The women employed are largely confined to monotonous, repetitive and demanding assembly-line jobs classified as unskilled. The work regime is harsh, and production targets qualifying for bonus payments practically unattainable. It is unusual for anyone to endure more than a couple of years of such employment, and in any case company practice is frequently to offer only short-term contracts in order to avoid legal commitments to long-term employees, and to lessen the prospect of labour organisation. Job security is low, therefore, turnover high, and prospects for promotion minimal. A full picture cannot be obtained, however, without examining the way in which contemporary employment practices intermesh with patriarchal structures in society. The women employed in these factories do not represent a random cross-section of adult women. They are overwhelmingly young and single, generally between the age of 18 and 24. For the most part they are resident in the family home, and are likely to be making a substantial contribution to the income of the household; in a significant number of cases, they will be the major (or only) wage-earner. This has two significant consequences. First, they are subject while active in the labour market to patriarchal controls within the family; the decision to take paid work may not be theirs, and they often do not control the wages earned. Secondly, their spell of employment in the 'global factory' will not present them with a life alternative; they will generally leave work and marry in their early 20s. Such work is therefore perfectly compatible with the patriarchal family and with a primary role as wife and mother. In this instance, at least, the situation in Latin America is directly comparable with that elsewhere in the Third World.[35]

A final factor which requires consideration is the apparently widespread existence of substantial numbers of female-headed households in Latin America (and generally throughout the Third

World). In much of the Third World, from a quarter to a third of households may be female-headed. For women heading a household which may contain a number of dependants, entry to the labour market is clearly a matter of survival. While not directly subject to patriarchal controls, such women suffer from the discrimination practised in the employment of women generally, the low level of wages (often defended on the grounds that women are earning only pin-money and do not 'need' a wage to maintain a family), and the need (in the absence of adequate social services) to combine running a household with paid work. They are faced, therefore, with a 'double burden' at its most extreme, and with the prospect of unremitting poverty.

For women in Latin America, then, entry to the labour market is likely to be a matter of necessity rather than choice. Employment opportunities are limited, and employment practices discriminatory. And in particular, greater access to the labour market does not of itself promise to generate substantial changes in the status of women. It takes place within a dependent capitalist society still dominated by patriarchal attitudes and values, and tends to fit in with those attitudes and values rather than to challenge them. It is not surprising, therefore, that the participation of women in conventional politics in Latin America also tends to confirm rather than to challenge the *status quo* in this respect. If paid work is seen as an indication of poverty and necessity – rather than a positive choice – it may lead to increased value being attached to 'leisure' as an index of social status. And if new industries employ single women for a period before marriage (as domestic service did in the past and may continue to do), their impact may easily be absorbed into traditional views of the 'domestic' role suitable for women. Contemporary research suggests that '*marianismo*' – the cult of feminine spiritual superiority and the celebration of the domestic sphere – remains powerful in Latin America,[36] and studies of women prominent in politics argue that they are channelled into (and generally welcome) public roles which reinforce their image as 'mothers'. Thus Chaney characterises female politicians in Chile and Peru as 'supermothers', transferring their caring and nurturant qualities deliberately and effectively to the public stage.[37] By opting for areas of concern connected with women's sphere as traditionally conceived, they reinforce rather than challenge the *status quo*. It is not surprising, faced with evidence such as this, that Western feminists have tended (though not without misgivings) to endorse the insistence of prominent women activists in Latin America that the 'separate sphere' inhabited by women is to be built upon rather than abandoned.[38]

4. The Middle East: the impact of Islam

Women's positions and their roles in the Middle East are widely attributed to the influence of Islam even though (in practical terms) the lives of poor Egyptian peasant women might not be so different from those of their non-Muslim counterparts in Africa with regard to domestic tasks, agricultural labour, child-rearing and community participation. The link between the subordinate status of women and Islam is complex and varied – in part because factors like regime ideology, power relations within the family, low literacy rates and employment opportunities also play a determining role, but also because Islam varies, and the way it is interpreted by individuals and regimes also varies considerably. The resurgence of Islamic fundamentalism in the Middle East and the establishment of the Islamic Republic in Iran has illustrated that development does not necessarily bring secularism in its wake.

Islam varies in several respects. There are different sects like Shi'ism and Sunnism, and there are different schools of legal interpretation within them. The weight and form of Islamic values also varies within particular social contexts: the folk Islam of the countryside is one of tradition and custom, and that of the urban educated more formal and intellectual. At the heart of Islam is the belief that the Quran is the word of God, and that the Quran and the *hadith* (the sayings of the prophet) comprise the basis for Islamic law. No distinction is made between religion and state and the duty of the good Muslim ruler and the function of the Islamic state is the implementation of *sharia* (Islamic holy law) codified some two centuries after the Quran. Since there are specific injunctions in the Quran concerning marriage and divorce, inheritance, modesty of dress and obedience to men, Islamic law enshrines the 'inequalities' of property inheritance, of legal witness and of rights in marriage and divorce. If, then, the historic

legal practice of Islam has created a framework of cultural preju-
dice against women, the varying ways in which regimes frame
their policy toward them is one index of the flexibility which
Muslims have to interpret Islam. But even where reforms in
personal status laws have taken place, change has generally been
justified by reference to Islam. Turkey has been unique in replacing Islamic personal status by a wholly secular civil code. The
most radical change in the Arab world took place in Tunisia in
1956 (although justification for the new laws was couched within
an Islamic tradition, albeit radically interpreted). The necessity to
justify change by reference to a pure or true Islam does set rather
strict limits on the debate about women's position and role.
Islamic feminists argue that the way the Quran has been interpreted is a deviation, and even a notable radical feminist such as
the Egyptian writer Nawal al-Saadawi links her critique of women's
subordination to a more pristine Islam. She emphasises the broad
ethical thrust contained in the Quran, rather than the detail of
the law:

> there have been religious thinkers and leaders who have insisted
> that Islam cannot be understood properly if it is taken simply
> as a conglomeration of unrelated precepts and statements.
> These brave people have opposed the isolation of sayings like
> 'And we have made you to be of different levels', or 'One
> above the other', or 'Men are responsible for women' from
> their general context and from the essential principles of Islam
> in order that they might be used to support backward interpret-
> ations of Islam.[39]

Whether such an approach to changing the position of women
will provide only a straitjacket of apologetics is a question for the
future, but the increasing political significance of Islam and the
popular mobilising potential of the various fundamentalist movements necessarily shape the context in which demands for reform
can be made. Changing women's position is not simply a question
of modifying customary and traditional practices, but an assault
on the heart of religion: the Quran as the message of God com-
municated through the prophet Mohammed. There are, however,
areas of law (other than personal status) which have been dispensed with. Civil and commercial law codes based on Islam have
been replaced by secular codes. However, where popular or legal

values relating to women and associated with Islam are operating in societies where men are in the ascendancy, change is more difficult. This is especially so when details of the law assign women an inferior position. Examining the real world of women in contemporary Islamic societies, it is nevertheless clear that Islam is not immutable. It is also clear that there is no unilineal progress whereby economic development goes along with secularism to the benefit of women, or even that economic exigencies necessarily bring increased employment opportunities for women.

The contrast between Iraqi and Saudi Arabian policies illustrate how regime ideology can act as a determining feature. Both states have labour-short economies. In Iraq, women were encouraged to seek employment at all levels. In Saudi Arabia, women's activities in all spheres (employment included) are heavily restricted, even though the Saudi Arabian government finds that the importing of foreign labour disrupts the conservative social values of the peninsular. The Ba'thist government in Iraq is avowedly modernist, but although women have increasingly moved into the labour market they are still very much dependent upon the goodwill of fathers and male relatives, and (given the high concentration of women in agriculture) still the source of cheap labour and subsidies to men working in urban centres. Although the Ba'thists have not radically changed personal status law the new code promulgated in 1979 emphasised criteria other than the Islamic principle, for the new amendments were based 'on the principle of the Islamic *sharia*, but only those that are suited to the spirit of today, and on legal precedents set in Iraqi courts . . . and on the principles of justice'.[40] These amendments guaranteed some rights for women in divorce, inheritance and marital choice, even though the extent to which the state would be able to intervene in such socially sensitive institutions as the family on behalf of women is questionable. Nevertheless it is in marked contrast to a state like Saudi Arabia, where women are forbidden to work, study in proximity to men or drive cars, and have only recently gained access at all to areas such as higher education.[41]

The contrast between these two societies is only partly a function of regime ideology. Iraq has undergone a prolonged process of change from the time of the late nineteenth-century Ottoman reforms, through colonialism and independence. Iraq, too, has a much lengthier history of urbanisation and modern education, whereas Saudi Arabia has undergone intensive change over a swift period and the changes have taken place in a society largely rural and pastoralist in character.

Perhaps the most dramatic impact of regime ideology on Middle Eastern women came with the establishment of the Islamic Republic in Iran and the consequent implementation of Islamic law and emphasis upon fundamentalist Islamic values. On the surface, it reversed what had seemed a gradual improvement in women's legal position over the previous fifty years of Pahlavi rule. After a visit to Turkey Reza Shah opened educational establishments to women, forbade discrimination in public places and forcefully abolished the veil, to the consternation of many. Although men's greater rights in inheritance and divorce were preserved, they were somewhat modified during the reign of Reza Shah's son, Mohammed. In 1967, the latter introduced the Family Protection Law, which gave the secular courts areas of jurisdiction over polygamous marriages and divorce; further measures extending these provisions were introduced in 1975. The Shah also launched campaigns against the wearing of the *chador* (the blanket-like outer garment). These reforms went along with a whole set of other secular measures, such as the replacement of the Islamic calendar with an imperial one. The clerical opposition to these changes was denounced as 'mediaeval black reaction'. The attack on tradition went along with the Shah's modernisation programme of industrialisation and agricultural reform. These latter processes, however, generally worsened the position of the great bulk of rural women, who were relatively untouched by the legal reforms or increased access to education. As Iran's national economy became more closely tied into the world economy and Iran's food imports soared, women contributed less and less to the family's food supply. For example, increased meat imports (along with erosion and overgrazing) brought a decline in herding, and with it the disappearance of women's traditional tasks such as milking, wool processing and rug weaving. Although there was an expansion in national education and employment, village girls and women rarely had access to schools and jobs. The Shah's modernisation programme shrank the world of village women, making them more dependent upon men. Furthermore, as men migrated to the towns women were forced to undertake rougher work like shovelling snow and squeezing rainwater out of the dirt roofs of houses.[42] Erika Friedl, who studied one Iranian village, summarised developments thus:

> Women . . . are edged out of production and are educated to become consumers ('homemakers'). The house is no longer where a woman's productivity is centred, but where the husband's economic success is demonstrated. Aside from her (unchanged) reproductive functions and such services as are necessary for the upbringing of her children, she becomes essentially part of the display.[43]

Even where women gain access to the sphere of production in the course of development, the effect (in the context of patriarchal control) may be to worsen rather than improve their situation. In the village of Asiaback, studied by Afshar, carpet weaving was introduced in 1967 after a man married a weaver and brought her to the village. By 1980, practically every household had a loom, and girls were beginning to weave at the age of six, and working full-time at weaving by the age of 12. Women who had previously spun their own yarn, collected natural dyes, and traded with weavers outside the village found themselves working as hands under their husband's or father's control. As they were excluded from the bazaar, they were unable to trade their produce. As a result of this new activity, a woman was able to earn a cash income over the year practically as large as that earned by a man, but in circumstances which increased rather than lessened her subordination:

> The rise in the contribution of women to the family income has not resulted in any improvement in their position. Women receive no payment for either spinning or weaving. The carpets are sold by the men in Saveh, where they also buy yarn and dyes. Women have no access to the sphere of circulation and do not own their produce nor their means of production. Neither are they able to sell their labour. Their ability to weave carpets has enslaved them even further in an unpaid relation of production which is kept separate from the money economy of the men.[44]

A further consequence of the introduction of carpet weaving was that fathers became reluctant to lose productive workers, and thus tended to marry their daughters later, at 18 or 19 rather than at 14 or 15 as before. A parallel can be drawn, therefore, between these young women and those who work in the Mexican assembly plants. In both cases, the situation is one of patriarchal control in which the woman does not enjoy independent use of the income she earns, and the system of control is strengthened rather than weakened.

In this case, the movement towards later marriage brought rural practice into line with the provisions of the Family Protection Code, but the effect was coincidental. In other areas, its effect has been minimal. One reason for this is that its provisions have simply been ignored (as are the provisions within Islamic law which give women some limited rights of inheritance and owner-ship). Another, however, is that such practices as polygamous marriage and divorce are rare, particularly in rural areas. An estimated 1 per cent of males are polygamous, and in Asiaback (to give one example) Afshar found that no divorce had occurred for 20 years. In general, the villages are not bastions of the ultra-conservative Islamic orthodoxy preached by the Ayatollah Khomeini. The influence of the mullahs is often remote, religious observance is lax, and social practices differ markedly from those prescribed. Afshar, again, reports that neither segregation nor the wearing of the *chador* are practised in Asiaback.[46]

There is, then, a marked contrast between the legal reforms introduced and the practical consequences of the Shah's moderni-sation programme. A limited number of middle-class women did gain some social and economic benefits, such as increased access to university education. But these women were alienated from the regime in the same way as their male counterparts by the chaos and inefficiency of the modernisation, the high level of repression and the excessive United States presence. In some ways, the cities have proved less hospitable for women than the villages. Hostility, aggression, and physical attacks from funda-mentalist males have been frequent, and (as we shall see) entry into the labour market has been made unattractive by the social and psychological pressures to which women have been subjected.

When the Iranian revolution broke out, there were high levels of female participation. Women, it seems, supported all groups: the secular *Fedayin*, the Islamic modernist *Mujahedin*, and the clergy. Middle-class and working-class women and students all joined the demonstrations and protests, and were frequently in the vanguard. Even some traditional village women (legitimated by religiously sanctioned opposition to the Shah) joined in demonstrations in nearby towns.[47] Donning the *chador* for demonstrations became symbolic of both secular nationalist and religious opposition.

The seizure of power by the fundamentalist wing of the clergy brought with it the implementation of an extreme interpretation of Islam based on assumptions of women's natural and biological inferiority. Because of family dependence upon women's wages, and because many of the working-class women who supported Ayatollah Khomeini worked, there has been no formal ban on female employment. Despite Khomeini's opposition to the extension of suffrage to women in 1962, women were not disenfranchised. Instead there has been a concerted propaganda drive directed against urban-educated women – that is, those from the strata most likely to oppose the regime. Khomeini has described women office workers as 'painted dolls who displace and distract men and bring sedition and degradation to the workplace'.[48] One further direct pressure driving women back to the home was the ban on nurseries at work places. These were considered 'dens of corruption'. Such propaganda has placed on men the onus of stopping the 'shame' of their wives and daughters working. Although many women have resisted the pressure to veil, those who are not modest in their dress have been harassed by the *hizballahis*, members of the party of God. The obsession with women's modesty and the stress on the necessity for domesticity and marriage has brought one Iranian feminist to comment that unmarried women are 'equated with terrorists', and to conclude that 'the effect of Islamic legislation has been to make women legitimate sex objects, excluded from most paid employment and chained with ever increasing social and ideological ties to the uncertainty of Islamic marriage'.[49]

Whether this Islam of Iran is the 'true' Islam or not is open to debate, but the Iranian experience illustrates that Muslim fundamentalists (and particularly the fundamentalist clergy) place a very great emphasis on the most conservative interpretation of Islamic textual sources relating to the position of women. Ironically, it is not only urban middle-class women who have been affected, but the urban poor and less well-off, and it is from these that the core of support for the clergy has derived. The regime appears to have greater control in the urban centres and although there is greater autonomy in the countryside it is here where the grip of the family and class has contained women within patriarchy. In Iran, then, change in urban society has produced improved access to employment and education, but the cities are more subject to the imposition of Islamic law and fundamentalist mores. In the villages, the prevailing values have sustained women's subordination as their roles changed with the expansion of capitalism and as industrialisation and construction in the towns attracted village men.

If the Iranian case illustrates the way in which regime ideology cuts against an improved position for women, developments in Egypt are less clear. As in Iran, a small but increasing number of women have sought employment in middle-class occupations and also as workers in textile factories. Interest in Egypt, however, has focused on the effects of the massive migration of Egyptian males from the countryside on the roles of the women left behind, particularly on the extent to which the absence of men has increased peasant women's independence. Recent research reveals rather mixed results. In general, though, it seems that migration has brought only limited changes in women's roles and positions. In most cases (in the absence of the male head of the family) an increasing burden falls on women, and girls are more likely to be taken out of the educational system than boys. Furthermore, male relatives from the extended family tend to make decisions concerning the spending of migrant remittances, the management of the plot of land and children's education. Yet increased autonomy depends very much on the stage women have reached in the reproductive cycle. At one extreme, the young childless married woman would be almost wholly under the public authority of the men of the family and the domestic authority of the mother-in-law. At the other extreme, a mature women in an established independent family – that is, one with sons or a son past infancy – would assume responsibilities for overall land management. In this case, she might control income from the land and her husband's remittances. Even so, it seems that such increased control is temporary:

On his return, he [the migrant male] resumes the patriarchal role he never fully relinquished. The months following his return are frequently ones of intense conflict . . . as he reappropriates what is socially his. The wife's resistance may well be tempered by the fear that his additional revenues may be invested in a new wife. In fact, this rarely happens, but it is a commonly expressed fear.[50]

The power to divorce in Islamic law is the prerogative of the male, and can clearly be used to ensure male ascendancy. Yet in her study of another Egyptian village, an Egyptian sociologist has suggested the potential for change, albeit within the context of woman's subordinate position within the extended family. The migration of young men has provided the finance for earlier marriage, and has thus increased the number of nuclear families at an earlier age. Within such families women have greater influence and participate more in family decisions.[51]

In summary, we can say that change has taken place in Muslim Middle Eastern societies. Girls and women have greater access to education and employment, although the length and nature of both tend to be determined by class position. In the rural areas, women have lost some of the small areas of independence, although there are varying effects on peasant women as a result of migration, be it to the towns or to oil-rich states. Contending interpretations of Islam do have an effect, but (as we have seen) the growth of fundamentalism – be it to produce an Islamic Republic or enhance the influence of its adherents – is unlikely to provide greater independence from men for women. Large-scale participation in the overthrow of the Shah was legitimated by the clergy. Yet even in Iran, the policies of the fundamentalist clergy have been tempered by political and social realities.

5. Conclusion: separatism, socialism and liberation

Our review of the situation of women in three regions of the Third World suggests that 'Westernisation' and 'modernisation' in themselves aré as likely to worsen as to improve the situation of women. This is in part a consequence of capitalist development and in part a consequence of the diffusion of 'Western' attitudes and practices regarding gender relations: whether or not the two are necessarily linked, they have historically gone hand in hand in the Third World.

In the light of the record we have documented, it is not surprising that prescriptions for the liberation of women in the Third World have been greeted with general scepticism.[52] Having distinguished between the impact of the penetration of capitalism and the impact of the diffusion of 'Western' attitudes and practices regarding gender relations, we shall conclude by examining in turn alternative strategies of liberation which relate to the rejection of these separate but connected phenomena. We look first at 'separatist' and culturally relativist positions (in relation to Islam), and second at socialist and socialist–feminist positions (in relation to Africa and Latin America).

In view of the deep penetration of Islamic values and social practices in the societies considered in the previous section, the degree of variety and flexibility in the Islamic tradition, and the hostility to Western influence in many areas, it is not surprising that a number of feminists have sought a way forward within the Islamic tradition rather than through its rejection. At one level (as we have seen) this effort may consist of rescuing that tradition from centuries of male domination and self-interested interpretation. At another, it may consist of proposing the sharp separation of male and female spheres already existing in these societies as a basis for independence and autonomy for women, and arguing that a strategy for 'liberation' in the Islamic context should build upon rather than reject the separateness of the male and female worlds. According to Higgins, 'Islamic feminists base their movement squarely on an ideology that stresses male and female distinctiveness and the desirability of separate spheres'.[53] There are echoes here of the position of some Latin American feminists (as regards the commitment to seeking a way forward within an indigenous cultural tradition), and also – superficially at least – of some radical feminist ideas. Within this approach, there is an attempt to re-evaluate the 'private sphere' of women. For example, in a study of religious observation, Beck argues that women inhabit and control a 'parallel world' of prayer meetings, cults, and spiritual advice which can function as a source of interaction and female solidarity.[54] The position is pushed to an extreme by Callaway, who sees seclusion as a possible basis for an autonomous women's realm, and Ahmed, who makes similar claims for the *harem* in Saudi Arabia.[55]

Insofar as this line of interpretation respects Islamic cultural traditions and avoids the trap of presenting Western practices as ideal, it is valuable. It becomes dangerously apologetic when it fails to incorporate a critique of present Islamic practice as a source of oppression, as when Wikan, for example, writes of Oman:

> There must be few contemporary societies where law and customary rules combine to define so powerless a position for women as in Oman. They have little say in the choice of spouse, cannot leave the house without the husband's permission, are debarred from going to the market to make a single purchase, often may not choose their own clothes, must wear masks before all males who are marriageable, and so forth. And yet I have never met women who seem so in control of themselves and their situation.[56]

Wikan argues that women judge themselves and each other not on the basis of imposed male values, but of values defined in their own world. But that world itself is the creation and reflection of male domination and female subordination. As other writers have pointed out, it is one thing to recognise that there may be elements in a particular situation which create space for a degree of autonomy and resistance (just as the generalisation of wage labour under capitalism creates the conditions for the overthrow of the system), and it may well follow from this that those elements should be built upon and transformed by revolutionary practice; but it is quite another thing – and quite mistaken – to claim that bondage should be celebrated because it is lived (as it will be until consciousness is revolutionised) as freedom.[57] Clearly, only an analysis which proposed a revolutionary transformation of the separate sphere of women could be described as radical feminist in orientation.

Although there is a basis in classical Marxism for the consideration of the 'woman question' as a specific and integral part of socialist revolution, the record of the existing socialist states suggests strongly that while the establishment of socialism leads to substantial advances for women (in comparison with their situation in capitalist society), organisation and mobilisation behind a separate feminist agenda is essential if such gains are not to be relegated to secondary status, or sacrificed as other priorities come to the fore. The clearest analysis of the merits and limits of a socialist rather than a socialist–feminist perspective is provided by Molyneux, who argues that 'the reforms of the socialist states in this area would form part of any feminist agenda for social change, and have done so in the past',[58] but goes on to discuss the problems that arise from the instrumental aspects of the socialist attachment to women's liberation, and the limitations of the manner in which it is understood within a socialist perspective. She argues that within that perspective there is a principled commitment to women's liberation, but that sexual equality is not a first priority; male and female roles are seen as complementary rather than hierarchically ordered; the primary goal is initially the destruction of the traditional social order, which entails substantial changes in the status of women; and the goal once the construction of a new stable order commences is socialist accumulation, which may at first prompt measures to open education and employment to women, but is likely to lead at a later stage to attempts to promote motherhood and the nuclear family, and to deny the need for a specific feminist agenda for reform. Without such a separate agenda (which has to be created and fought for), specifically feminist goals will be forgotten, or denied priority.

The accuracy of this analysis is confirmed by the experience of socialist states in the Third World. Reviewing the experience of Cuba, for example, where there has been a consistent commitment to advancing the status of women, Nazzari concludes that

> Material constraints to the solution of the woman question in Cuba originate in the drive for socialist accumulation and the development of the country's productive forces. These concerns have led the Revolution to make policy decisions that preserve women's inequality in the labour force, perpetuate the personal dependence of women on men, and thus work against the equal sharing of housework and child care as decreed by the Family Code.[59]

She points out in addition that the impact of the renewed emphasis on wage labour and material incentives in the 1970s, after the abandonment of the 'moral incentives' approach associated with

Guevara in the 1960s (particularly in combination with the appearance of unemployment as a problem later in the decade and the resulting pressure on women to leave the labour market) has been to reinforce this tendency. The Cuban experience reminds us, therefore, that within a socialist framework (as within a capitalist framework), the choice of a particular strategy of development may have unforeseen consequences as far as women are concerned.

Evidence from Mozambique, too, tends to confirm this picture. Urdang reports that although FRELIMO has been consistently committed to women's liberation – in principle, and in practice – it sees the oppression of women as arising from the traditional social order rather than from the structure of gender relations as such. Traditional practices such as child marriage, forced marriage, bride price and polygamy are attacked, but the alternative that is advanced is monogamy, and a campaign to incorporate women into production.[60] As a consequence, nothing is done to alleviate the 'double burden' which women suffer, and their traditional role in production is disregarded. Examining the activities of the state-sponsored Organisation of Mozambican Women (OMM), Urdang found that its plan of action for 1981 centred around the mobilisation of women to contribute to the consolidation of the revolution, but offered no programme relating to the particular needs of women themselves.

Even in socialist states in the Third World which make an explicit commitment to women's liberation, the obstacles to meeting the goals expressed do not lie only (as is sometimes suggested) in the reluctance of men brought up in a patriarchal society to give up their privileges, although this is part of the problem; they arise also from the tendency, within a socialist perspective, to associate the subordination of women exclusively with the capitalist system. Blindness to the separate impact of patriarchy leads to an inadequate understanding of the problem, and a deficient approach to its solution.

7

The International Context

1. Introduction

A state's international bargaining position depends on the character of the regime in control of the state and – especially in the Third World context – on the personality of the leader; on its economic resources and the extent of external control over them; on the alliances which the state makes with its neighbours and the intergovernmental organisations to which it belongs; and on the state's strategic importance. Virtually all Third World regimes have close links with the industralised West, conservative and traditional regimes by choice and revolutionary regimes (which otherwise gravitate towards the Soviet Union) out of military and economic need. The pull of the West is understandable: Western states (and the United States particularly, and Western-dominated institutions such as the World Bank and the International Monetary Fund (IMF)) have the resources to assist in a way that the Soviet Union, with its shortage of foreign exchange, does not; this is important for rulers who wish to survive – the state is the source of their own power and must be maintained.

Even those rulers who ally with the West out of choice rather than necessity may retain strong nationalist sentiments, leading them to take, for example, action in favour of indigenous entrepreneurs at the expense of foreign capital. However all rulers, whatever their ideological orientation, who indulge in too strident a nationalism face the danger of cutting themselves off from external support; their foreign policy will be designed to strengthen rather than erode their domestic power base. Ironically, the rulers of a poor state may be more secure than those who rule a wealthy state but squander its resources, or whose policies create grave social inequalities; such rulers may survive only if they are underpinned by an external power.

The extent to which the Great Powers interest themselves in the affairs of Third World states will depend on the geographical location and strategic importance of the latter, and on considerations such as the size of markets and investments. States particularly susceptible to external intervention will be those which are in 'the backyard' of a great power (the Latin American states in relation to the United States) and those which have a commodity for export (notably Middle East oil) which is vital to the industrial and military wellbeing of one or more of the Great Powers. For these reasons, Latin America and the Middle East have been of much greater importance than Africa to the Soviet Union, the United States and the industrialised countries of the West. However, since 1974 the Horn of Africa has become the cockpit of Great Power rivalry. The West remains determined to protect its investments in South Africa and in Namibia, which has rich deposits of uranium, despite mounting international criticism of South Africa's repressive apartheid policies.

The different international context of the three regions is reflected in this chapter, which gives more attention to external interference in the affairs of Latin America and the Middle East than of Africa and devotes correspondingly greater space in the Africa section to the institutions designed to promote political and economic co-operation among the region's 51 states. Least attention to such institutions is given in the section on the Middle East, since they have not been of much significance in that region. By the same token, the important role played by multinational companies in Latin America receives considerable attention.

2. The international context in Africa

Until 1974 (when military coups occurred in both Portugal and Ethiopia), Africa south of the Sahara was not a theatre of paramount concern for the two superpowers. With an eye primarily to Western security interests, the United States intervened in Congo–Léopoldville in the early 1960s, gave military support to Portugal (a NATO ally) in its fight against liberation forces in its African colonies, extended support to South Africa, and gave low-level backing (for a time) to the Smith regime in Rhodesia. After the Cuba missile crisis of October 1962 the volume of United States aid to Africa (which was already small) decreased further.[1] The Soviet Union, for its part, was not wholly impressed by the socialist rhetoric of African leaders such as Nkrumah of Ghana, Sékou Touré of Guinea, and Modibo Keita of Mali, but regarded them nevertheless as 'progressive' leaders who deserved encouragement. However, it gave minimal amounts of economic (as distinct from military) aid even to the radical states. Between 1954 and 1983 Soviet economic aid to sub-Saharan African states totalled only US $836 million; Western aid disbursements in 1983 alone, to the same area, were worth over $8000 million ($8 billion). Where the Soviet Union did score was in providing a model of what could be achieved through centralised economic planning; it also gained much credit for the financial and material support which it gave to the liberation movements in southern Africa.

In the late 1960s, both the superpowers supported the federal government in the Nigerian civil war. In the next decade (as the influence of middle-level powers increased and the voice of the People's Republic of China – which in 1970 began building a 1000-mile railway between Tanzania and Zambia on terms very favourable to these two states – carried greater weight in world affairs) bipolarity gave way to multipolarity. Soviet foreign policy was greatly affected by the Sino–Soviet split, and the Soviet Union's policy towards Africa (like that of the United States) became more pragmatically based than formerly.[2] Both sides now recognised the complexity of African politics, and the Soviet Union (more clearly than the United States) appreciated that socialism in Africa (even when it was expressed in Marxist–Leninist terms) was heavily overlaid with nationalism. Moreover, in both Angola and Ethiopia after 1974 the two superpowers avoided direct confrontation, and opted instead for proxy conflict – the Cubans (it would seem of their own volition) became the Soviet surrogates in both countries, while the United States backed the dissident forces championed by South Africa in Angola and from 1977 befriended Somalia rather than Ethiopia (its former ally) in the Horn of Africa. The latter became the cockpit of Great Power rivalry: both the United States and the Soviet Union had a strong strategic interest in the Indian Ocean. Under an agreement made with the Kenyan government in 1980, the

United States undertook a massive restructuring of the port of Mombasa, making it ready for use in an emergency.

In southern Africa, the policy of the United States government has been dictated by the very high level of Western financial investment in the Republic of South Africa – approximately US$25 billion in 1982, of which the US's share was $14 billion – by strategic and mineral resource considerations, and by a desire to halt the spread of Communist influence in the southern African sub-region – felt to be imminent following the establishment of Marxist–Leninist regimes in Angola and Mozambique in 1974–5 and of a radical regime in Zimbabwe in 1980. While condemning the white minority government's apartheid policies and stressing the need to moderate them, the United States has backed South Africa's attempt (in the face also of mounting domestic political pressure) 'to establish a "cordon sanitaire" along its northern borders by replacing the former white buffer with a stable ring of black buffer states'.[3] In recent years, South Africa has abandoned the détente policy pursued in the 1970s, whereby the National Party government sought to open a 'dialogue' with Black Africa, in favour of a military policy designed to curb the activities of the ANC and a destabilisation policy which aims ultimately to replace the revolutionary and radical regimes in the sub-region with moderate, pro-Western ones. South African troops have launched direct military attacks on ANC facilities in Mozambique and Lesotho and have penetrated deep into Angola, allegedly in pursuit of SWAPO guerillas. South Africa has also provided both military training and equipment to dissident groups in Angola and Mozambique. In defiance of the United Nations, it has continued to rule Namibia, where (by consolidating power in the hands of a multi-ethnic, puppet government) it is trying to prevent a SWAPO takeover.

As we note below, the South African government has continued to pursue its destabilisation policy despite the non-aggression and security pacts signed with the governments of Mozambique and Angola in 1984. Though a substantial segment of the business community within the Republic is convinced that this policy is mistaken and that it is damaging to the South African economy, the United States government has supported it, even to the extent of announcing publicly (early in 1986) that it would give military aid to the UNITA rebels in Angola. Unrealistically, the United States has linked the withdrawal of Cuban troops from Angola with the independence of Namibia and has refused to recognise Angola's MPLA government. The Soviets continue to station advisers in Angola and to provide military aid to the various national liberation movements in southern Africa. In this way, the Soviet Union and its eastern bloc allies build up political credit for the future at minimum cost to themselves – and thereby, ironically, contribute to the very outcome (the spread of Communist influence in the sub-region) that United States policy is largely designed to prevent. (However, the Soviets backed the wrong side in the Rhodesian liberation struggle – the Zimbabwe African People's Union (ZAPU) rather than the Zimbabwe African National Union–Patriotic Front (ZANU–PF), the present ruling party – and have little influence in Zimbabwe today). Moreover, though the Western powers are being forced to reappraise their attitudes to the white minority regime in the light of political upheavals and police repression within South Africa, where is at present scant prospect of their responding fully to the call made early in April 1986 by Desmond Tutu, then Anglican Bishop of Johannesburg, for the imposition by the international community of economic sanctions on South Africa. 'The United States does not believe that punitive sanctions will help promote change in South Africa', said a spokesman for the Reagan Administration in rejecting Bishop Tutu's call. 'In the US view, punitive sanctions would hurt South Africa's economy, which is central to the region's stability and a major force for change domestically'.[4]

If we exclude certain areas of the continent – notably the Horn of Africa and much of southern Africa – the predominant influence of external powers in Africa is exerted by neither the United States nor the Soviet Union (nor China, for that matter) but by the former colonial powers, especially Britain and France. Following independence, the 'mother country' was normally the new state's principal trading partner. African leaders sought to diversify their countries' trading links, the principal beneficiary being the European Economic Community (EEC); the volume of trade which even Africa's revolutionary states conduct with the eastern bloc's Council for Mutual Economic Assistance (or Comecon) is still very small. In February 1975 African, Caribbean and Pacific (ACP) states joined together in signing the Lomé convention with the EEC; this convention has been renegotiated by the ACP countries on two subsequent occasions. Under the most recent agreement, signed at Lomé on 8 December 1984 between the EEC and 65 ACP countries, European development aid was virtually doubled. Despite these new multinational ties, the economic, financial, military and cultural links between France and most of its former African colonies remain particularly close. The ex-British colonies are members of the Commonwealth and this (probably more than their membership of the United Nations) enables them to exercise some leverage in world affairs. However, the extent of the influence of African states is circumscribed by their continuing economic dependence.

This dependence was very real at the time that political independence was formally achieved, especially for those countries (such as copper-rich Zambia and Zaire) whose economies were based overwhelmingly upon the raw materials produced for export by multinational mining companies. From about 1965 onwards, a strong sense of economic nationalism led several African governments to take total (or majority) ownership of these extractive industries; however, the lack of indigenous managerial and technological skills meant that effective control still lay with the foreign companies. These and other African governments used the revenue accruing from the export of primary produce to launch modest industrialisation programmes, initially of the import-substitution variety. Many of these ventures – to produce cement, cigarettes, tyres and textiles, for example – were begun in conjunction with foreign companies. African governments tended to adopt an ambivalent attitude towards the latter: on the one hand, they sought to attract foreign investment through the grant of 'tax holidays' and other concessions and, on the other, they nationalised or (as in Kenya and Nigeria) 'indigenised' foreign-owned enterprises, either fully or in part. While major aspects of the economic organisation of states as ideologically divergent as Nigeria and Angola are still subject to foreign control, the ruling élites of these states are not mere puppets on foreign strings. This was shown when, in 1979, the Nigerian military government seized BP holdings as a punishment for the company's dealings with South Africa. Again (as we noted in Chapter 6) the Angolan government has not moderated its internal policies, which are based substantially upon Marxist–Leninist doctrine, in deference to Gulf Oil, an American multinational company which extracts Angola's oil from the Cabinda enclave. Moreover, no African country has been more assertive in its foreign policy than Tanzania, showing that even a very poor country can exercise a degree of political autonomy: President Nyerere at various times defied Britain and the United States, and from 1979 onwards strongly resisted the dictates of the IMF. Most African states (including Mozambique and Zambia) have been wary of coming under the exclusive domination of a particular superpower.

President Nkrumah of Ghana believed that a united Africa, subject to a single government, was the only effective way of ending external dependency; he was convinced that without unity neocolonialism and racist minority rule in Africa would continue. Julius Nyerere also favoured African unity but was not equally convinced that sub-regional blocs were incompatible with it; indeed, in the same year (1963) that the Organisation of African Unity (OAU) was formed, Nyerere was working hard to establish an East African federation linking Kenya, Tanganyika and Uganda. Though this move failed, the East African Common Services Organisation (a sub-regional functional union between the three states) survived and was transformed into the East African Community in 1967.

The Organisation of African Unity[5]

Since its formation, the OAU has registered some modest successes: it has provided a meeting ground for African leaders and has acted as an umbrella for sub-regional organisations and UN agencies, such as the Economic Commission for Africa (ECA); it has tried to settle interstate disputes and its liberation committee has to an extent helped several countries to throw off the colonial yoke. But there have been significant failures and numerous problems, of which some are due to the Organisation's cumbersome structure (which works against swift decision–making), its insecure financial base and its lack of a groundswell of popular support. The OAU also suffers from an excess of politics, as was shown in the secretary-general elections at the summit conferences held in June 1983 and November 1984. The underlying principles of the Charter have themselves contributed to the Organisation's difficulties. The clause stating that each independent African state has the right to join the Organisation has proved problematic in recent years, most acutely over the seating of a delegation from the pro-Western government of Chad, headed by President Hissene Habré, and the recognition as the Organisation's 51st state of the former Spanish Sahara under the title of the Saharan Arab Democratic Republic. The prolonged period of crisis over these issues (from 1982–4) threatened the OAU's very existence. Further difficulties have arisen over the principles of non-interference in the internal affairs of member states and non-alignment; neither principle has been strictly applied.

In respect of the major areas of activity established by the Charter, the Organisation's record is mixed. In promoting the liberation of southern Africa – always its principal area of concern – the OAU has worked through the African Liberation Committee (ALC), though never exclusively. In 1970 it adopted the Lusaka Manifesto of 1969, and thereby declared its preference for achieving independence in southern Africa through negotiation rather than armed conflict. It came to rely increasingly on the initiatives taken by a group of states – the 'Front-Line States' (FLS) – with a primary interest in the sub-region,[6] though these states were themselves sometimes divided over the best course to pursue in their handling of issues, such as those relating to Rhodesia and Namibia. Since the FLS operated on behalf of the OAU, the Organisation can claim to have played some part in the achievement of independence by Portugal's African colonies in the mid-1970s and by Zimbabwe in 1980. However, as far as the OAU itself is concerned, the Organisation's moral backing always counted for more than its financial support.[7]

In settling inter-African disputes, the mediatory efforts of the OAU have counted for much less than the mediation of individual African heads of state – the Organisation's projected Commission of Mediation, Conciliation and Arbitration was in fact never formed. The OAU, under cover of the principle of non-interference, has also failed to condemn the glaring atrocities which have occurred in several Black African states, and has been slow to act over explosive issues such as the Spanish Sahara and Chad. This is mainly because it is difficult for the Organisation (given the often divergent interests of its members) to agree on a common policy – most unanimity was achieved over attitudes towards South Africa.

Sub-regional economic co-operation

From the 1970s the OAU has shown an increasing concern with economic affairs. Economic resolutions were passed at several of the annual summit conferences, but the Organisation has lacked the financial and other resources to implement them. It has also often had to give prior attention to urgent (and frequently divisive) political issues. In April 1980 the economic summit in Lagos produced the Lagos Plan of Action, which sought to achieve collective self-reliance for the continent by the turn of the century, but the Plan has largely been ignored. The 21 heads of state and other African leaders who attended the 1985 summit adopted an 'Addis Ababa Declaration' on fighting drought and reducing tropical Africa's US$170 billion debt, but whether anything will come of this Declaration is another matter. The importance of economic co-operation is widely recognised and a large number of sub-regional groups exist in various parts of the continent for this purpose. Organisations with limited objectives, such as the Conseil de l'Entente between Benin (the former Dahomey), the Ivory Coast, Niger and Burkina Faso (the former Upper Volta), have a long survival record, while other small sub-regional groupings have collapsed, though some of them have subsequently resurfaced. In this section we focus on the two major existing associations (a third, the East African Community, collapsed in 1977): the Economic Community of West African states (ECOWAS) and the Southern African Development Co-ordination Conference (SADCC).

ECOWAS[8] The Treaty of Lagos, which was signed in May 1975, established a 15- (subsequently 16-) nation economic community of predominantly English- and French-speaking West African states which pledged themselves to work towards the free movement of goods and people throughout the community area, with the object of promoting trade between themselves and increasing their independence, as a group, from the rest of the world. The Community began functioning early in 1977 and set up its headquarters in Lagos, the Nigerian capital. Since then progress in certain directions has been achieved: for example, a common customs nomenclature has been drafted, an energy programme has been formulated and partly funded, a major communication project has been launched, and a comprehensive trade liberalisation and promotion programme covering a ten-year period from May 1978 has been agreed (the first phase of this programme was completed in 1981). On the other hand, the agricultural programme (which aims to make the Community self-sufficient in foodstuffs) was set back by severe drought that again, especially in 1984–5, afflicted the whole of the Sahel belt, and there have been serious delays in reaching decisions on such emotive issues as the member-states' contributions to the common fund based in Lomé. Economic co-operation has been hampered by the linguistic and ideological differences and poor communications between member states, and the proliferation of currencies, and of foreign exchange restrictions and controls, in the West African sub-region. Other difficulties have arisen because member states retain a strong sense of economic nationalism, and a majority of them are also simultaneously members of other West African sub-regional groups. Six Francophone West African states belong to the Communauté Economique de l'Afrique de l'Ouest (CEAO); some of the aims of CEAO, which has made remarkable progress in interstate trade since it began to function on 1 January 1974, conflict with those of ECOWAS. A weakness of ECOWAS is the extent to which it is dominated by Nigeria, which accounts for a third of its total budget, 60 per cent of its trade and two-thirds of its GNP.[9] The fact that Nigeria, an oil-producing state with a population of some 100 million, is facing major financial problems as a result of the sharp fall in the price of oil in recent years has serious knock-on effects for the Community. Because of all these impediments, only halting progress has so far been made towards achieving ECOWAS's primary goals.

SADCC[10] This sub-regional group came into being in 1979, but was not formally established until April of the next year. It has nine member states – Angola, Botswana, Lesotho, Malawi, Mozambique, Swaziland, Tanzania, Zambia, and Zimbabwe – which between them have a population of about 60 million. With substantial energy resources, rich mineral deposits and abundant agricultural land, the sub-region has great economic potential, but needs external finance, technology and manpower to supplement limited local resources in these fields. The stated aims of SADCC are to co-operate in designated areas in order to secure the equitable development of the sub-region as a whole and reduce the economic dependence of member states, especially on the Republic of South Africa. (In 1979, the South African government itself proposed a 'Constellation of Southern African States', the latest of its schemes for forging closer economic links with the black states to the north.) The areas of co-operation are: transport and communications, agriculture, industry and trade, energy, manpower development, mining, tourism, and finance. Individual member states are to co-ordinate functional activities within a specific area: Angola is responsible for co-ordinating energy and conservation, Mozambique for transport and communications, and Tanzania for industry and (from July 1984) trade. Food security is assigned to Zimbabwe but the co-ordination of agriculture generally is a shared responsibility, thereby underlining the vital importance of agriculture to the sub-region, parts of which have suffered from serious drought over the past three years.

Trade within the sub-region (which is at present limited) is to be encouraged, but – in the conviction that common markets and customs unions lead to the uneven development of member states – there is no intention within SADCC of establishing a free-trade area. Moreover, the creation of an integrated and balanced industrial economy is seen as a long-term, rather than an immediate, goal. Though many industrial projects have been formulated (to produce, for example, cement, paper and packages, textiles and farm equipment), the emphasis is on non-industrial areas of co-operation, with priority given to improving transport and communications as a means of stimulating production and facilitating trade. A development fund has been set up, with finance supplied mainly by Organisation for Economic Co-operation and Development (OECD) governments (especially governments in the Scandinavian and Benelux countries); most of the technology comes from the same sources. The Soviet Union has shown little interest in SADCC and has not supported its projects. By mid-1984 SADCC had generated some 250 projects costed at approximately US$5 billion; however, funding was sufficient for the completion of only 16 per cent of them.[11]

The fact that SADCC relies so heavily on external aid, even for co-operative projects, is a major drawback since it means that outside interests will influence (and may determine) project-choice and long-term strategy (SADCC member states themselves are committed to providing just under one-quarter of the total funds required). There is an obvious contradiction inherent in the position of most OECD governments (including those in the EEC, which is said to have been instrumental in the creation of SADCC): they are the chief financial backers of SADCC, but remain deeply involved in the South African economy. Notwithstanding the agreements reached by both Mozambique and Angola with South Africa in 1984 (the Nkomati Accord and the Lusaka Agreement respectively), South Africa still supports dissident groups in both countries: Nkomati has not brought peace to Mozambique, while the Lusaka Agreement has been rendered even more of a dead letter than it already was by the United States pledge (made early in 1986) to provide UNITA with military aid. The South African cabinet has also blocked the revised Southern African Customs Union agreement negotiated with the BLS countries (Botswana, Lesotho and Swaziland) in 1982, thus denying these countries the substantial increases in revenue to which they are entitled.[12] All the present indications are therefore that South Africa will continue to use its economic and military strength to maintain the *status quo* in southern Africa. Again, the economic nationalism of SADCC member states may lead some of them to retain (or develop) trade links with South Africa, thereby impeding the realisation of SADCC's aims. In 1980 South Africa sold US$1.3 billion worth of goods and services to 40 African countries – a huge increase on the $300 million worth of South African exports to the rest of Africa 10 years earlier;[13] and (in the wake of the Nkomati Accord) Mozambique entered into a number of co-operative enterprises with South Africa. SADCC's structure is still sufficiently flexible to allow a member state to pursue policies which it conceives to be in its own national interest: Zimbabwe has decided to expand the domestic production of coal-powered electricity at Wankie rather than to meet its additional electricity requirements by purchase from the Kariba–Kafue hydroelectric facilities in Zambia and/or the Cabora Bassa facility in Mozambique. This example underlines the difficulty which SADCC will face in achieving the equitable distribution of benefits. This is likely to become a real problem when in due course SADCC gives major attention to the industrial development of southern Africa; it has already become an issue in relation to the planned production of steel by four SADCC states.

Sub-regional political co-operation

The touchstone of what can be achieved through groups such as ECOWAS and SADCC will be the political leaders' perception of what is in their own and the national interest. Take, for example, the attitude of Félix Houphouet-Boigny, the veteran President of the Ivory Coast. A lukewarm supporter of the OAU (whose meetings he never attends), he participates actively in ECOWAS, serving as an elder statesman of the group and playing a key role in removing misunderstandings between member states. He is also a firm supporter of the annual Franco–African conferences, which deal with issues such as collective security and economic co-operation. One thing is certain: given the conflicting interests of African states and the political instability from which many of them suffer, it will be impossible in the forseeable future to form a continent-wide political union, subject to a common government, such as Nkrumah advocated. The OAU itself has been too internally divided to take any initiative in this direction (and, indeed, has also done next to nothing to promote political co-operation among small groups of member states). The record in the latter sphere is not encouraging. Of the many attempts which have been made (both before and after the establishment of the OAU in 1963) to form political unions, only a small number have been successful: the union of Ghana and British Togoland in 1957, Italian and British Somaliland in 1960, Southern Cameroons and the Republic of Cameroon in 1961, and Tanganyika and Zanzibar in 1964. Perhaps to these should be added the confederal association of Senegambia, linking Senegal and the Gambia in 1981, though this association falls short of full political union. The parties concerned freely entered into these unions; however, except in the case of Tanganyika and Zanzibar, each union was achieved before the independence of one or both parties. In the exceptional case, Chinese and East German influence in Zanzibar was a factor taken into account by President Nyerere's government.

Against these successes must be set a number of failures, important reasons in each case being institutional incompatibility and the perception of incumbent leaders that their political power base was being (or would be) eroded. These were the main cause of the early collapse of the Mali Federation formed in 1959 between Senegal and the French Soudan (later Mali),[14] while they proved a major stumbling bloc to the formation of an East African federation in 1963. No comparable attempts at achieving small-scale political union have been made in the subsequent period and (with the main exception of Somalia in the Horn of Africa) African states now accept the interstate boundaries established at independence.

3. The international context in Latin America

For the Latin American states, and particularly for the smaller states of Central America, the overwhelming presence of the United States to the north has been the most significant defining factor in the international context throughout the present century. Our first consideration, therefore, must be with the role played by the United States. Secondly, we should consider the role of international organisations and multinational corporations. Finally, we shall be able to assess the extent to which a collective Latin American voice independent of the United States is emerging in the region.

Ever since 1823, when President James Monroe warned the European powers to keep out of the Americas, the United States has claimed the right to exert exclusive authority in its own 'back yard'. Although its economic and military power was not initially equal to the task, by the turn of the century the occupation of Cuba (1898), the annexation of Puerto Rico (1898) and the sponsoring of the breakaway Republic of Panama, formerly a province of Colombia (1903), signalled US readiness to back up its claims with forceful action. Active intervention was officially endorsed in 1904, when President Theodore Roosevelt announced that his country would exercise 'international police power' in cases of 'chronic wrongdoing or an impotence which results in a general loosening of the ties of civilised society'.[15] Over the following three decades Central America and the Caribbean became a familiar stamping ground for United States troops, deployed at various times in Mexico, Cuba, Panama, Haiti, the Dominican Republic and Nicaragua, while the United States government made (and unmade) governments throughout the area. In addition, Mexico (which had suffered considerable territorial losses to the United States in the nineteenth century) suffered intervention during the revolutionary period. At first such interventions were justified (as by President Taft in 1912) on moral and racial grounds; inevitably, however, the strategic and economic self-interest which had been present from the start came increasingly to the fore as United States business interests followed the flag: looking back on his military career in 1935, General Smedley Butler candidly described himself as 'a high class muscle man for Big Business, Wall Street, and for the bankers'.[16]

In the 1930s, when the 'Good Neighbour' policy announced by President Franklin Roosevelt in 1933 began to operate, emphasis was switched away from armed intervention to the promotion and support of local dictators, throughout Central America and the Caribbean. Some, such as Rafael Trujillo in the Dominican Republic and Anastasio Somoza in Nicaragua, got their start as commanders of a United States-created National Guard. Others, such as Fulgencio Batista in Cuba and Hernandez Martinez in El Salvador, became dependable allies of the United States after making their own way to office. All proved harsh and intolerant, and in the end ruled without any semblance of popular support.

During the Second World War and its immediate aftermath, a number of important developments occurred. First, the United States emerged as a world power. Secondly, it began to define its interests (in global terms) in opposition to those of the Soviet Union as it perceived them, and to assess conflicts within the Americas in the context of the Cold War. Thirdly, it sought to extend its diplomatic and economic power further across mainland South America. And, fourthly, it began to find ties with dictatorships south of its borders increasingly counter-productive, given the need to defend the values of democracy against the challenge of the Soviet Union, and to respond to pressure throughout the 'Third World' for social reform and political freedom. Fifthly, however, it found that its strategic and economic interests were frequently tied to anti-democratic forces, and in this context a number of serious dilemmas arose.

Nationalist governments which put United States economic interests at risk in their pursuit of social justice were denounced as communistic and Soviet-controlled – as with the government of Jacobo Arbenz in Guatemala, overthrown in a coup organised and funded by the CIA.[17] But in the same period the United States threw its support behind democratisation in Brazil in 1945, and in Bolivia after the revolution of 1952. A consistent pattern seemed to be emerging when Colombia and Venezuela were prompted toward democracy under moderate leadership in 1958, but the situation in the region changed dramatically at the end of that year, when Fidel Castro swept to power in Cuba as Batista's dictatorship crumbled while the United States dithered in the wings.[18] The consolidation of the Cuban Revolution and its rapid shift into the Soviet orbit has been the major factor behind United States intervention in the region ever since. For the last 25 years the United States has been the prisoner of its own perception that a confrontation between the superpowers has been playing itself out in Latin America, and its policy has been pulled in two opposing directions. On the one side is the awareness that social reform and democratisation are essential in the long run if the underlying conditions of poverty and repression which make revolution attractive are to be removed. On the other is the perceived need to support conservative allies and build up friendly armies in order to protect United States interests in the short term, and prevent radical opponents from gaining ground. This is a 'two-track' policy, in which one track persistently runs foul of the other.

The problems the United States has faced are clearly seen in the failure of the Alliance for Progress, launched by President Kennedy as a direct response to the Cuban Revolution. Its reformist impulse was rapidly lost as the armies built up across Central and South America and trained in the task of counter-insurgency tired of the moderate politicians sponsored by their paymasters, and took power for themselves, urging the need to adopt drastic methods to root out the guerrilla movements which sprang up across the continent in the wake of Castro's success in Cuba. The threat these movements posed was rarely substantial, but the United States soon abandoned its commitment to reform as the strategic perspective which had initially inspired it underwent a reorientation. In the wake of the botched attempt to defeat the Cuban Revolution at the Bay of Pigs, President Kennedy sponsored the overthrow of the democratically-elected President Bosch of the Dominican Republic, while his successor (President Johnson) supported and swiftly welcomed the coup which overthrew President Goulart of Brazil in 1964, and sent 20 000 troops to the Dominican Republic in 1965 to prevent Bosch from returning to power.[19]

Developments such as these, in response to the Cuban revolution, set the scene for United States relations with Central and South America in the 1970s and 1980s. The overriding goal became to prevent at all costs the appearance of another Cuba in the Americas, and sporadic attempts to promote or support reform broke down as old allies reacted with hostility, or new forces threatened too radical a departure from the *status quo*. The situation was further complicated by suspicion arising out of long-standing United States links with the most conservative business and political interests throughout the region, and by the refusal of local armies (greatly strengthened by United States aid and by the licence given them by the doctrine of counter-insurgency to play a dominant role in domestic affairs) to heed the urgency of social reform. Given its record, it was not easy for the United States to pose in the region as the agent of democracy and progress.

The dilemmas facing the United States in South America over the last two decades are best seen in the case of Chile. In the early 1960s, concern that the Conservatives who ruled the country would prove unable to resist the power and appeal of the left coalition headed by Salvador Allende (a socialist doctor with lengthy parliamentary experience) led the United States to back the newly prominent Christian Democratic leader Eduardo Frei, in the hope that he would provide an attractive reformist alternative to socialism. To this end, millions of dollars were poured into the country to back Frei's presidential campaign in 1964, and in the wake of his resounding victory he was encouraged to pursue land reform and other progressive measures. The eventual outcome was unfortunate, from the United States point of view. Frei's 'Revolution in Liberty' weakened under pressure from the right in the country and from conservative elements in his own party, the most committed reformers moved to the left as they saw their hopes frustrated, and in 1970 the Chileans elected Allende (by the narrowest of margins) as their president. Although the Allende government had been democratically elected, and was committed to a reform programme broadly similar to that adopted by Frei with United States blessing in 1964, his government faced unremitting hostility from the United States. United States agencies promoted economic destabilisation and funded civil disorder, while stepping up aid to the armed forces, and had their reward in September 1973, when General Augusto Pinochet seized power at the head of a military junta which continues to rule the country today.[20] The bloodshed which accompanied and followed the coup, along with the curtailing of civil liberties and the widespread use of repression and torture, inevitably reinforced the impression that (despite lip service paid to democratic reform) the United States would tolerate any action (and any regime) however harsh, which could present itself as fundamentally opposed to Communism. The recent record of the United States in Central America – and in particular its lawless campaign against Nicaragua – strongly reinforce this impression.[21]

If the United States is indisputably the major external governmental actor in Latin America, it is by no means the only major international force. In terms of the economic development of the region and its foreign policy orientation, as important a role has been played by multinational or transnational corporations. Up until the Second World War, the major foreign corporations engaged in the region were concerned above all with the exploitation of natural resources, and primarily with minerals. The activities of primary commodity-producing multinationals (generally but not universally of United States origin) produced a nationalistic reaction of particular intensity from the 1960s onwards, but at the same time the very governments which were reacting with hostility to the activities (and sometimes the presence) of those corporations concerned primarily with the extraction of raw materials were actively promoting the entry into their economies of a new wave of multinational corporations engaged in manufacturing activity. The result, over recent decades, has been a weakening of the hold of foreign corporations in the raw materials field, and their replacement with state monopolies or joint ventures of various kinds, and a shift of the bulk of multinational activity into the areas of manufacturing – again commonly on the basis of joint ventures either with the state itself or with private companies of indigenous origin. As a result, the issues involved in multinational investment have changed. Concern over the national control of sources and production of raw materials (with its accompanying nationalism) has tended to give way to an increasingly sophisticated process of bargaining with mining and manufacturing multinationals over such issues as investment programmes, rates of profit, levels of taxation, transfer of technology, and access to overseas markets. For the mining multinationals in particular, direct ownership is largely a thing of the past, but access to technology, markets and foreign finance has enabled them (in many cases) to accept 'nationalisation', often in return for generous compensation, but to continue to reap handsome profits from service contracts and other continuing links with their former properties.[22] Additionally, in the most developed countries of the region (notably in Brazil and Mexico) the multinationals are only a part of a diversified and advanced modern industrial sector in which their practices differ little (if at all) from those of the largest nationally-owned enterprises and the companies owned and operated by the state.

The heyday of nationalist confrontation over foreign monopoly extraction of raw materials came from the later 1960s onwards. There had been earlier confrontations (such as the nationalisation of foreign-owned oil companies in Bolivia and Mexico in the 1930s), but it was in the atmosphere of developmentalism and the assertion of national sovereignty in the period of global decolonisation after 1960 that the major confrontations occurred. In 1968, the incoming Peruvian generals nationalised the International Petroleum Corporation, and the Venezuelan-based companies passed into national ownership under agreed terms in 1976. By this time, as the role played by Venezuela in the development of OPEC testified, the act of nationalisation *per se* was not necessarily the major element in a strategy of extracting greater benefits from natural resource endowments.[23] In the meantime protracted negotiations with the copper companies active in Chile had led to the taking of a majority share by the state under Frei in 1967 (under terms substantially modified in 1969), and to outright nationalisation (with the unanimous support of Congress, and without compensation) under Allende in 1971.[24] In the same period, Peru nationalised the Cerro de Pasco Corporation, but its different treatment of the Southern Copper Corporation (engaged in a large-scale long-term investment programme) gave an indication that the nature of the issues was changing.[25]

The major change came, however (as noted above) with the arrival of the major manufacturing multinationals in the region. The process began in earnest after the Second World War with the arrival of European car manufacturers in Brazil, keen to break the American grip on assembly operations and on imports. Volkswagen was swiftly followed by Ford and General Motors, and over the ensuing three decades manufacturers moved into a number of countries in the region.[26] Today the major economies of the region are able to play one company and one country off against another, acquiring commitments to long-term investment and to greater transfer of technology after short periods of in-country production. One consequence has been the divergence of the interests of different countries on such issues. In Central America, individual corporations involved in the production of raw materials or agricultural commodities (such as bananas) may still present a substantial obstacle to national sovereignty; in the middle-ranking countries of the region the struggle to attract manufacturing investment may prove an unequal one (as Chile has found over the last decade, despite its unprecedented concessions to prospective investors); for the major emerging industrial powers of the region (Brazil and Mexico) access to foreign technology and investment is a key component in their development strategy. Advanced manufacturing industry in Mexico is still dominated by United States capital, whereas Brazil has attracted investment in fairly comparable proportions from the United States, Europe, and Japan;[27] both have found the goal of national independence an elusive one, as links with multinationals prove a necessary avenue to modern technology and international finance. At the same time, the high levels of capital investment (and foreign exchange spending) required to set up sophisticated modern industries commit them to develop these new industries as exporters and foreign exchange earners, and expose them to the competition of similar producers elsewhere (and the footloose global sourcing policies of the modern multinationals). Dependency, reduced in one area, is created in another.[28]

The difficulties caused for economic co-operation at the regional level by uneven industrialisation are clearly seen when we turn to the final topic covered in this section, that of the role of regional and international organisations in the area. On economic issues, the most significant venture has been the creation of the Andean Common Market (or Andean Pact), set up under the Cartagena agreement of 1969. First of all, anticipated economic integration has failed to materialise, as each of the participating countries has entered long lists of exceptions and protected lines of production, thus greatly weakening the impact of general plans for reduced tariff barriers. Secondly, the apparent virtual unanimity of the early 1970s over the issue of strict national control over foreign investment has disappeared, all but wrecking the organisation as a consequence. A decision was taken in 1971 that all member countries would adhere to a set of common practices – the most important of which related to maximum rates of profit repatriation, and protection of particular areas of production for national or joint ventures, or mandatory movement towards joint venture status.[29] As economic circumstances and governments have changed, regional solidarity on the issue has dissolved. Both Chile and Colombia have broken with the organisation over Decision 24 (as the foreign investment code of practice is known). Interstate rivalry and anxiety to offer attractive terms to foreign investment has precluded any consistent concerted action to establish better bargaining positions where the entry of multinationals to local economies is concerned. The distinction between national and foreign capital is not so significant (to policymakers in these capitalist-oriented economies) as the imperatives of global capitalist competition. National capital increasingly adopts the character of foreign capital and seeks links with it, so that the end result is one in which the multinationals embed themselves deeply into the national economy, reshaping it in their own image. As a result, the whole economy – rather than simply that part of it directly controlled by foreign capital – becomes 'internationalised'.[30]

On the other hand, the emergence of Mexico and Brazil as industrial giants south of the Rio Grande has been a central element in a steady shift of diplomatic power in the region away from the United States. One forum in which this has been particularly clear has been the Organisation for American States (OAS), founded in 1948 and soon enlisted by the United States into its global Cold War effort. For the first two decades of its existence it proved highly biddable by the United States, expelling Cuba after the revolution, for example, and endorsing the invasion of Guatemala in 1954 and that of the Dominican Republic in 1965. But in the 1970s Mexico's long-standing independent foreign policy began to gather support in the region, particularly as Brazil (committed to an independent foreign policy from 1960) began to develop its links with Black Africa. The first sign that a major shift had occurred came in 1979, when the United States was unable to win support at the OAS for a regional policy of hostility to the Sandinista regime in Nicaragua, and the subsequent emergence of the Contadora Group of Latin American countries (led by Mexico and Venezuela and committed to finding a peaceful solution to the Central American situation) confirmed the United States' weakened diplomatic power. The group – named after the Panamanian island on which the foreign ministers of Colombia, Mexico, Panama and Venezuela met in January 1983 to set it up, in an effort to find a political solution to conflicts in Central America – swiftly established a diplomatic position independent from that of the United States. In January 1986 along with the Lima Support Group (the South American democracies of Argentina, Brazil, Peru and Uruguay), it issued the Caraballeda Message for Peace, Security and Democracy in Central America, calling for a Latin American solution based on self-determination, non-intervention, pluralism, the departure of all foreign troops, the closure of military bases, and the ending of international military manoeuvres in the region.[31]

Over the last two decades, then, economic interests have diverged sufficiently to make united action difficult, while the growing power of states in the region has reduced the historic predominance of the United States. The evidence of the reorientation of the OAS and the activity of the Contadora Group suggests that Latin America is beginning to find a voice of its own; but the United States remains the major obstacle to the establishment of an authoritative and independent regional perspective.

4. The international context in the Middle East

The Middle East has been subject to extensive external intervention. Religion, strategic importance and oil have provided the major motives for foreign powers to seek political influence and a military presence in the area. In the past, the Western powers have sent crusaders and colonial armies and more recently the United States has established a Rapid Deployment Force (RDF, renamed US Central Command in 1983) to ensure access to oil supplies. Imperial Russia and the Soviet successor state have been concerned to exert influence in a region on which it abuts. In turn, the West has been keen to contain Russia's influence in the area: in the nineteenth century, it was through supporting Turkey, 'the sick man of Europe'; in the twentieth, by building regional alliance systems.

Tension and conflict between the states in the region have facilitated external powers' search for influence and allies. The Arab–Israeli conflict and the Palestinian problem, the tension between conservative monarchical and radical republican regimes in the 1950s and 1960s and, between radical Islamic and conservative and secular ones in the 1980s, have resulted in Middle Eastern states relying on Eastern and Western Europe for arms and security. The alignment of states with different superpowers has frequently increased interstate tensions. Yet there has also been a great deal of fluidity in the foreign alignment of states in the area, and notable dramatic realignments. Whilst Africa and Latin America generally remained immune from the repercussions of the Cold War, détente and the New Cold War, the Middle East has been very much entangled in it.

Neither the Soviet Union nor the United States had a colonial past in the Middle East. It was France and Britain which sought to defend their remaining economic and military interests against the rising nationalist tide in the post-Second World War period.[32] The most stalwart supporter of nationalism and independence was the Nasser regime in Egypt. Egypt's support for Algerian independence from France, opposition to regional states joining Western military pacts, its arms purchase from Czechoslovakia and nationalisation of the Suez Canal culminated in the joint Israeli, British and French invasion in 1956. The failure to bring down the Egyptian regime marked the end of significant European influence in the Middle East and a complete identification of these powers with the Israeli enemy. The Egyptian arms purchase from the Eastern bloc alienated the United States which (with Britain) refused to fund the Aswan dam, a project crucial for the agricultural and industrial development of Egypt. Nationalist –

and increasingly neutralist – Egypt accepted Soviet aid for the dam project and conducted a militant propaganda campaign against the pro-Western regimes of Iraq, Jordan and Lebanon. The United States replaced Britain and France as the architect of a pro-Western regional alliance system, a policy crystallised in the 1957 Eisenhower doctrine: an offer of US economic and military aid against 'armed aggression from a nation controlled by international communism', namely Egypt.[33] By 1958, the pro-Western Iraqi monarchy had fallen, Lebanon was undergoing a civil war, the Jordanian monarchy had come under severe internal threat and Egypt and Syria had formed a United Arab Republic. Although Lebanon and Jordan stabilised, Syria, Iraq and Egypt (the most populous of the Arab states) were receiving arms and aid from the Soviet Union.

Western pressures against nationalist regimes (against Egypt in particular) had undermined the broad policy of containing the Soviet Union with United States-sponsored military pacts with the Northern Tier, Turkey, Pakistan and Iran, and British-sponsored pacts with the Arab states, targeted at the Soviet Union's 'soft under-belly'. In the jargon of the time the Soviet Union had 'leap-frogged' the encirclement, but at the request of the states of the area rather than through any purposeful expansion. The Soviet Union became identified as a supporter of republican Arab nationalism, and (indirectly) of the Arab side in the Arab–Israeli conflict. The increased links between the Soviet Union and radical nationalism encouraged the more conservative Arab monarchies (like Saudi Arabia and Libya) and Iran to seek stronger ties with the West, as it encouraged the United States to bolster Israel with direct governmental economic and military aid.

Although the United States was able to support Israel (on the basis of a shared opposition to radical nationalism), and the conservative Arab states (on the basis of anti-Communism), there were tensions with the latter because of United States support for Israel. The Soviet Union had its own problems with the Arab nationalist states because it had recognised Israel's right to exist in 1948 and (although the USSR opposed Zionism) never withdrew its acceptance of Israel within the 1948 boundaries. A further constraining factor on Soviet influence was the popular view that although the USSR was a useful supplier of arms and aid, it was a Communist state adhering to an atheistic ideology. Radical nationalist regimes regarded Communism as alien – and, certainly, the bulk of their Muslim populations did.[34]

Despite these tensions, the superpowers supported their regional allies in the 1967 and 1973 wars, both of which threatened to embroil them directly in the conflict. Middle East conflicts clearly had the potential to become global ones, since (in the last resort) the only way the superpowers could sustain their influence to realise their interests in the area was through the provision of military and diplomatic aid which enhanced the ability of the states to act independently of a superpower ally. The dual consequences of the 1967 war acted as a spur to independent action. On the one hand, the fear of global confrontation led to a form of détente between the United States and the USSR in the area but, on the other hand, Israel's victory resulted in the occupation of Syrian, Egyptian and Jordanian territory and a group of states opposed to the post-1967 *status quo*. Egypt and Syria launched the 1973 war to draw the Powers into the Arab–Israeli conflict.

Events subsequent to the 1973 war showed that the alignment of states in the region with any particular superpower is not fixed. Desperate to recover Sinai and reopen the Suez Canal, Egypt turned to the United States with a view to generating diplomatic pressure on Israel from the latter's most powerful supporter. The United States government took the opportunity to take Egypt (the most powerful of the Arab states) out of the Soviet orbit and ultimately out of the conflict with Israel. The Camp David Accords of 1978 and the Egypt–Israel Treaty of 1979 (both mediated by the USA) brought together the two strongest protagonists in the Arab–Israeli conflict. Indicative of the importance of the region for the United States was the fact that Israel and Egypt were the two largest recipients of military and economic assistance by the mid-1980s.

Despite the fact that oil came largely from the Arab states, it was not until 1973, with the embargo of that year, that the United States' involvement with Israel affected her access to oil. The main producers of the 1950s and 1960s were non-Arab Iran, states under British protection like Kuwait and Bahrein, or states like Saudi Arabia whose major foreign policy goal was to prevent the radical republicanism of Nasser spreading to the Arabian Peninsular. The only real divergence of interests between the Arab oil-producing states and the United States concerned the

Arab–Israeli conflict. Otherwise, they were agreed on combating Communism and the influence of the Soviet Union and nationalist states aligned with the Soviet Union. The succession of President Sadat in 1970, his shift toward the West and his expulsion of Soviet advisers brought the 1973 oil embargo as the *quid pro quo* from the conservative oil-producing states. Israel's military predominance and the indirect involvement of the oil states in the 1973 war through the oil embargo caused the latter to view Israel as a real threat. Because the United States had become dependent on oil imports after 1970, both the United States and Saudi Arabia had a vested interest in ending the major issue between them: the lack of a solution to the Arab–Israeli conflict and the Palestinian problem.

Events in the region were to play into the hands of the United States toward the end of the decade. In 1979, the Soviet Union invaded Afghanistan at the request of a government which had come to power through a coup; in 1979, the Shah of Iran was replaced by an Islamic fundamentalist government, and in 1980 Iran and Iraq went to war. Fearful of a threat from an Islamic regime which was 'anti-imperialist', anti-monarchist and favoured the 'oppressed and the downtrodden', the Saudi government turned to the United States for the weaponry to withstand the Iranian challenge. Regional tensions gave the United States the opportunity to reconsolidate an influence over Saudi Arabia which would put aside the divergence on the Arab–Israeli conflict. Advanced Warning Aircraft (AWACs) were supplied under contract terms which made them wholly dependent on US personnel for their operation and maintenance.[35] Although the states of the Gulf have emphasised their unwillingness to accept American military bases on their territory and that the unresolved Palestinian problem and the Israeli enemy are their major problems, the United States government has continually pressed a policy of 'strategic consensus': that the USSR is the major threat to regional stability and the supply of oil. With the exception of Oman, the states of the area have not accepted this image of an aggressive, expansionist Soviet state threatening the 'free movement of Middle Eastern oil', as expounded in the Carter Doctrine of 1980. Yet the very weakness of the sparsely populated and politically underdeveloped states of the Gulf prevents any capacity for self-defence against an Israel or an Iran.

Although militarily dependent, it might have been expected that the vast revenues accruing to states like Saudi Arabia would have enhanced their economic independence. Yet the oil price increases of 1973–4 and 1978–9 resulted in such massive reserves that only the United States economy could absorb them. United States banks, investment funds, and government bonds effectively recycled the large amounts of surplus, and the development and consumer boom and welfare spending brought in a flood of Western multinationals and expatriate labour.

Despite the persistent involvement of the superpowers in the region neither has been able effectively to control their allies in the area, and it is thus inaccurate to describe Middle Eastern states as surrogates. It is a coincidence of interests between regimes and a particular superpower which has resulted in a harmonious relationship. In the short term, however, there has been a great degree of independence of action. The Soviet Union was unable to prevent Egypt and Syria from going to war in 1967 and 1973, Syria invading Lebanon in 1976 or Egypt and Iraq from imprisoning Communists. Even though the United States created Israel as the most effective military power in the region, Israel has acted independently in crises ranging from the bombing of the Iraqi nuclear reactor in 1982 to the bombing of Beirut in 1983. Supplying arms secures influence for the superpowers, but within circumscribed limits. It has rarely secured control over their use, and in times of war the superpowers have always resupplied their allies.

One result of the strategic and economic importance of the Middle East has been the very large-scale military expenditure by the governments of the region. In terms of world military spending *per capita*, six of the top seven states are in the Middle East. Between 1962 and 1980 spending has increased from $4.7 billion to $46.7 billion.[36] Fuelled by the Arab–Israeli conflict and the Shah of Iran's megalomania and funded by the superpowers and oil wealth, the Middle East has become one of the most heavily-armed areas of the world. Not only is it a great drain on resources but highly dangerous in an area where volatile interstate relations are linked to interests identified by the superpowers as vital.

Political co-operation

In the previous section tensions between states in the area have been highlighted. There have also been attempts at union and unity between the Arab states, although differences in foreign alignment, regime ideology and relative level of involvement in the Arab–Israeli conflict have frequently placed severe limits on such co-operation. Leaving aside Israel and Iran (although the latter is Islamic, albeit of the Shi'a variety) the states of the region seem well fitted to organise regional political and economic co-operation. Despite the diversity there is a common language and a sense of common history and culture. There is a degree of economic complementarity: the oil states with capital but a limited capacity to invest it domestically because of the lack of human and agricultural potential, on the one hand, and states like Egypt and Syria with limited capital but manpower resources and an agricultural and industrial potential.

The earliest institutional form of co-operation was the Arab League which was established in 1945. Based on a general sentiment for Arab unity, there has been hardly any movement toward greater unification under the aegis of the Arab League since its formation. Arab states have been jealous of their sovereignty and the main expansion of Arab League activities has been in specialised functional areas like law, health, education and culture. The Arab League (or rather its Secretary-General) has frequently been involved in solving disputes between member nations, but these interventions have generally enhanced the personal presence of the Secretary-General and the symbolic role of the Arab League. With a few exceptions the Arab League has been unable to press sanctions on member states which have been in conflict with each other. Even where Arab states have been in conflict with non-Arab states (as in the Iraq–Iran war) the Arab League has remained very much on the sidelines. When Egypt signed the peace with Israel and moved outside a broad Arab consensus, the removal of the Arab League headquarters from Cairo to Tunis was emotive and symbolic rather than effective and Egypt was easily able to tolerate the feebly co-ordinated ostracism.

Steps toward Arab unity have been made bilaterally rather than under the auspices of the League. Such unity attempts have generally been ill-prepared and disorganised, and have ended in failure. In 1961 the union of Egypt and Syria in the United Arab Republic ended with Syria's secession after three years of an uneasy relationship between the two states. Other unity agreements have remained on paper only: the 1969 Tripoli Charter signed by Sudan, Egypt and Libya; and the 1973 and 1974 agreements between Libya and Egypt and Libya and Tunisia respectively, came to nothing. States with similar political regimes have tended to form more lasting unions. The United Arab Republic unified two republican and nationalist regimes and lasted three years. Syria, however, had a factionalised officer corps and a society where landlords and merchants were socially and politically dominant. Egypt's political order was more stable: the army was united, society was relatively homogenous and President Nasser's leadership was unchallenged. Despite the Arab nationalist impulse, even Syrian Arab nationalists came to resent Egyptian administrators and officers exercising control.[37]

The United Arab Emirates (UAE), formed under British influence to guarantee a pro-Western stability in the Gulf after the British departure in the late 1960s, has proved a longer-lasting union. It was a confederation of tribal societies agreed between the heads of ruling families in the lower Gulf and lay on a firm financial basis of oil wealth. Despite tensions between the emirates of Abu Dhabi and Dubai, Abu Dhabi's financial support for the poorer emirates and a similarity of social and political structure between them all have served to maintain the UAE and preserve the role of the ruling *shaykhs*. A more recent form of political co-operation has emerged in the Gulf area: the Gulf Co-operation Council (GCC). It includes all the states of the Gulf, and although the members emphasise economic co-operation and co-ordination, the impetus for its formation was the threat from the radical Islamic republic in Iran and the desire to establish some form of military and intelligence co-operation between the states of the Gulf. This was a means of securing independence of the United States, which is seen by some as determined to secure access to oil regardless of the interests of the regimes in the Gulf region.

Oil and politics

Whereas the impetus for co-operation in the 1950s was Arab nationalism, by the 1980s it was oil. The history of oil in the Middle East provides one of the few examples where Third World states have been able to shift the balance of power away from the industrialised world and its largest multinational corporations and shift it to their advantage. Until the early 1970s, the oil-producing states had given control over exploration drilling, production, pricing and exporting to the oil companies. By the end of the decade all of the Middle Eastern states had taken full control over their oil industries and had increased the price of a barrel of oil from around $3 in 1972 to around $34 in 1983. In 1980 Arab proven reserves were 52 per cent of the world total, production was 36 per cent of the world total and the Arab share of the Organisation of Petroleum Exporting Countries (OPEC) production exceeded 71 per cent. In the same year Arab oil provided 71 per cent of European and 47 per cent of American oil imports.[38]

A complex combination of factors produced this dramatic change, which launched relatively poor desert states into the centre of political and economic international affairs.[39] Briefly and simply, the producer states had slowly gained increasing control over supply and production levels from the oil corporations which had previously kept oil prices low. Cheap oil had encouraged the Western economies to become highly dependent on it as a source of fuel and energy. A shifting imbalance between supply and demand (in part a result of an increasing American need to import oil from the beginning of the 1970s) provided the opportunity for oil-producing states to secure what they believed a realistic price. The 1973 war gave the political motivation and the size of Arab production within OPEC provided the economic capacity to raise prices. The fall of the Shah of Iran in 1978–9 and dislocations in Iranian oil production brought the second opportunity for the oil states to increase prices. Although the supply and demand ratio is important, for there has been a fall in the price of oil in the mid-1980s because of the world recession, it was the forging of a connection between oil and politics which began the process in 1973.

Although some of the surpluses accruing to the oil states have been recycled through trade and investment, there has been some benefit for the poorer states of the area. The demand for labour has meant that tens of thousands of Egyptians, Palestinians, Jordanians, Syrians and Yemenis have gone to work in the expanding economies of the Arabian peninsula since 1973. By the mid-1970s, migrant labour constituted nearly half of all those actively employed in the oil-producing states and in a state like the UAE more than 80 per cent. Much of the labour is Middle

Eastern, although a proportion comes from Pakistan and there has been a recent trend toward contract labour from south-east Asian states like South Korea.

Egypt is a major source of migrant labour, with numbers abroad rising from about 10 000 in the 1950s to 500 000 in the late 1970s. The incentives are clear. Given the skill structure, population size, wealth and commitment to rapid development by the governments of the oil-producing states, the demand for labour is there. Egypt has a large and poor population, limited domestic capital and, by the mid-1960s, large-scale industrialisation had come to an end. For the Egyptian migrant, work in an oil state is lucrative. A university teacher could earn twice his lifetime earnings in four years of secondment to Kuwait. If the benefits for some individual incomes from this vast increase in regional wealth are obvious, the ultimate benefits for Egyptian society and economy are less so. Although remittances from migrant labour have become Egypt's largest foriegn currency earner, some of the other consequences have not been so beneficial. There has been a boom in consumer spending which has increased imports dramatically: from £E133 million in 1975 to £E1224 million in 1979. Skilled labour and professionals have migrated, creating labour shortages crucial for Egypt's own development programmes. One leading Egyptian social scientist has argued convincingly that Egypt did not export its 'negative': 'it was not surplus labour or surplus population that was tapped by migration . . . it was the high level of manpower, the trained, and the most skilled medium-level manpower of Egypt's labour force'.[40] It seems unlikely that the flow of wealth to the region will aid the poorer states in any significant way without greater unity, and (as we have seen) the emphasis on unity has declined considerably from the heady days of the 1950s, while the impact of external events tends to act as a divisive force in the 1980s as much as it did in the Cold War of the 1950s.

5. Conclusion

Latin America and the Middle East have been subject to considerably more external intervention than Africa, an important reason for this being the geographical proximity of Latin America to the United States and of the Middle East to the Soviet Union. The Middle East especially – because of its oil, strategic importance and religion – has become the cockpit of international competition – competition in which Britain and France (the former colonial powers) joined in the post-1945 period in order to defend their remaining economic and military interests against the rising tide of Arab and Iranian nationalism. The Middle East became entangled in Cold War politics and was (and remains) a vast powder keg with the potential of exploding at almost any time into a major global conflict. The tension and competition between states in the region have facilitated the external powers' search for influence and allies; however, the states' alignment has not been unidirectional – and has, moreover, changed over time. In the 1950s Egypt, under President Nasser, accepted Soviet aid for the Aswan dam, but 20 years later, under President Sadat, was allied with America in the search for agreement with Israel. This example illustrates a further point, namely that the alignment of different states in the region with different superpowers has added to the tensions between states – Egypt was ostracised by the more radical Arab states and by non-Arab Iran for its apparent abandonment of the Palestinian cause.

In Latin America, since the Monroe Doctrine of 1823, the United States has sought to safeguard its interests – if necessary by the use of force – in the states to the south. Especially after the Cuban revolution the United States, Janus-like, has faced in two directions: on the one hand (as it had shown in its post-war dealings with Bolivia, Colombia and Venezuela) it encouraged democratisation and social reform, and, on the other, it supported repressive counter-revolutionary regimes like those of the Somoza family in Nicaragua. The dilemma facing the United States can best be seen over Chile – support for the reforming Eduardo Frei but also for the repressive General Augusto Pinochet against Salvador Allende, a reformer of socialist persuasion. While in Latin America the alignment of most states remains with the United States and the Soviet Union has minimal influence in the region, diplomatic power has shifted away from the United States to Brazil and Mexico, the region's industrial giants.

Until about 1974 Africa was not a theatre of paramount concern for the two superpowers. The United States extended support to the South African government (which she saw as a bulwark against communism and a guarantor of Western business interests, gave moral backing to Ian Smith, the rebel Prime Minister of Rhodesia, and worked for the establishment of pro-Western governments in the southern African sub-region. The Soviet Union encouraged what she regarded as 'progressive' governments (such as those of Nkrumah in Ghana and Sékou Touré in Guinea), and backed liberation movements – notably ZAPU in Rhodesia and the MPLA in Angola – in their struggle against white minority rule. China's involvement in African affairs – of which the building of the railway linking Tanzania and Zambia was the high water mark – was limited, but had the effect of increasing the pragmatic base of Soviet policy. In Angola and Ethiopia after 1974 the two superpowers avoided direct confrontation with each other and opted instead for proxy conflict. The strategic importance of the Indian Ocean meant that the Horn of Africa was an area of concern for both. The United States urged the South African government to moderate its apartheid policies, but has made no attempt to dislodge the white minority regime; it rejected out of hand Bishop Tutu's call in April 1986 for the imposition of economic sanctions on South Africa.

African states differed widely in their external alignments and, except towards South Africa, did not share a common foreign policy. Their governments, like governments in the other two regions, wished to assert their independence of outside control. Marxist-led Angola allowed an American multinational company to extract its oil and neither Angola nor Ethiopia (which was also under Marxist rule) would allow the Soviet Union to establish a military base on its soil, though the French were given this right by several African Francophone countries. In the Middle East, Saudi Arabia and the Gulf states turned to the United States to withstand the radical challenge from Iran, but they refused to accept American military bases in their territories. Again, the Soviet Union was unable to prevent Egypt and Syria from going to war against Israel in 1967 and 1973. In Latin America, the OAS defied the United States government by adopting (in October 1983) a resolution calling for the withdrawal of all foreign troops from Central America.

In Africa – and substantially in the Middle East – multinational companies have been concerned above all with the exploitation of natural resources, principally minerals. In all three regions, from the 1950s in Latin America and the Middle East and from a decade or more later in Africa, nationalist pressure has forced the corporations to relax their hold in the raw materials field in favour of state monopolies or joint ventures. In Latin America especially, the multinationals have increasingly turned their attention to manufacturing, often again on the basis of joint ventures, and new issues (including the transfer of technology) have come to the fore. Brazil and Mexico have highly sophisticated modern industrial sectors which are under the control of state companies and large indigenous privately-owned companies. Middle-ranking countries such as Chile are anxious to attract manufacturing investment, while the dependence of poor Central American states on multinationals extracting raw materials or providing agricultural products like bananas is such that their autonomy is somewhat eroded.

In the post-1973 period oil (and the lack of it) has come to play an increasingly important role in the politics of all three regions, and of the Middle East especially. It has brought a vast increase in the wealth of the Middle East, enabling individual governments in the region to commit large sums to military expenditure and capital works. In the international sphere the oil weapon made it possible for members of OPEC – including Nigeria in tropical Africa and Mexico and Venezuela in Latin America – to shift for a decade the balance of power away from the industrialised world; however, OPEC's leverage has declined with the world recession of the 1980s and the fall in the price of oil.

In Africa especially the fact that a small number of states have oil and others have not has increased the differences in their levels of development. Uneven development – caused in Latin America by the extent of industrialisation which the various states have achieved – impedes effective political and economic co-operation at regional level. The prospects of such co-operation have been most favourable in the Middle East, where there is a common language, a sense of common history and culture, and a degree of economic complementarity – though in fact probably the best results have been achieved in Africa, the region least favoured in these respects. In none of the three regions has the regionwide organisation – the OAU in Africa, the OAS in Latin America, and the Arab League in the Middle East – been a particularly effective body. In the Middle East the main expansion

of Arab League activities has been in specialised functional areas
like law, health, education and culture; in Africa, the OAU has
served as a forum for the exchange of views between African
leaders, and has shown most unanimity in its attitude towards
South Africa; and in Latin America, the OAS was used by the
United States as an instrument to further its own foreign policy
until (in recent years) Brazil and Mexico emerged as industrial
powers capable of challenging US dominance.

In the sphere of political unification, the results have been
rather disappointing. The union between Egypt and Syria (leading
to the formation of the UAR) foundered for the same sort of
reasons as did the union in West Africa between Senegal and the
(French) Soudan to form the Mali Federation – namely, the conviction on the part of the incumbent leadership of Syria and
Senegal that they (and their countries) would be disadvantaged
by the continuance of the union. The United Arab Emirates is a
successful confederation of tribal societies in the lower Gulf
which was formed before the British departed in the late 1960s
and is based on oil wealth. In Africa, the 1964 union between
Tanganyika and the tiny state of Zanzibar has survived as the
United Republic of Tanzania, if sometimes precariously; a number
of other unions – such as that between the Southern (British)
Cameroons and the Republic of Cameroon in 1961 – have also
survived, though in these cases (discounting the 1981 confederation between Senegal and the Gambia) union took place before
the independence of one or other of the contracting parties. As
to sub-regional functional associations, probably the best results
have again been achieved in Africa: EACSO and its successor the
East African Community (EAC) provided for many years (until
the EAC finally collapsed in 1977) a wide range of common
services between Kenya, Tanzania and Uganda, the member states.
ECOWAS in West Africa and SADCC in Southern Africa are
more recent functional associations of considerable potential
influence; a number of smaller groupings, such as the six-state
Francophone CEAO, have already proved their worth. In Latin
America, uneven industrialisation has worked against sub-
regional economic co-operation, as the history of the Andean
Group shows: it has proved impossible to agree on reduced tariff
barriers or the extent of national control over foreign investment.
In the Middle East, the Gulf Co-operation Council emphasises

economic co-operation between its (Gulf) member states, but is more political than economic. Functional co-operation elsewhere has been hampered by differences in foreign alignment, regime ideology, and the relative level of involvement in the Arab–Israeli conflict.

8

Famine, Petrodollars and Foreign Debt

1. Introduction

The history of the Third World is to a large extent the history of its incorporation into a global economy dominated by the 'core' industrialised countries of Western Europe and the United States. In their colonies, the imperial powers imposed taxes, deprived indigenous farmers of land, and sought to stimulate new 'needs' by introducing consumer goods, all in an effort to raise revenues and force local populations into providing labour for commercial farming and export-oriented production. In time the process of incorporation became largely self-propelled as new local élites sought to extend and deepen the process of development, and opportunities for survival entirely outside the market economy were eroded. In the twentieth century, mineral or agricultural export-based orientation has begun to give way (in Latin America in particular) to industrialisation based (initially at least) on import substitution. In this chapter we consider some contemporary manifestations and consequences of this incorporation.

Throughout most of the Third World malnutrition and starvation affect substantial groups of the population. In part this is a result of population growth and pressure on resources and the environment over time, and natural disasters such as drought or flood can bring tragic consequences where the balance is fragile. But it is also a consequence of the impact upon domestic food production and consumption of the shift of resources into export crops and industry, and international and national income distribution patterns which deny to hundreds of millions of people the ablity to command an adequate diet. We focus primarily on the case of Africa, where the crisis is deepest and most dramatic.

250

We turn then to the problems of export-led development. At first sight, the oil price rises of the 1970s represented a victory for primary commodity producers over their historically more powerful customers. They seemed to overturn a pattern within which exporters of primary commodities were the victims of foreign control of production or marketing, and low returns to their national economies. But the temporary (albeit spectacular) gains of the oil states reinforced their nature as monodependent primary exporters, while the consequences of the price rises themselves on the international economy into which the producers were locked were eventually negative in a number of ways for the oil producers.

Finally, we examine the predicament of the more advanced Third World countries, which have sought to pursue programmes of industrialisation funded by extensive foreign borrowing in a highly unstable world economy. Here we examine the 'debt crisis', created in part at least as a result of the effects of the rises in oil prices on financial markets, and subsequently upon world trade.

If in one sense these case studies illuminate different aspects and stages of the process of incorporation into the world economy, in another they reflect the interdependent nature of processes taking place simultaneously around the Third World. They show, too, that perhaps the most lasting legacy of the 'West' in the Third World has been the creation of economies and élites oriented toward capitalist development, at once dependent upon and allied to the developed countries themselves. Third World leaders and policy-makers have not simply been the victims of international market forces, or the impositions of more powerful states. Events have taken the course they have (very often) because of the commitment of Third World states to patterns of development which have tightened their links with the international market and reinforced their status as primary commodity producers or their need for foreign capital and technology. In this chapter we explore, then, the politics of economic development in the context of an interdependent but unequal world economy.

2. Famine

There is no general shortage of food in the world. Nor is there an overall shortage in many Third World countries which experience chronic problems of malnutrition on a massive scale. Both Zimbabwe and Brazil, for example, are major food exporters, yet between 25 per cent and 30 per cent of their populations suffer from malnutrition. Nor is it the shift from subsistence production to commercial agriculture and exports alone which leads to malnutrition – and, in severe cases, to famine – in the Third World. It is the combination of this shift with highly unequal distribution of income which leads to hunger on a massive scale. Cuba, for instance, is heavily dependent upon imported food, but its distributional policies have eliminated hunger and malnutrition. What is more, the virtually total elimination of malnutrition since the revolution has taken place despite the fact that food production overall has barely kept pace with population growth.[1] Dependence upon imported food, in combination with an inability to buy it on the part of substantial proportions of the population, creates a 'silent famine' of persistent malnutrition throughout large parts of the Third World. And where access to food is precarious, 'natural disasters' such as drought or flood can rapidly lead to crisis as small farmers without reserves lose their crops and animals, or labourers fail to find work and are therefore unable to afford food. Crises of this kind have ravaged Africa in recent years.

In the decade before independence and until approximately 1965 both agricultural exports and food production for local consumption increased in Africa. In the 1970s, however, with only a few exceptions, the volume of agricultural production (food and non-food) declined and the population increased at a faster rate than food was produced. Drought conditions in many parts of Africa in the 1980s have made it impossible to reverse this trend. Nor is Africa alone in this regard. In Central America and the Caribbean, food production for the domestic market failed to keep pace with population growth between 1950 and 1975, with the result that between 1960 and 1980 total food system imports (including fertilisers and agricultural machinery) rose from $306 million per year to $3.434 billion per year, more than doubling in real terms.[2]

It is in Africa, though, that the crisis in agriculture has been most acute. A World Bank study published in 1981 attributed it to five complementary trends: a declining growth rate of agricultural production overall, bringing it below the rate of population growth in the 1970s; stagnant agricultural exports and a decline in the African share of world trade for many commodities; stagnant *per capita* food production in the 1960s, falling in the 1970s; commercial imports of grains rising at more than three times the rate of population increase; and, as a consequence of all these developments and a change in consumption habits, an increase in the overall level of food dependency.[3] Some of the blame for the poor performance of African agriculture over the last twenty years must lie with the ruling élites – for example, in preferring, as the Zambian government still does, and as the Mozambican government did until the fourth FRELIMO Congress of April 1983, to invest in the huge, highly-capitalised agricultural scheme where help for the small rural producer might have made more sense, in not providing the latter with the market incentives to produce more, and in persisting on ideological grounds with rural experiments, such as *ujamaa vijijini* in Tanzania, long after they have failed economically. The provision of market incentives is very important: while Goran Hyden is right to suggest that considerations of family and kinship do count with the African peasantry,[4] it is also true that rural producers will step up their marketable output if they are provided with credit, fertilisers, improved storage, collection and transport facilities, and if (above all) they are given good prices for their produce. If these things are absent, and if there is not also an adequate supply in the local shops of goods for the peasant to buy, peasant farmers may produce only enough to meet their own immediate needs. Another consequence will be a drift to the towns, thereby reducing the ratio of food producers to consumers. A policy of incentives to peasant producers alone, however, is insufficient. Even in areas of the Third World where a large majority of the population is rural, large numbers commonly depend (in part at least) upon earning a wage to survive. Loss of earning capacity can lead to starvation in the midst of plenty. As the proportion of rural dwellers depending on money income for survival rises, the problem becomes as much one of guaranteeing minimum year-round incomes as of providing incentives for peasant producers.

As well as natural disasters such as flooding and drought, the poor performance of agriculture in certain parts of the continent is also due to the adoption of bad farming practices over an extended period. This is recognised by the Ethiopian Government's Relief and Rehabilitation Commission, which has blamed the Ethiopian famine of 1973–4 not on drought but on 'a combination of long continued bad land use and steadily increasing human and stock populations over decades', thus making people and animals vulnerable when drought struck. There is no doubt that the southward movement of the Sahara, causing increased 'desertification' in West Africa's Sahel belt, is caused in part by deforestation and overgrazing, though the carrying capacity of the land could probably be improved if better management practices were adopted. But while 'desertification' certainly reduces farming yields, there is no exact correlation between agricultural output and rural poverty; indeed, agricultural success – through the adoption, for example, of commercial farming in central Kenya and eastern Botswana – may cause land shortage or even landlessness among rural villagers. There is, therefore, a link between the spread of commercial farming and the incidence of bad farming and grazing practices. These may be forced responses to circumstances which make survival impossible otherwise, as pastoralists and subsistence oriented farmers are pushed on to marginal land. For example, the group hardest hit in the Ethiopian famine of 1972–4 – the Afar pastoralists – had been pushed off good riverside land in the Awash valley by the spread of commercial cotton and sugar cultivation, and forced to shift their herds on to land which could not support them. This greatly reduced their ability to withstand the drought when it came.[5]

In looking at famine, then, it is not enough to focus on the food supply. We need to look at the erosion of self-sufficient peasant production as incorporation into national and international markets proceeds. One of the constant features of colonial policy in Africa (as elsewhere) was to undermine the self-sufficiency of the indigenous population. Revenues had to be raised, so that the administration of the colony should not be a drain on the resources of the metropolis. And beyond that, labour had to be forced or tempted into the mines or on to the farms of settlers, or into types of indigenous production that could be traded for profit.

In Southern Rhodesia (now Zimbabwe) in the early years of the twentieth century, over 90 per cent of marketed food came from independent Shona producers, subject to increasingly onerous taxes but preferring farming on their own account to migrant labour. After 1908, however, a series of measures was taken to weaken African farming and provide opportunities for white settlers. Lavish credit was provided for the latter, and denied to African farmers; new rents and fees were levied, and Africans forced off good land and into distant reserves. Overall, Palmer observes, 'African farmers faced the full blast of competition from heavily subsidized European farmers while simultaneously being pushed away from easy access to markets, a process greatly facilitated by the work of the 1914–15 Native Reserves Commission, which reduced the reserves by a million acres and took from them much of the best land within easy reach of the main centres'.[6] In subsequent years, white settlers pressed the colonial authorities for an end to agricultural extension work among African farmers, as it made them stronger competitors. The crowning glory of the policy of destruction of indigenous agriculture came with the Maize Control Act (1931) and the Maize Control Amendment Act (1934), which excluded African farmers from the best markets, imposed low prices for their produce, and forced them into a role of suppliers of cheap maize to the mines and other European concerns. In conjunction with the Land Apportionment Act (1934), this produced a situation in which land once farmed by Africans was kept idle under European control, while African farmers were denied free access to remunerative markets. White settlers felt they could prosper only if African agriculture was undermined; Africans were to labour for settlers, and eke out a precarious living on overcrowded reserves. By the end of the 1930s 'the agricultural economy of the Shona and the Ndebele, like that of the Kikuyu and most Southern African peoples, had been destroyed'.[7]

Even where the need to favour settler agriculture or mining operations did not lead to policies aimed at undermining African agriculture, the imposition of taxes and the extension of cash-cropping could weaken the ability of the peasantry to survive. In Nigeria, for example, where white settler agriculture was never allowed to develop, the spread of cash-cropping in northern Hausaland (in part in response to the need to meet tax payments) along with the weakening of the bonds of social responsibility between local rulers and their peoples, led to the undermining of 'precautionary mechanisms' such as the keeping of common foodstocks. As land was taken out of diversified food production and put under groundnuts and cotton, dependence upon the market increased, leading to what Apeldoorn has described as the 'atrophy of the defences of the poor'.[8]

As the case of Nigeria suggests, the policies which weaken the ability of populations to respond to crises of drought or famine are often pursued after colonial rule has given way to independence. On Vail's evidence, Malawi (formerly Nyasaland) is a striking case in point, notwithstanding the high level of agricultural production achieved by the Banda government. In the colonial period, policy towards African agriculture fluctuated in accordance with changing needs, and the interests of neighbouring mining areas, powerful railway companies, and the interests of the weak local white settler farmers. The latter experimented successively with coffee, cotton and tobacco, before concentrating in the main on tea production made viable by a virtually captive labour force of migrants from neighbouring Mozambique and a system of forced labour known as *thangata*. Elsewhere, however, peasant agriculture was relatively stable, though forced by freight costs to concentrate upon the production of cotton rather than maize. In the wake of independence in 1964, President Banda's government adopted certain colonial-type measures aimed at developing the estate sector of the economy. New taxes and charges for schooling and other services made the earning of a cash income essential and led many peasants to seek work on the tea plantations and newly-established tobacco plantations; the alternative of migrating to the mining areas of neighbouring states was subject to tight government control and approval. In addition, much of the surplus realised by government-created marketing boards from the sale of the crops of peasant producers was channelled into the estate sector. These various policies, Vail remarks, were 'highly reminiscent' of those pursued by the British colonial government, but were 'carried out with a thoroughness that only an independent government without local political opposition could dare'.[9]

A historical perspective is essential. We need also to find out how food is distributed, and what determines its distribution between different members of the community. That food is available does not mean that all persons can gain access to it. These points are made by Amartya Sen in his illuminating study, *Poverty and Famines*, and are substantiated by a number of case studies, including one on the Ethiopian famine (1972–4) and another on drought and famine in the Sahel (1968–73). The famine in Ethiopia was not accompanied by any significant reduction in food output; even at its height in 1973 there was no abnormal drop in the consumption of food per head. It hit the north east (especially Wollo) in 1972–3, and provinces further south (particularly Hararghe) in 1973–4. The relative incidence of starvation was probably greatest among the pastoral people, who had lost some of their traditional dry-weather grazing land to commercial agriculture, as we saw above; many of their animals perished in the drought and the terms of trade of animals for grain turned against them. However, a majority of the famine victims in absolute numbers came from the agricultural community in the north east. Sen writes:

> While the food output in Wollo was substantially reduced in 1973, the inability of Wollo to command food from outside was the result of low purchasing power in that province. A remarkable feature of the Wollo famine is that food prices in general rose very little, and people were dying of starvation even when food was selling at prices not very different from pre-drought levels. The phenomenon can be understood in terms of extensive entitlement failures of various sections of the Wollo population.[10]

Sen points out, then, that the problem may not be one of an absolute food shortage, but a lack on the part of sectors of the population of the means to command (or obtain) an adequate share of the food available. As the process of commercialisation proceeds, peasant producers tend to lose access to land on which they might grow food of their own, without gaining sufficient access to money earnings to enable them to enter the market to buy food in sufficient quantity to survive. Once they fall below a level at which survival is possible, they are forced into practices which worsen their situation: overfarming of tired and marginal land, slaughter or sale of animals which could have provided future food or income, and consumption of portions of seed which should be retained for future planting. Sen comments, in relation to the Sahel, that 'recent developments such as the growth of cash-cropping . . . have added to the country's overall earning power but seem to have led to a decline in the exchange entitlement of particular sectors of the population'. Thus 'while commercialization may have opened up new economic opportunities, it has also tended to increase the vulnerability of the Sahel population'.[11]

The situation in the Sahelian countries of Mauritania, Senegal, Mali, Upper Volta (now Burkina Faso), Niger and Chad was comparable in many ways to that in Ethiopia: both pastoralists, who went south in search of fodder for their animals and paid employment for themselves, and agriculturalists suffered severely from the drought, especially in 1973, the worst year. A large number of animals (perhaps half the total) were lost and crops were destroyed, leading to a decline in the income and purchasing power of both groups. The people affected could not therefore command food, either through their own output or through exchange, and the number of those who died in 1973 alone was estimated at 100 000. Again, the critical factor was not so much the shortage of food – food supplies were adequate in nearly all the Sahelian countries to prevent starvation – but the inequality of distribution and the inability of many people to establish entitlement to it.

Additional lessons, some reinforcing those learned from the experience of 1973, have emerged from the famines in Ethiopia, Somalia, the Sudan, Mozambique and other parts of Africa in 1984–5. All the signs of impending famine were evident in Ethiopia and Somalia months (even years) before the main crisis occurred, but Western governments ignored the early warnings of the aid agencies. In the Sudan, the problem was accentuated because the government's reluctance to admit that a famine existed (as in Ethiopia in 1973) caused food to be hoarded and its price to rise sharply. In both the Sudan and Ethiopia, food was available in the country. In the Sudan at least grain merchants had good stocks at the end of 1985, but the starving had no money with which to purchase it. And in both cases, the problem was one of distribution across difficult and sometimes wartorn terrain with inadequate transport. By the time relief did reach the distant villages, the many people (such as farm labourers and dependants) who could not establish a claim to such food as was available locally had left their homes and become socially dislocated migrants; the number of deaths among agriculturalists was very large. Again (as in 1973) the pastoralists suffered severely; many of their animals died and they obtained poor prices for those which they sold in order to obtain food. The structures were virtually non-existent to help the nomads and others living outside village settlements.

By mid-July 1985, when the enormously successful Live-Aid concert was held in London and Philadelphia, the main short-term problem across the Sahel belt was no longer one of food supply, but the shortage of trucks to transport the food – for example, to Darfur in western Sudan and Wollo in northern Ethiopia. Unfortunately, extensive flooding was impeding relief work, as was also the Ethiopian regime's continuing preoccupation with the war against rebel forces in Eritrea and Tigré. Seeds for replanting were everywhere scarce, having been eaten by hungry farmers and their families.

3. Petrodollars

Between November 1973 and April 1974, world oil prices rose fourfold. In 1979 a second sharp rise took place. The world is still living out the consequences. The initial success of OPEC was made possible by the dependence of the advanced Western economies as a whole upon imported oil, and the central role of oil as a source of energy in modern industrial society. It seemed to strike a blow for primary exporters against their generally more powerful international trading partners, and promised to bring about a permanent shift in power relations in the international market. To a certain extent, it did so. But, more than a decade on, it is hard to say where the advantage now lies. In many ways the results have been negative for the oil producers themselves, while the worst hit have not been the advanced nations, but non-oil-producing Third World states. This is not to say that the oil producers were wrong, or foolish, to seek a better return for their oil. It suggests that the forcing up of prices in the short term was not in itself sufficient to overcome the liability of dependence on a single primary commodity, or to alter their subordinate position in the international economy. Indeed, their actions reinforced their status as primary producers, and increased their dependence on flows of goods and services from the advanced economies. It produced, therefore, in an exaggerated form, a set of circumstances which have bedevilled all developing countries in recent decades: rapid development requires foreign exchange for necessary imports of equipment and technology; efforts to boost export returns to provide the foreign exchange lead to a bias against domestic agriculture as land and investment is switched to exportable crops; foreign borrowing creates a need for further expansion of exports to meet repayment schedules; and the dependence eliminated at one level is continually recreated at another. This is a consequence of increasing integration into a capitalist-dominated international economy. But it is one in which Third World leaders and policy-makers, even in states of a declared socialist orientation, have enthusiastically participated.

The change in the relationship between the oil-producing states, the oil companies and the consumer nations since the early 1970s has produced one of the most dramatic reversals in contemporary international economic relations. It has brought to the centre of international politics and finance a group of desert kingdoms which have small populations, extremely limited agricultural potential, and in the main scanty technically skilled personnel. Indicative of the growth of these states is Saudi Arabia's increase in oil revenue from $0.6 billion in 1965 to about $70 billion in 1979.

The years 1973 and 1974 were the crisis years for the Western economies and the Third World. There were gunfights in American petrol queues and strict rationing of kerosene in impoverished states like Sudan. The fall of the Shah and the Iranian revolution of 1978–9 brought another jump in the price of oil. There were other factors at work which caused the world recession: the collapse of currency agreements, uneven balance of payments spread among OECD countries and growing protectionism. Even so, the higher price of oil was a very important feature of the world slump of the 1970s and 1980s and it is ironic that the benefits for this new set of Third World states had such negative effects on non oil-producing states in the Third World. Although some of the latter, like Pakistan and Bangladesh, were able to recoup some of the greatly increased outflow of foreign exchange by exporting labour to the oil rich states and a few others, like South Korea and Brazil, developed their trade with OPEC countries, the broad effects were negative.

It has, however, been a considerable achievement for OPEC to have secured control over the pricing and supply of their natural resources from some of the largest and richest MNCs. Clearly, oil is a commodity unlike those possessed by other Third World states. Initially, it was the domination by the oil MNCs which made oil so cheap and caused the industrialised states to be dependent on it as a source of energy. By the 1970s OPEC had become the swing producer and was able to increase prices. Within OPEC it is a handful of Arab states in the Gulf, led by Saudi Arabia, which are the swing producers, largely because they are 'low absorbers', that is, unable to spend the vast revenues for reasons of demography and geography. An oil producing state like Nigeria with its 100 million population has no difficulty spending on development. On the other hand, states like Saudi Arabia, Kuwait and the United Arab Emirates, without agricultural potential, have small populations and large surpluses held in Western economies. In 1982 these were estimated at between $200 billion and $400 billion in the United States alone.[12] Furthermore these states have had to import labour for development projects to such an extent that the United Arab Emirates and Qatar rely on non-nationals for over 80 per cent of their labour force.[13] They also rely on imported consumer goods, manufactures, and civil and military technology. Between 1974 and 1980 imports from OECD countries have increased by between 300 per cent and 400 per cent.[14] Even oil-producing states with a significant agricultural sector, like Iraq and Iran, have had to import basic foodstuffs. Although OPEC members have gained control over their major export, there has not been any qualitative increase in their independence. The freezing of Iranian assets in American banks outside the United States during the embassy hostage crisis was a clear indication of the leverage held by recipients of oil investments. It is also important to point out that OPEC is not a proper cartel as the price of oil is a function of demand. Depressed demand in the 1980s has brought down the price of oil as increased demand in the early 1970s was an important factor in its increase. Since the oil-producing states depend on imports from the industrialised West, they have been made to pay a high price for these imports as the OECD states recycled the oil surpluses through trade.

If some OECD states have not performed so badly after the oil price increases, the Third World, particularly the least developed states, has been quite seriously affected. One of the main consequences of the two oil price increases and the subsequent world recession has been to worsen sharply the import capacity of non-oil Third World states. In his address to the nation of 9 December 1981, President Julius Nyerere of Tanzania pointed out that 'for the amount of money with which we used to buy thirteen barrels of oil, we now only get one', and that his country had 'to give about four times as much cotton to buy a 7-ton lorry as we had to give in 1972, or ten times as much tobacco or three times as much cashew'.[15] Thus the poorer Third World countries were led into debt in the wake of the oil crisis, or sank further into poverty if they were unable to attract funds. They tended not to benefit from the surplus capital available, and to suffer further as the developed countries changed the patterns of their imports to respond to the crisis themselves. The countries of the industrialised West have attracted the OPEC surpluses, cut raw material imports, and concentrated on improving their trading positions with the OPEC states. Non-oil exporting Third World states were excluded from this recycling process. Most of the surpluses were placed with Western financial institutions, in part a function of the large scale expansion of Western banks which were making most of their profits by the mid-1970s from overseas earnings.[16] Ironically the oil-producing states have done rather poorly out of the process. One economist has estimated that the rate of return on their investments between 1972 and 1979 was between zero and −3.4 per cent. For the Third World the result has been increased indebtedness with its attendant problems of high interest rates and debt servicing. Many economists have recommended direct investment in the Third World as a means of enhancing economic growth, reducing the necessity to borrow on the international capital market and achieving a higher rate of profit for the oil states' investment.

Recycling to the Third World has taken place through trade and migrant labour. OPEC's imports increased from $20 billion in 1973 to $226 billion in 1981, and with the erosion of OPEC's surpluses by the mid-1980s, trade had become even more central. The trend in the 1970s did not favour the developing countries. In 1973 advanced industrial countries accounted for 77 per cent of OPEC's imports and non-oil developing countries for

16 per cent. By 1979 their respective shares were 75.5 per cent and 14.2 per cent.[17] The fact that manufacturing is concentrated in a handful of Third World states has limited the number of beneficiaries even though it has been demonstrated that the expansion of OPEC imports from the advanced industrial states has been a costly process with OPEC 'importing inflation rather than real goods and services'.[18] The weak trading relationship with the non-Muslim Third World has not been accorded much sympathy from Arab circles. Abd-al Aziz Sowayegh writes that 'their development plans will . . . depend to a large extent on their ability to adjust to and comply with the new reality of limited, costly energy supplies'[19]

The oil surplus states have given aid, some most generously. While United States aid was 0.27 per cent of GNP in 1985, in the mid-1970s Qatar gave 15 per cent, the UAE 11 per cent and Kuwait 8 per cent. Despite this high proportion of aid, derived from a depletable resource, the pattern of donations has benefited the poorer Arab states, other states with sizable Arab or Muslim populations, or states being weaned away from links with the Soviet Union. For example, between 1973 and 1977 Egypt, Syria and Jordan received 51.8 per cent of OPEC aid.[20] The next largest recipient was Pakistan, with 9.5 per cent. Rather than giving for projects the largest proportion during this period has gone for balance of payments support. Because only a few of the OPEC states have surpluses the pattern of OPEC giving has reflected the foreign policy goals of conservative states like Saudi Arabia, Kuwait, and the UAE. The provision of Saudi aid to Sudan, Somalia and Egypt was based on their break with the USSR. In the case of Egypt, its later withdrawal was a result of the peace treaty with Israel.

A further means of recycling has been through remittances transferred by migrant workers. Given the small populations, the lack of skills and the magnitude of expenditure by the oil states, there has been massive labour migration. The chief labour importers have been Bahrein, Kuwait, Libya, Qatar, Saudi Arabia and the UAE. In 1975 Saudi Arabia had 773 400 migrant workers, of whom 90 per cent were Arab, and the UAE had 251 500, of whom 65 000 were Asian. For the poorer states these remittances are an important source of foreign currency. By 1980 Egyptians were sending back $2.69 billion, Pakistanis $2.03 billion, Indians

$3 billion, and Filipinos $376 million.[21] Remittances to Pakistan were equivalent to all her exports of raw cotton and cotton textiles or one-third the value of all exports. Remittances were Egypt's largest foreign currency earner.

Remittances help the balance of payments, but have a negative side. It is well documented that Pakistan and Egypt have lost highly educated technical, managerial and medical personnel, as well as skilled workers. Furthermore, remittances are frequently spent on consumer goods which are a further drain on foreign exchange.

The consequences of the oil price increases have been somewhat mixed, particularly when taken with the reactions of governments, banks and exporters of OECD countries. There has been increasing debt and decreasing raw material exports. Although the OPEC states have benefited and some in particular have quadrupled per capita income and spending on welfare, they have not benefited as much as they might. Relying on imports for consumer goods and development projects has increasingly eroded capital surpluses. Surpluses of the 'low absorbers' have frequently gained a negative return and because they are so dependent on imports from and investments in Western capitalist systems, they have produced more oil than they require to stabilise Western economies. But the recession in the West and the overproduction of oil in the mid-1980s has led to a fall in the price of oil and cuts in production. Saudi Arabia, a state which can draw on foreign assets, was producing around 9 million barrels per day between 1979 and 1981, but by the summer of 1985 was producing only 2 million barrels. Between 1981 and 1985 its revenues fell from $108 billion to $47 billion.

The dual process of a falling price and production cuts has also had its effect on OPEC solidarity. Member states have increasingly disagreed on pricing policy and production levels. While Saudi Arabia has been able to manage, budgets have been cut from $84 billion in 1981–2 to $60.4 billion in 1984–5. Saudi Arabia has a per capita income fifty-five times that of Nigeria, which with its large population and their expectations based on the boom of the 1970s, has found the drop in income a very bitter pill to swallow. The result has been very sharp divisions at the regular OPEC meetings. In the 1970s the OPEC states became the haves of the Third World, but by the 1980s OPEC itself had become divided between the 'haves' and the 'have-nots', with countries like Nigeria and Indonesia becoming indebted to maintain development programmes.

4. The debt crisis

The 'debt crisis' of the 1980s was a consequence of the oil price rises of the 1970s and their repercussions first in international financial markets and later in the area of international trade. In the first stage, after 1973, the foreign currency earnings of the major oil states found their way into the United States and European money markets, and were channelled from there, in large part, to sovereign Third World states in large syndicated loans. United States banks in particular competed aggressively for business in this area, convinced that sovereign borrowers were safe customers. There were six important characteristics to the lending which took place. Firstly, it multiplied the amount of debt in the hands of Third World states. Secondly, the rate of borrowing far outran the rate at which foreign-exchange generating capacity could be developed; it would therefore need to be 'rolled over' (refinanced by new lending as it became due) in part at least for the forseeable future. Thirdly, it went above all to the largest and most developed Third World states, with Brazil, Mexico and Argentina being the leading recipients. Fourthly, it came primarily from commercial sources rather than from the governments and official agencies which had been the major lenders before. Fifthly, it was made at floating rather than fixed rates of interest at times when inflation was rendering rates of interest low or even negative in real terms. And sixthly, although large numbers of banks were involved as a consequence of raising loans through 'syndicates', the largest lenders by far were the nine major United States banks and two British banks (Lloyds and Midland). All of these accumulated obligations well in excess of their total capital reserves.

This was primarily, then, a business which involved the big banks on the one hand, and the 'big' developing countries on the other. In March 1985 the debts of Mexico and Brazil were well over twice those of South Korea, the next largest borrower, virtually three times those of Argentina and Venezuela, and five times those of Indonesia and the Philippines. In addition, the larger Latin American debtors had proportionately greater exposure to commercial bank debt, and were therefore paying high rates of interest: 10.8 per cent in 1983, for instance, whereas low-income countries owing primarily to official lenders were paying 3.7 per cent.[22] The risks on the other side were just as great. At one stage, the nine leading United States banks had Third World debt on the books to the extent of two-and-a-half times their total capital and assets; in June 1984, the same banks held debt in Mexico, Brazil, Argentina and Venezuela alone well in excess of their total capital and assets.[23]

If interest rates had remained stable while the major borrowers had been able to expand their exports and foreign exchange earnings sufficiently to meet the bulk of their repayment liabilities, and banks had been willing to provide fresh money to cover remaining needs, a crisis could have been avoided despite the highly unstable situation that resulted. But such an outcome became impossible in the wake of the second phase of the oil crisis. After the second wave of price increases in 1979 real interest rates climbed until they reached record levels as the United States tried to finance its deficit without relaxing its tight monetary policy. Similarly tight monetary policies in the advanced countries around the world led to recession, falling demand for the exports of Third World countries, and sharply declining terms of trade. The result was a ferocious 'scissors effect' as interest rates floated up, raising the payments due on Third World debt, while export revenues dropped, reducing their ability to pay. If new loans could not be secured, the major debtors were bound to fail to meet their debts as interest and amortisation payments fell due. It was at this point that the significance of the shift towards commercial lending revealed itself. Just when new money was needed to sustain the stability of international financial markets, and when sovereign or official lenders would have been able to take a longer-term view and grant more credit, the commercial banks, concerned for the security of the massive loans they had made in the past in new circumstances which threatened this new business, began to draw back. The new situation reflected changes in the pattern of lending since 1978. By that time, the OPEC surpluses that had been channelled into international lending by the commercial banks had begun to dry up as the price of oil fell back in relative terms, and OPEC imports increased. As a consequence, there was a shift toward shorter term loans, and hence more rapid maturing of liabilities. By the early 1980s, countries were borrowing in order to meet repayment demands, rather than to fund new investment.

The crunch came in late 1982. On Friday, 13 August, Mexican Finance Minister Jesus Silva Herzog informed Mexico's creditors that Mexico was unable to meet due payments on its debt. In the wake of that announcement, a number of fundamental and virtually unprecedented changes occurred in international financial markets. In a panic reaction, all the more powerful because of uncertainties prompted by the hostilities in the South Atlantic earlier in the year and the manifest instability of military governments in Argentina and Brazil, the banks cut off flows of finance to Latin America. Henceforth, commercial banking was to be 'involuntary', prised out of banks which had previously participated in syndicated loans, generally in proportion to their exposure, solely for the purpose of helping debtors to meet interest payments as they fell due. It had hitherto been accepted as axiomatic by all participants that flows of money into borrowing countries would always be positive, with new lending outweighing the return flow of interest and principal due. But now, year after year, the flow was negative. The Latin American debtors faced a need to pay out far more than they were receiving, while levels of trade and export prices remained depressed. Had they been unable to do so, or chosen not to do so, a collapse of the international financial system, or at least major parts of it, would have ensued. That it did not was entirely due to the ability of the major debtors to restructure their foreign trade in order to release foreign exchange to meet their mounting liabilities. This was achieved primarily, in the absence of favourable export prices, by sharply increasing the volume of exports, and by cutting imports even more sharply. Thus Brazil, for example, managed a small trade surplus of US$780 million in 1982, slightly down on 1981. In 1983 this widened to US$6500 million, largely due to reduced imports, and doubled again to US$13 100 in 1984. Mexico's performance was even more dramatic. With the average value of exports stagnant between 1981 and 1983 at around US$20 billion, and rising only slightly to some US$24 billion in 1984, imports were slashed from a peak of US$24 billion in 1982 to just over

US$8 billion in 1983, and rose to US$11 billion in 1984. This in turn meant the imposition of patterns of austerity which brought recession in the domestic economy and severe cuts in the standard of living of populations already suffering hardship. The debtors, and particularly their poorer citizens, were to pay the price of collective recklessness for which the foreign banks and largely unaccountable leaders were jointly responsible. In Mexico, for example, the purchasing power of wages fell by half between 1976 and 1984, and similar patterns were repeated throughout the area.

To a certain extent, all parties have been caught out by the unprecedented rise in real interest rates, but there was recklessness on all sides too. The borrowers had accumulated foreign exchange far more rapidly than they could hope to invest it productively, and had kept little track of the ends to which it was devoted. As much as 40 per cent of the flow of dollars to Mexico, for example, is reckoned to have found its way out into private bank accounts overseas, while it was becoming clear in the winter of 1985 that the fraudulent issuing of import licences in Nigeria had been a channel for the diversion of vast sums of currency abroad. The bankers had indulged in competitive lending on the basis of poor research and little knowlege, in the hope that the snowball would continue to roll. The international authorities, meanwhile, had stood back and left the commercial banks, unsuited for long term lending to sovereign borrowers, to cope with the situation created by the oil price rises and the resultant disturbances to financial markets. The consequences were catastrophic for the debtors, potentially so for the banks, and negative for the developed countries. However the blame was to be allocated, the costs were to be borne by the debtors. In the words of one commentator, 'The IMF set itself up to save the system, organising banks into a lender's cartel and holding the debtor countries up for a classical mugging.'[24]

The ability of the most indebted Latin American regimes to generate large surpluses on their balance of trade was a major surprise. Perhaps even more of a surprise, though, was their willingness to accept the major programmes of austerity that this effort implied, and their ability to impose them on their citizens. It is necessary, therefore, to consider these two issues in greater depth.

The most radical option would have been repudiation. In other words, the debtors could have gone beyond declarations, to which the greater majority of them were forced in the wake of the Mexican announcement, that they needed to come to new terms with their creditors, and simply stated that they would not honour their debts. This course of action was urged most strongly, as the only equitable solution to the crisis, by Fidel Castro. The idea was canvassed in a series of meetings held in Havana during the course of 1985, and backed up by a sophisticated analysis of the origins of the crisis, set in the context of the North-South debate, and a call for the establishment of a New International Economic Order.[25] Despite the popularity of the repudiation option with radicals and with opposition groups quite widely across Latin America, it was not seriously considered by any of the governments of the area. A number of the considerations involved were practical. In the short term there would necessarily be considerable disruption to trade if normal trade credits and other sources of finance for day-to-day international transactions were cut off.[26] Equally, if the crisis were seen as a passing manifestation of extreme instability in international markets, it would seem shortsighted to threaten future flows of investment and loan capital from the developed world far into the future in order to overcome it. More significantly, the decision-makers involved, in Mexico as much as in Brazil and Argentina, were the beneficiaries and the representatives of a pattern of growth which was both highly dependent upon access to international markets, and highly unequal in its impact over time on their populations. Even after the ending of military rule in Brazil and Argentina, the leaders of the major debtors, Miguel de la Madrid Hurtado in Mexico, José Sarney in Brazil, and Raul Alfonsín in Argentina, had no wish to break with the banks. Nor did they wish to mount a noisy international campaign against the banks themselves; they were hardly in a position to have the issue of equity raised in connection with their own domestic policies.

In general, the countries which came closest to confrontation were the weakest. More than anything, this reflected the balance of power between debtors and creditors. Mexico and Brazil, each owing something in the region of US$100 billion to the banks, were perfectly aware of the bargaining power that their enormous debts gave them. The smaller debtors, equally, were aware of their lack of bargaining power, and more likely to be unable to raise covering finance. They tended, also to have less authority at home, and to fear more the consequences of attempts to impose austerity policies. It is not surprising, therefore, that the most intransigent response came from Peru. Its debt, something over US$13 billion in 1985, was low by the standards of the major debtors. At the same time, though, the best efforts of a government whose Prime Minister and Finance Minister from December 1982 until March 1984 had been a former IMF official and a top executive of the Wells Fargo bank were able to generate a trade surplus of only US$1000 in 1984.[27] This reflected a cut of over 40 per cent in imports, against a background of poor prices for mineral exports, and unfavourable conditions for agricultural production. Due to channel over half the proceeds from exports to debt servicing and repayment in 1985, the incoming government of APRA leader Alan Garcia simply announced that it would limit its payments on the debt to 10 per cent of export proceeds. This highlighted the link between prices for exports and ability to repay debt, and gave a boost to the popularity and legitimacy of Garcia's government. It was less defiant an attitude than it appeared, though. First of all, it was a position taken in response to opposition calls for repudiation, an option which Garcia emphatically rejected when Castro proposed it. And secondly, it was essentially making a virtue of necessity. In practice, Peru had been paying roughly the same proportion of its export proceeds on the debt in recent years, and was not in a position to do more.

What is significant is that despite their attempts to canvass support from other governments in the region, the Peruvians were no more successful than Castro had been in winning adherents to their cause. Among the major debtors there were clear differences of emphasis in policy. Alfonsín, in Argentina, aware of the strength of the opposition Peronists in the unions and among the working class in general, and conscious that the sharp slump in the economic fortunes of the country during the period of military rule had made the imposition of further austerity virtually unthinkable, stated vigorously that he would not reach an agreement with the IMF which implied such an outcome. At the same time, though, he applied radical measures to bring inflation under control. Sarney, in Brazil, continued the practice of previous military governments, playing for time and resisting the more strenous dictates of the bankers, but making it quite clear at the same time that repudiation was out of the question, and that Brazil would not line up alongside Peru and present the bankers with a unilateral ultimatum. It was Mexico, though, with its 'popular' PRI government and its more durable hold, through the official trade union structure, over the organised working class, which adapted most readily to the demands for austerity of its international creditors. The ability of the Mexican government to impose such measures reflected first of all a capacity to exert authority greatly in excess of that of the military governments of Argentina and Brazil which gave way to civilian rulers in 1983 and 1984.[28] It is not credible, in any of these cases, to argue that the measures taken have been forced upon governments entirely unwilling to accept them. In every case, élites pursuing capitalist development have found themselves facing severe domestic economic crises, and have been able to use the 'external threat' of the IMF and the banks to justify economic policies which have favoured their class interests. It is not surprising, therefore, that Roett, in an account of the collective efforts of the 'Cartagena group' of eleven leading Latin American debtors, has been able to report that 'the meetings of the political leaders of the hemisphere have been a model of reasoned and highly concerned analysis'.[29] The group came together in June 1984 in Cartagena, Colombia, following the January 1984 'Declaration of Quito', which drew attention to the social, economic and political consequences of the debt crisis. Subsequent meetings during 1984 and 1985 failed to produce a common Latin American response, and in general the meetings of the major debtors generated statements of concern for the impact of repayment, particularly upon the fledgling democracies of the region, and assurances that repudiation and similar unilateral responses were not under consideration. The conservative regimes that have come to power throughout the region in the wake of the retreat of the generals are unlikely candidates for a crusade against the banks and the international order upon which they depend.

By the end of 1985, the discussions between the debtors and their creditors had come to focus on the 'Baker plan', a minimal programme for readjustment over the following three years proposed by United States Treasury Secretary James Baker at the October 1985 meeting of the IMF/IBRD in Seoul. This was essentially a suggestion that the commercial lenders should come forward with a further US$20 billion over three years to ease the strain on debtors. These funds were to be matched by official lenders, led by the World Bank. Firstly, the banks proved reluctant to comply. Secondly, even if such funds had been forthcoming they would not have reversed the negative net flow of funds from debtors to creditors. And thirdly, this did nothing to remedy the prospect of negative flows throughout the 1980s. However, the response of the Cartagena group was habitually cautious. Meeting in Montevideo late in December, they argued, as they had done before, that the measures did not go far enough, and pressed for a package of minor measures aimed at softening the impact of repayment and spreading it more evenly.

On the broader economic policy front, the major debtors have proved more resistant to pressure from the IMF and similar bodies than might have been supposed. They have persistently reminded the representatives of the banks and of the developed countries that in the absence of fresh loans or renegotiated terms they can only meet their obligations by generating trade surpluses. With imports cut back as far as possible (and incidentally thereby damaging the trade and growth prospects of the developed countries themselves), this means in practice raising export earnings. But declining terms of trade, increasing levels of protection against Third World exports in developed countries and the diversion of funds which could otherwise be invested in foreign exchange-generating activity to debt repayment have put serious obstacles in the way of such a course of action. As a consequence, the austerity policies promoted by the IMF have been widely resisted. The clearest example is that of Brazil, which pursued through 1984 and 1985 a policy of expansion despite inflation of well over 200 per cent per year.

As always a historical perspective is informative. Since before the Second World War Brazil has been embarked, whether under civilian or military rule, upon an ambitious programme of economic development and diversification which has made it a leading industrial power. From the 1950s onwards, when first European and then United States car makers were attracted to the country, this programme has been highly international in orientation, and has tied the country ever more closely into the world economy. Two further characteristics of Brazilian development are relevant here. Firstly, it has been highly energy- and import-intensive. Hence the enormous expansion over recent decades of oil and capital goods imports.[30] And secondly, it has meant a consistent pursuit of growth to the detriment of both equitable income distribution, and orthodox economic policy of the kind favoured by such international bodies as the IMF.[31] The posture of the civilian regime in Brazil in the mid-1980s perfectly reflected this persistent policy orientation: strongly committed to the international economy and to maintenance of access to required imports of fuel and capital goods, and therefore opposed to the dislocation that repudiation would imply, but equally determined to resist pressure to abandon expansionary policies in favour of austerity and recession.

5. Conclusion

Our examination of three facets of the international economy has revealed the complex intertwining of social and economic issues and international and domestic policies in the Third World. Arguably, food production in Africa, oil revenues in the Middle East, and the debt crisis in Latin America are the most vital issues affecting those areas today. To a certain extent, though, as some of the discussion above reveals, the separation between them is an artificial one. A brief consideration of the way in which all the issues discussed above come together in two widely contrasting cases – Brazil and the Sudan – illustrates the connections between them.

Brazil enjoys enormous agricultural potential, exports massive quantities of food, and suffers high levels of chronic malnutrition. This is a grim reflection of the literally fatal combination of highly unequal income distribution and outward-oriented growth. Throughout the recent decades of headlong expansion the shortage of foreign exchange has constituted a severe constraint. Agricultural policy has therefore concentrated upon the development of export potential, and credit and other forms of support have been channelled primarily into large commercial farms in the south and south-east, using capital intensive methods and producing soya, coffee, sugar-cane and cotton in the main for export. The staple foods of beans and manioc have been ignored.[32] The consequence has been a massive shift of land use away from traditional food crops towards crops for export or for industrial processing, as exemplified in recent years by the spread of orange groves (making Brazil the world's largest exporter of orange juice) and cane plantations in the state of Sao Paulo. The spread of sugar cane cultivation reflects most strikingly the links between oil, famine and debt. Throughout the late 1960s and the 1970s, and particularly after 1973, the cost of Brazil's imported oil, greatly in demand as a consequence of the type of development pursued, escalated rapidly. One response was a search for indigenous oil deposits, rewarded with offshore finds of considerable potential off Rio de Janeiro in the early 1980s. Another was an equally successful development of alcohol production from cane to provide a substitute. This was at first mixed with petrol at the rate of one part to four, but subsequent technological developments led to the introduction of engines consuming 100 per cent alcohol which were standard in Brazil's substantial domestic output of motor vehicles by the mid-1980s. The other side of an apparent success story in terms of innovation and increased national autonomy was a severe worsening in the availability of food as small producers in Sao Paulo state in particular lost their land to the larger recipients of subsidised state credits who put together cane plantations linked to processing plants in the countryside.[33] For as long as Brazil pursues its current course of development, preferring energy- and capital-intensive areas and methods of production, promoting its deeper integration into international markets and allowing grossly unequal levels of income and access to resources to persist, it will generate hunger and malnutrition along with dynamic growth under civilian and military rulers alike.

Brazil, with its strong state, its dynamic capitalist economy and its powerful internationalised domestic capitalist class, is at one end of the spectrum of Third World states. The Sudan is at the other, but in a different way its situation encapsulates the cycle of underdevelopment, poverty and debt; in April 1985 the political repercussions of the combination of these factors were illustrated with the fall of President Ja'far Numeiri. The regime, established in 1969 through a military coup, was toppled after widescale popular demonstrations. The president's unpopularity was in part due to a singular political ineptness: with his country in a state of famine he made a speech blaming excessive consumption and asked why the Sudanese needed to eat three meals a day. Drought certainly played a role in producing food shortages and engendering opposition, but it was only the last straw. The oil price rise of 1973 hit the Sudan badly as an importer, but also spurred a massive development programme on the basis of attracting foreign investment, particularly from oil producing states. Loans were to be repaid out of increased production in agriculture and industries based on agriculture. Between 1978 and 1985 the foreign debt increased from US$3 billion to US$10 billion. Projects were poorly planned, subsistence agriculture was neglected, and infrastructural support was weak. The neglect of peripheral regions brought armed rebellion in the south and further expenditure for the government. Skilled and technical labour migrated to the oil producing states, and salary increases to deter migration fuelled inflation as the remittances spent on cars and consumer durables became a further drain on foreign exchange. IMF pressure for austerity measures resulted in the removal of subsidies and the doubling and tripling of the prices of basic necessities. The drought and subsequent famine brought the final collapse as starvation hit the east and the west, and the rural poor fled to the cities and urban centres. The distortions generated in the economy by the oil boom in neighbouring Middle Eastern states and the inflow of loans and remittances had greatly impaired the ability of substantial portions of the population to resist the drought and its consequences. Ironically, a record harvest was reported in late 1985, but in the western region production remained poor, and the starving lacked the resources to buy the food that was available.

Our exploration of the issues of famine, oil, and debt reveals the need for a global perspective in the analysis of Third World politics. It also reveals the complex inter-linking of issues, and the enduring disadvantages which Third World states suffer vis-à-vis the developed world. An historical perspective and a focus upon the manner in which Third World states are integrated into the global economy make indispensable contributions to our understanding of Third World politics today. Four essential points should be made in conclusion. First of all, it is a mistake to believe that the development of the world economy is directed (or in any sense controlled) by any group of individuals or countries. Practically all the developments reviewed in this chapter were unintended and unforeseen by the major protagonists, whether they were bankers, oil shaykhs, or development planners in Africa. And frequently – as with the current state of the debt crisis and the world recession – everyone loses. A distinction needs to be made, therefore, between the day-to-day decisions which individuals make in their own interests, the broader consequences of outcomes which they cannot predict, and the ability of particular countries to pursue (and protect) their own interests in the world economy. Secondly, however, the major losers are always those least able to take action to protect their own interests, and in the global economy those are the Third World states. Even the apparently powerful oil states discovered the limits of their power as the consequences of their pre-emptive raising of oil prices revealed themselves. Thirdly, one cannot attribute all the actions of Third World governments to pressure from outside. A focus upon the nature and historical development of the global capitalist economy – as distinct from the current ability of particular states to exert influence over others (which is of course considerable) – shows that the process of incorporation into the global economy has created within most Third World states élites highly supportive of integration, and anxious to deepen it rather than see it reduced. As the case of Brazil shows, they act under structural constraints, but in their own interests. And these interests may entail the pursuit of policies of economic nationalism inimical to their international backers. Finally, our depiction of the negative consequences of the promotion of export capacity under colonial and independent governments alike – and preference for high-technology, capital-intensive farming methods in general – should not be read as a plea for a return to subsistence agriculture. It is not the availability of technology itself that is to blame, but the distribution of wealth and power, and the way in which resources are allocated. Hunger has been with us throughout world history, but it is only in this century that the resources to banish it have been available. On the whole, the record of productivity is better in capitalist oriented economies, but the record of distribution is better where socialism has been adopted as a guiding principle. It is only recently, however, that socialist countries in the Third World have begun to emphasise basic needs over large-scale and energy-hungry investment projects. Attention has to be paid not only to the type of system, but also to the income and investment strategies pursued within it.

Notes and References

1. The Heritage of the Past

1. The main sources for this section are: T. Hodgkin, *Nationalism in Colonial Africa* (London: Frederick Muller, 1956); R. Oliver and J. D. Fage, *A Short History of Africa* (Harmondsworth: Penguin, 1962); M. Crowder, 'Indirect Rule – French and British Style', in M. Crowder (ed.), *Colonial West Africa: Collected Essays* (London: Frank Cass, 1978) ch. 9; and C. Clapham, *Third World Politics. An Introduction* (London: Croom Helm, 1985).
2. See J. Iliffe, *A Modern History of Tanganyika* (Cambridge University Press, 1979) ch. 2.
3. W. Rodney, *How Europe Underdeveloped Africa* (Dar es Salaam: Tanzania Publishing House, 1972, and London: Bogle-l'Ouverture, 1972) p. 162.
4. As well as Crowder, 'Indirect Rule', this discussion of French Africa is based on K. E. Robinson, 'Political Development in French West Africa', in C. W. Stillman (ed.), *Africa in the Modern World* (University of Chicago Press, 1955) pp. 140–81.
5. B. B. Schaffer, 'The Concept of Preparation: Some Questions about the Transfer of Systems of Government', *World Politics*, XVIII, 1 (October 1965) p. 59.
6. See R. S. Morgenthau, *Political Parties in French-Speaking West Africa* (Oxford: Clarendon Press, 1964), Part Eight. For a new and thoughtful perspective on decolonisation, see R. C. Crook, 'Decolonization. The Colonial State and Chieftaincy in the Gold Coast', *African Affairs*, 85, 338 (January 1986).
7. C. Stevens, *The Political Economy of Nigeria* (London: The Economist Newspaper Ltd, 1984) stimulated my thinking on this issue.
8. R. B. Collier, *Regimes in Tropical Africa. Changing Forms of Supremacy, 1945–1975* (Berkeley: University of California Press, 1982) ch. 3.
9. See D. Austin, 'The Trinitarians: the 1983 South African Constitution', *Government and Opposition*, 20, 2 (Spring 1985).
10. For an authoritative introduction to the period discussed here,

consult L. Bethell (ed.), *The Cambridge History of Latin America* (Cambridge: Cambridge University Press, 1984–5) vols I–III. For a reliable single-volume study, see J. Lockhart and S. Schwartz, *Early Latin America* (Cambridge: Cambridge University Press, 1983). For a set of readings on the period, see E. Archetti, P. Cammack and B. Roberts (eds), *Latin America* (London: Macmillan, 1987) Part II.

11. For evocative accounts of the experiences of Mexico, Peru and Brazil respectively, see M. Leon-Portilla, *The Broken Spears* (London: Constable, 1962); N. Wachtel, *The Vision of the Vanquished* (Hassocks: Harvester Press, 1977); and J. Hemming, *Red Gold: The Conquest of the Brazilian Indians, 1500–1760* (London: Macmillan, 1976).

12. See Bethell (ed.), *The Cambridge History*, vol. II, chs 1–2.

13. See S. Stein and B. Stein, *The Colonial Heritage of Latin America* (New York: Oxford University Press, 1970); C. Prado Jr, *The Colonial Background of Modern Brazil* (Berkeley and Los Angeles: University of California Press, 1967); and F. Knight, *Slave Society in Cuba during the Nineteenth Century* (Madison: University of Wisconsin Press, 1970).

14. The best overall account of independence is J. Lynch, *The Spanish American Revolutions: 1803–1826* (London: Weidenfeld and Nicolson, 1973).

15. T. Halperin-Donghi, *The Aftermath of Revolution in Latin America* (New York: Harper and Row, 1973).

16. L. Bethell (ed.), *The Cambridge History*, vol. III, chs 8–9; 16.

17. For a splendid comparative essay, see B. Albert, *South America and the World Economy from Independence to 1930* (London: Macmillan, 1983).

18. The most stimulating general discussion is provided by F. H. Cardoso and E. Falatto, *Dependency and Development in Latin America* (Berkeley and Los Angeles: University of California Press, 1979).

19. There are excellent case studies of the process of proletarianisation in the period by Albert, Fernandez and Munck, on Peru, Chile and Argentina respectively, in M. H. J. Finch and B. Munslow (eds), *Proletarianisation in the Third World* (London: Croom Helm, 1984).

20. See K. H. Karpat, 'The Transformation of the Ottoman State', *International Journal of Middle East Studies*, 3 (1972); K. H. Karpat, 'The Land Regime, Social Structure and Modernization in the Ottoman Empire' in W. Polk and R. Chambers (eds), *The Beginnings of Modernization in the Middle East* (Chicago: Chicago University Press, 1968); A. Hourani, 'The Ottoman Background of the Modern Middle East' in K. H. Karpat (ed.), *The Ottoman State and its Place in History* (Leiden: Brill, 1974).

21. R. L. Tignor, *State, Private Enterprise and Economic Change in Egypt 1918–52* (Princeton: Princeton University Press, 1984) pp. 59–77.

22. See N. van Dam, 'Minorities and Political Elites in Iraq and Syria', in T. Asad and R. Owen (eds), *Sociology of 'Developing Societies': The*

Middle East (London: Macmillan, 1983); A. Hourani, *Syria and Lebanon: A Political Essay* (London: Oxford University Press, 1954) ch. VII.

23. R. Owen, *The Middle East in the World Economy 1800–1914* (London: Methuen, 1981) pp. 154–67.
24. K. Salibi, *The Modern History of Lebanon* (London: Weidenfeld and Nicolson, 1965).
25. See H. Batatu, *The Old Social Classes and the Revolutionary Movements of Iraq* (Princeton: Princeton University Press, 1978) pp. 13–50; D. Pool, 'From Elite to Class: The Transformation of Iraqi Political Leadership', *International Journal of Middle East Studies* 12 (April 1980).
26. Based on E. Abrahamian, *Iran Between Two Revolutions* (Princeton: Princeton University Press, 1982).

2. State and Society

1. See R. H. Jackson and C. G. Rosberg, 'Why Africa's Weak States Persist: The Empirical and the Juridical in Statehood', *World Politics*, XXXV, 1 (October 1982).
2. Stevens, *The Political Economy of Nigeria*, p. 11.
3. M. F. Lofchie (ed.), *The State of the Nations: Constraints on Development in Independent Africa* (Berkeley: University of California Press, 1971) Conclusion, pp. 272–3.
4. In the section which follows I have drawn substantially upon John Iliffe's illuminating study, *The Emergence of African Capitalism* (London: Macmillan, 1983) pp. 1–113.
5. See Iliffe, *The Emergence*, pp. 46–8, 51.
6. For an informed study of MNCs, see C. Kirkpatrick and F. Nixon, 'Transnational Corporations and Economic Development', *Journal of Modern African Studies*, 19, 3 (September 1981).
7. In 1977 the NNOC was amalgamated with the Ministry of Petroleum to form the Nigerian National Petroleum Corporation (NNPC). See A. Kirk-Greene and D. Rimmer, *Nigeria Since 1970. A Political and Economic Outline* (London: Hodder and Stoughton, 1981) p. 86.
8. For a fuller discussion, see my introduction to W. Tordoff (ed.), *Administration in Zambia* (Manchester University Press, 1980) pp. 31–3.
9. M. Szeftel, 'Conflict, Spoils and Class Formation in Zambia' (Ph.D. thesis, University of Manchester, 1978) p. 455.
10. R. Sandbrook, 'Patrons, Clients, and Factions: New Dimensions of Conflict Analysis in Africa', *Canadian Journal of Political Science*, V, 1 (March 1972) p. 107.
11. C. L. Baylies and M. Szeftel, 'The Rise of a Zambian Capitalist Class in the 1970s', *Journal of Southern African Studies*, 8, 2 (April 1982) p. 212. The authors' observation is limited to Zambia, but has a wider application.

280 *Notes and References*

12. This point is made by G. Hyden, *Beyond Ujamaa in Tanzania. Underdevelopment and an Uncaptured Peasantry* (London: Heinemann, 1980) p. 30.
13. See D. Rock, *Argentina 1516–1982* (Berkeley and Los Angeles: University of California Press, 1985).
14. Good case studies are Steve Stein, *Populism in Peru* (Madison: University of Wisconsin Press, 1980); L. Aguilar, *Cuba 1933: Prologue to Revolution* (Ithaca: Cornell University Press, 1972); and D. Levine, *Conflict and Political Change in Venezuela* (Princeton: Princeton University Press, 1973).
15. On Bolivia, see H. Klein, *Parties and Political Change in Bolivia, 1880–1952* (Cambridge: Cambridge University Press, 1969) and J. Dunkerley, *Rebellion in the Veins: Political Struggle in Bolivia, 1952–1982* (London: Verso, 1984).
16. For a set of readings on populism, see E. Archetti, P. Cammack and B. Roberts (eds), *Latin America* (London: Macmillan, 1987), Part IV.
17. On Argentina, Brazil and Mexico respectively, see S. Baily, *Labor, Nationalism and Politics in Argentina* (New Brunswick: Rutgers University Press, 1967); K. Erickson, *The Brazilian Corporative State and the Working Class* (Berkeley and Los Angeles: University of California Press, 1977); and N. Hamilton, *The Limits of State Autonomy: Post-Revolutionary Mexico* (Princeton: Princeton University Press, 1982).
18. R. Collier, 'Popular Sector Incorporation and Political Supremacy' in S. Hewlett and R. Weinert (eds), *Brazil and Mexico: Patterns in Late Development* (Philadelphia: ISHI, 1982).
19. For a useful collection, see J. Malloy (ed.), *Authoritarianism and Corporatism in Latin America* (Pittsburgh: University of Pittsburgh Press, 1977).
20. G. O'Donnell, 'Corporatism and the Question of the State', in Malloy (ed.) *Authoritarianism*.
21. See F. H. Cardoso, 'On the Characterization of Authoritarian Regimes in Latin America', in D. Collier (ed.), *The New Authoritarianism in Latin America* (Princeton: Princeton University Press, 1979).
22. For the background on Brazil see P. Flynn, *Brazil: A Political Analysis* (London: Ernest Benn, 1978); T. Skidmore, *Politics in Brazil, 1930–1964* (New York: Oxford University Press, 1967); and R. Roett, *Brazil: Politics in a Patrimonial Society* (Boston: Alleyn and Bacon, 1972).
23. See D. Hopwood, *Egypt: Politics and Society 1945–81* (London: Allen & Unwin, 1982).
24. See P. E. Haley and L. W. Snider, *Lebanon in Crisis* (New York: Syracuse University Press, 1979).
25. For Syria and Iraq see T. Petran, *Syria* (London: Ernest Benn, 1972); N. van Dam, *The Struggle for Power in Syria: Sectarianism, Regionalism and Tribalism in Politics, 1961–78* (London: Croom

Helm, 1979); and C. Helms, *Iraq, Eastern Flank of the Arab World* (Washington: Brookings Institution, 1984).
26. See C. Dunbar and S. Nasr, *Les Classes Sociales au Liban* (Paris: Presses de la Fondation des Sciences Politiques, 1976).
27. H. Batatu, 'Some Observations on the Social Origins of Syria's Military Ruling Group', *Middle East Journal*, XXXV (1981).
28. See D. Warriner, *Land Reform and Development in the Middle East* (2nd edn) (Oxford: Oxford University Press, 1962).
29. J. Waterbury, *The Egypt of Nasser and Sadat* (Princeton: Princeton University Press, 1983) p. 211.
30. Waterbury, *The Egypt of Nasser*, p. 222.
31. Abrahamian, *Iran Between Two Revolutions*, p. 431.
32. M. G. Weinbaum, *Food, Development and Politics* (Colorado: Westview Press, 1982) p. 27.
33. B. Hansen and S. Radwan, *Employment Opportunities and Equity in a Changing Economy: Egypt in the 1980s* (Geneva: International Labour Organisation, 1982) pp. 99–111.
34. R. L. Sklar, 'The Nature of Class Domination in Africa', *Journal of Modern African Studies*, 17, 4 (1979), p. 537.
35. R. Melson and H. Wolpe (eds), *Nigeria: Modernization and the Politics of Communalism* (East Lansing: Michigan State University Press, 1971), p. 28.

3. Political Parties and Participation

1. The early part of this chapter draws especially on Hodgkin, *Nationalism in Colonial Africa*, ch. 5.
2. D. Austin, *Politics in Ghana, 1946–60* (London: Oxford University Press, 1964) ch. VII.
3. Collier, *Regimes in Tropical Africa*, chs. 2 and 3.
4. The Brong-Ahafo Region was established in 1959. See W. Tordoff, 'The Brong-Ahafo Region', *The Economic Bulletin*, 3, 5 (Accra, May 1959).
5. See Austin, *Politics in Ghana*, ch. VI, which brilliantly captures the excitement of the struggle for power in Ashanti between 1954 and 1956, and D. Austin and W. Tordoff, 'Voting in an African Town', *Political Studies*, VIII, 2 (June 1960).
6. A. R. Zolberg, *One-Party Government in the Ivory Coast* (Princeton University Press, 1964) pp. 129, 185; R. Tangri, *Politics in Sub-Saharan Africa* (London: James Currey, 1985) p. 40.
7. See J. S. Coleman and C. G. Rosberg, Jr (eds), *Political Parties and National Integration in Tropical Africa* (Berkeley: University of California Press, 1964), introduction, especially p. 5.
8. See J. Mende, 'Senegal: Diouf's New Directions', *Africa Report*, 27, 6 (November–December, 1982).
9. See C. Pratt, *The Critical Phase in Tanzania, 1945–1968. Nyerere and the Emergence of a Socialist Strategy* (Cambridge University

Press, 1976) p. 238, and passim.
10. The tripartite system of policy-making in Tanzania is stressed by Jeannette Hartmann in *Development Policy-Making in Tanzania, 1962–1982: A Critique of Sociological Interpretations* (Ph.D. thesis, University of Hull, 1983).
11. The remainder of this discussion of policy-making in Tanzania is based on A. J. Liviga and J. K. van Donge's valuable paper, 'Tanzanian Political Culture and the Cabinet' (University of Dar es Salaam, December 1983) (mimeo).
12. For a fuller discussion, see Tordoff (ed.), *Administration in Zambia* (1980) pp. 15ff.; 272–4; and ch. 10, and C. Gertzel, C. Baylies and M. Szeftel (eds), *The Dynamics of the One-Party State in Zambia* (Manchester University Press, 1984), esp ch. 4. For the food riots, see *The Guardian* (London), 18 December 1986.
13. A. R. Luckham, 'A Comparative Typology of Civil–Military Relations', *Government and Opposition*, 6, 1 (Winter 1971) p. 13.
14. Szeftel, 'Conflicts, Spoils and Class Formation in Zambia', p. 282.
15. D. B. Cruise O'Brien, *Saints and Politicians: Essays in the Organisation of a Senegalese Peasant Society* (London: Cambridge University Press, 1975) p. 156.
16. See P. Smith, *Labrynths of Power: Political Recruitment in Twentieth Century Mexico* (Princeton: University of Princeton Press, 1979), and J. Reyna and R. Wainert (eds), *Authoritarianism in Mexico* (Philadelphia: Institute for the Study of Human Issues, 1977).
17. See K. Johnson, *Mexican Democracy: A Critical View* (revised edn) (New York: Praeger, 1978), ch. 4, and J. Hellman, *Mexico in Crisis* (New York: Holmes and Meier, 1978).
18. W. Little, 'Party and State in Peronist Argentina, 1945–1955', *Hispanic American Historical Review*, 53, 4 (1973).
19. R. Munck, 'Democratization and Demilitarization in Argentina, 1982–1985', *Bulletin of Latin American Research*, 4, 2 (1985).
20. T. Skidmore, *Politics in Brazil, 1930–1964* (New York: Oxford University Press, 1967) chs 7–8.
21. See A. Valenzuela, *The Breakdown of Democratic Regimes: Chile* (Baltimore: Johns Hopkins University Press, 1978), ch. 1, and M. Fleet, *The Rise and Fall of Chilean Christian Democracy* (Princeton: Princeton University Press, 1985).
22. J. Martz, *Colombia: A Contemporary Political Survey* (Chapel Hill: University of North Carolina Press, 1967), and P. Oquist, *Violence, Conflict and Politics in Colombia* (New York: Academic Press, 1980).
23. See D. Levine, *Conflict and Political Change in Venezuela* (Princeton: Princeton University Press, 1973).
24. See J. Linz and A. Stepan (eds), *The Breakdown of Democratic Regimes: Latin America* (Baltimore: Johns Hopkins University Press, 1978), and J. Peeler, *Latin American Democracies: Colombia, Costa Rica, Venezuela* (Chapel Hill: University of North Carolina Press, 1985).
25. See H. Penniman (ed.), *Venezuela at the Polls* (Washington:

American Enterprise Institute for Public Policy Research, 1980).
26. Peeler, *Latin American Democracies*, p. 121.
27. For early contributions to the debate, see E. Herman and J. Petras, 'Latin American Democracy: Rhetoric and Reality', *New Left Review* 135 (1985), and P. Cammack, 'Latin American Democracy: Threat or Promise', *New Left Review* 137 (1986).
28. Abrahamian, *Iran Between Two Revolutions*, p. 450.
29. L. Binder, *In a Moment of Enthusiasm: Political Power and the Second Stratum in Egypt* (Chicago: Chicago University Press, 1978) p. 42.
30. Waterbury, *Egypt under Nasser and Sadat*, p. 322.
31. Waterbury, *Egypt under Nasser and Sadat*, p. 355.
32. C. H. Moore, 'Authoritarian Politics in an Unincorporated Society, The Case of Nasser's Egypt', *Comparative Politics*, 6 (April, 1974) p. 197.
33. See J. Devlin, *The Ba'th Party: A History from its Origins to 1966* (Stanford: Hoover Institution, 1976); I. Rabinovitch, *Syria Under the Ba'th 1963–66* (Jerusalem: Israel Universities Press, 1972).
34. H. Batatu, *The Old Social Classes*, p. 1072 and *passim*.

4. The Military

1. S. E. Finer, *The Man on Horseback. The Role of the Military in Politics* (London: Pall Mall, 1962) pp. 21–2; 84–5; and chs 7–9.
2. R. Luckham, 'French Militarism in Africa', *Review of African Political Economy*, 24 (May–August 1982) p. 70.
3. A. Hughes and R. May, 'Armies on Loan: Toward an Explanation of Transnational Military Intervention among Black African States: 1960–1984', paper presented at the 21st Anniversary Conference of the African Studies Association of the United Kingdom, University of York, 19–21 September 1984.
4. J. R. Cartwright, *Politics in Sierra Leone, 1947–67* (University of Toronto Press, 1970) p. 255; T. S. Cox, *Civil Military Relations in Sierra Leone: A Case Study of African Soldiers in Politics* (Cambridge: Cambridge, Mass.: Harvard University Press, 1976) p. 135 and *passim*.
5. See W. Tordoff, *Government and Politics in Africa* (London: Macmillan, 1984), ch. 7, where full references are given to the Nigerian and Ghanaian case studies included in that chapter. On Nigeria, see especially R. Luckham, *The Nigerian Military: A Sociological Analysis of Authority and Revolt, 1960–67* (Cambridge: Cambridge University Press, 1971) ch. XI and *passim*.
6. Radio Accra announcement by the army, 24 February 1966, and broadcast by Major-General J. A. Ankrah, 28 February 1966, quoted in D. G. Austin, 'The Ghana Case', *The Politics of Demilitarisation* (Collected Seminar Papers, Institute of Commonwealth Studies, University of London, April–May 1966) pp. 41–6. See also A. A. Afrifa, *The Ghana Coup* (London: Frank Cass, 1966), and R. First,

The Barrel of a Gun: Political Power in Africa and the Coup d'Etat (London: Allen Lane, 1970) pp. 169–201.

7. See M. F. Lofchie, 'Uganda Coup: Class Action by the Military', *Journal of Modern African Studies*, 10, 1 (May 1972) pp. 19–35. For critical comments on Lofchie's article, see J. D. Chick, 'Class Conflict and Military Intervention in Uganda', *Journal of Modern African Studies*, 10, 4 (December 1972) pp. 634–7, and I. Gershenberg, 'A Further Comment on the 1971 Uganda Coup', *Journal of Modern African Studies*, pp. 638–9. See also S. Decalo, *Coups and Army Rule in Africa: Studies in Military Style* (New Haven: Yale University Press, 1976) ch. 5.

8. See Decalo, *Coups*, ch. 2; First, *The Barrel of a Gun*, pp. 212–3.

9. Clapham, *Third World Politics*, p. 143.

10. See S. P. Huntington, *Political Order in Changing Societies* (New Haven: Yale University Press, 1968) ch. 4.

11. M. J. Dent, 'Corrective Government: Military Rule in Perspective', in S. K. Panter-Brick (ed.), *Soldiers and Oil: The Political Transformation of Nigeria* (London: Frank Cass, 1978) ch. 4.

12. First, *The Barrel of a Gun*, p. 22; R. W. Jackman, 'Politicians in Uniform', *The American Political Science Review*, LXX, 4 (December 1976) p. 1097.

13. See Collier, *Regimes in Tropical Africa*, ch. 5.

14. See Clapham, *Third World Politics*, p. 157.

15. W. Little, 'Military Power in Latin America: An Overview', Working Paper 4, University of Liverpool, Institute of Latin American Studies (1986) p. 11.

16. J. Dunkerley, *The Long War: Dictatorship and Revolution in El Salvador* (London: Junction Books, 1982) ch. 1.

17. See F. Nunn, *Yesterday's Soldiers: European Military Professionalism in South America 1890–1940*, (Lincoln: University of Nebraska Press, 1983).

18. E. Lieuwen, *Mexican Militarism: the Political Rise and Fall of the Revolutionary Army, 1910–1940* (Albuquerque, University of New Mexico Press, 1968).

19. See H. Klein, *Parties and Political Change in Bolivia, 1880–1952* (Cambridge: Cambridge University Press, 1971) chs 5–6.

20. For a detailed account, see G. Kolb, *Democracy and Dictatorship in Venezuela, 1945–1958* (Connecticut: Archon Books, 1974).

21. See R. Potash, *The Army and Politics in Argentina, 1928–1945* (Stanford: University of Stanford Press, 1969) and *The Army and Politics in Argentina, 1945–1962* (London: Athlone Press, 1980).

22. For the data for the 1930–1964 period, see W. Little, 'Military Power', p. 20.

23. See A. Angell, 'The Soldier as Politician: Military Authoritarianism in Latin America', in D. Kavanagh and G. Peele (eds), *Comparative Government and Politics: Essays in Honour of S. E. Finer* (London: Heinemann, 1984).

24. For an account of the origins and application of the doctrine in Brazil,

see A. Stepan, *The Military in Politics* (Princeton: Princeton University Press, 1971), and M. H. M. Alves, *State and Opposition in Military Brazil* (Austin: University of Texas Press, 1985) Part I.
25. For a comparative account and a set of case studies, see P. O'Brien and P. Cammack (eds), *Generals in Retreat: The Crisis of Military Rule in Latin America* (Manchester: Manchester University Press, 1985).
26. See G. O'Donnell, *Modernisation and Bureaucratic Authoritarianism, Studies in South American Politics* (Berkeley: University of California Press, 1973). For a summary critique, see P. O'Brien and P. Cammack (eds), *Generals in Retreat*, ch. 1.
27. For a fuller discussion, see P. Cammack and P. O'Brien, 'Conclusion', in P. O'Brien and P. Cammack (eds) *Generals in Retreat*.
28. For this early period in Syria see P Seale, *The Struggle for Syria* (London: Oxford University Press, 1965) and G. Torry, *Syrian Politics and the Military* (Columbus: Ohio State University Press, 1964).
29. U. Dann, *Iraq under Qassem, A Political History* (New York: Praeger, 1969).
30. See H. Dekmejian, *Egypt under Nasir* (Albany, New York: State University of New York, 1971), ch. 11.
31. Petran, *Syria*, ch. 5.
32. See Rabinovitch, *Syria under the Ba'ath*; van Dam, *The Struggle for Power*, and Devlin, *The Ba'ath Party*.
33. van Dam, *The Struggle for Power*, p. 127.

5. Revolution

1. T. Skocpol, *States and Social Revolution* (Cambridge: Cambridge University Press, 1979) p. 4.
2. C. G. Rosberg and T. M. Callaghy (eds), *Socialism in Sub-Saharan Africa: A New Assessment* (Berkeley: Institute of International Studies, University of California, 1979) p. 5.
3. L. Adamolekun, 'The Socialist Experience in Guinea', in Rosberg and Callaghy (eds), *Socialism*, p. 77.
4. Quoted in P. Chabal, *Amilcar Cabral, Revolutionary Leadership and People's War* (Cambridge University Press, 1983) p. 66.
5. See Clapham, *Third World Politics*, pp. 164–5 and ch. 8 on 'The Revolutionary State'. On Zimbabwe, see A. Astrow, *Zimbabwe: A Revolution that Lost its Way?* (London: Zed Books, 1983).
6. *Sunday Mail* (Zimbabwe), 29 July 1984, quoted in B. Munslow, 'The ZANU Party Congress of 1984', *Journal of Communist Studies*, 1, 1 (March 1985) p. 78.
7. On Mozambique generally, see especially B. Munslow, *Mozambique: The Revolution and its Origins* (London: Longman, 1983), and J. Hanlon, *Mozambique: The Revolution under Fire* (London: Zed Books, 1984).
8. R. Hallett, 'Mozambique', in H. V. Hodson (ed.), *The Annual*

Register. A Record of World Events, 1984 (Harlow: Longman, 1985), pp. 249–52; *The Guardian* (London), 15 March and 7 November 1986, and *The Observer* (London), 16 March and 26 October 1986.

9. On Angola generally, see especially J. Marcum, *The Angolan Revolution*, vol. I: *The Anatomy of an Explosion (1950–1962)* and vol. II: *Exile Politics and Guerrilla Warfare (1962–1976)*, both volumes published by Massachusetts Institute of Technology Press (Cambridge, Mass.) vol. I in 1969 and vol. II in 1978; and M. Wolfers and J. Bergerol, *Angola in the Frontline* (London: Zed Press, 1983).

10. For an informed discussion of the continued militarisation of the African continent, see R. Luckham, 'Armaments, Underdevelopment and Demilitarisation in Africa', *Alternatives: A Journal of World Policy*, VI, 2 (July 1980).

11. On Ethiopia generally, see especially F. Halliday and M. Molyneux, *The Ethiopian Revolution* (London: Verso, 1981).

12. This suggestion is made by J. W. Harbeson, 'Socialist Politics in Revolutionary Ethiopia', in Rosberg and Callaghy (eds), *Socialism*, pp. 345–6; 352 ff.

13. See Clapham, *Third World Politics*, pp. 171–2, and 'The Workers' Party of Ethiopia', *Journal of Communist Studies*, 1, 1 (March 1985) pp. 76–7.

14. See B. Loveman and T. Davies (eds), *Che Guevara: Guerrilla Warfare* (Lincoln and London: University of Nebraska Press, 1985) for basic texts and a review of developments into the 1980s.

15. For a history, see A. Knight, *The Mexican Revolution, 1908–1920* (Cambridge: Cambridge University Press, 1986), 2 vols.

16. See N. Hamilton, *The Limits of Autonomy: Post-Revolutionary Mexico* (Princeton: Princeton University Press, 1982).

17. See R. Anderson, *Outcasts in Their Own Land: Mexican Industrial Workers, 1906–1911* (DeKalb: University of Northern Illinois Press, 1976), and A. Knight, 'The Working Class and the Mexican Revolution, c. 1900–1928', *Journal of Latin American Studies*, 16, 1, 1984.

18. For a history, see J. Dunkerley, *Rebellion in the Veins: Political Struggle in Bolivia 1952–82* (London: Verso, 1984).

19. For a debate, see B. Useem, 'The Workers' Movement and the Bolivian Revolution', *Politics & Society*, 9, 4, 1980, and P. Cammack, 'The Workers' Movement and the Bolivian Revolution Reconsidered', *Politics & Society*, 11, 2, (1982).

20. R. Immerman, *The CIA in Guatemala: The Foreign Policy of Intervention* (Austin: University of Texas Press, 1982) and S. Schlesinger and S. Kinzer, *Bitter Fruit: The Untold Story of the American Coup in Guatemala* (London: Sinclaire Brown, 1982).

21. For general accounts of the revolution, see H. Matthews, *Revolution in Cuba: An Essay in Understanding* (New York: Charles Scribner's Sons, 1975), and K. S. Karol, *Guerrillas in Power: The Course of the Cuban Revolution* (London: Jonathan Cape, 1971).

22. J. Benjamin, *The United States and Cuba: Hegemony and Dependent Development, 1880–1934* (Pittsburgh: University of Pittsburgh Press,

1977), and J. O'Connor, *The Origins of Socialism in Cuba* (Ithaca: Cornell University Press, 1970).

23. R. Debray, *Revolution in the Revolution?* (New York: Monthly Review Press, 1967).

24. R. Debray, *A Critique of Arms* (Harmondsworth: Penguin, 1977) and Loveman and Davies, *Che Guevara*, provide critiques of the original 'foco' theory.

25. See R. Millett, *Guardians of the Dynasty* (Maryknoll: Orbis Books, 1977).

26. See G. Black, *Triumph of the People: The Sandinista Revolution in Nicaragua* (London: Zed press, 1981).

27. M. Dodson, 'Nicaragua: The Struggle for the Church', in D. Levine (ed.), *Religion and Political Conflict in Latin America* (Chapel Hill and London: University of North Carolina Press, 1986).

28. *Nasser Speaks, Basic Documents* (London: Morsett Press, 1972) p. 17.

29. *Nasser Speaks*, p. 40.

30. R. Mabro, *The Egyptian Economy 1952–72* (Oxford: Oxford University Press, 1974) pp. 56–7.

31. *Nasser Speaks*, p. 66.

32. See I. Harik, *The Political Mobilization of Peasants* (Bloomington: Indiana University Press, 1974) and R. Baker, *Egypt's Uncertain Revolution under Nasser and Sadat* (Cambridge, Mass.: Harvard University Press, 1978).

33. F. Halliday, 'Yemen's Unfinished Revolution', *Middle East Information and Research Project* (October 1979).

34. For the Iranian revolution see Abrahamian, *Iran Between Two Revolutions*; R. Graham, *Iran Illusion of Power* (London: Croom Helm, 1979); F. Halliday, *Iran: Dictatorship and Development* (Harmondsworth: Penguin, 1979); N. Keddie, *Iran: The Roots of Revolution* (New Haven: Yale University Press, 1981).

35. J. Bill, *The Politics of Iran: Groups, Classes and Modernization* (Colombus, Ohio: Merrill, 1972).

36. Abrahamian, *Iran Between Two Revolutions*, p. 431.

37. Abrahamian, *Iran Between Two Revolutions*, p. 435.

6. Women in Third World Politics

1. M. Etienne and E. Leacock, 'Introduction', in M. Etienne and E. Leacock (eds), *Women and Colonization: Anthropological Perspectives* (New York: Praeger, 1980) p. 7.

2. K. Sacks, *Sisters and Wives: The Past and Future of Sexual Equality* (Westport: Greenwood Press, 1979) p. 110.

3. P. Roberts, 'Feminism in Africa; Feminism and Africa', *Review of African Political Economy*, 27/28 (February 1984) p. 176.

4. C. Robertson, 'Ga Women and Socioeconomic Change in Accra, Ghana', in N. Hafkin and E. Bay (eds), *Women in Africa: Studies in*

Social and Economic Change (Stanford: Stanford University Press, 1976).

5. E. Boserup, *Women's Role in Economic Development* (New York: St Martin's Press, 1970) p.16.

6. R. S. Oboler, *Women, Power and Economic Change: The Nandi of Kenya* (Stanford: Stanford University Press, 1975) p. xxx.

7. K. Crehan, 'Women and Development in North Western Zambia: from Producer to Housewife', *Review of African Political Economy*, 27/28 (February 1984).

8. M. Etienne, 'Women and Men, Cloth and Colonization: The Transformation of Production–Distribution Relations among the Baule (Ivory Coast)', in Etienne and Leacock, *Women and Colonization*.

9. R. S. Rattray, *Ashanti Law and Constitution* (London: Oxford University Press, 1929) p. 88.

10. K. Okonjo, 'The Dual-Sex Political System in Operation: Igbo Women and Community Politics in Midwestern Nigeria', in Hafkin and Bay (eds), *Women in Africa*.

11. C. Ifeka-Moller, 'Female Militancy and Colonial Revolt: The Women's War of 1929, Eastern Nigeria', in S. Ardener (ed.), *Perceiving Women* (London: Dent, 1977).

12. J. Van Allen, ' "Aba Riots" or Igbo Women's War? Ideology, Stratification, and the Invisibility of Women', in Hafkin and Bay (eds), *Women in Africa*.

13. P. Hill, *Studies in Rural Capitalism in West Africa* (Cambridge: Cambridge University Press, 1970) p. 62.

14. Hill, *Studies*, ch. 3, especially pp. 35–40. A 'company' of men was made up of the core of the group that operated the beach-seine net. The women were always referred to as 'the wives'; while most women were wives, some unmarried company members brought single women (such as sisters) with them.

15. K. Arhin, *West African Traders in Ghana in the Nineteenth and Twentieth Centuries* (London: Longman, 1979) p. 127.

16. P. C. Garlick, *African Traders and Economic Development in Ghana* (Oxford: Clarendon Press, 1971) p. 49; the author draws upon the findings of Gloria Addae, 'The retailing of imported textiles in the Accra markets', Proceedings of the West African Institute of Social and Economic Research, 3rd Conference (1954), as confirmed by European businessmen.

17. C. Dennis, 'Capitalist Development and Women's Work: A Nigerian Case Study', *Review of African Political Economy*, 27/28 (February, 1984) p. 11.

18. Robertson, 'Ga Women and Socioeconomic Change in Accra'.

19. E. Chaney and M. Schmink, 'Women and Modernization: Access to Tools', in J. Nash and H. Safa (eds), *Sex and Class in Latin America* (South Hadley: Bergin, 1980).

20. B. Rogers, *The Domestication of Women: Discrimination in Developing Societies* (London: Tavistock, 1980).

21. S. Jacobs, 'Women and Land Resettlement in Zimbabwe', *Review of*

African Political Economy, 27/28 (February 1984) p. 48.

22. J. Nash, 'Aztec Women: The Transition from Status to Class in Empire and Colony', in Etienne and Leacock (eds), *Women and Colonization*.

23. I. Silverblatt, 'Andean Women under Spanish Rule', in Etienne and Leacock (eds), *Women and Colonization*.

24. S. Brown and E. Buenaventura-Posso, 'Forced Transition from Egalitarianism among the Bari', in Etienne and Leacock (eds), *Women and Colonization*.

25. K. Young, 'Modes of Appropriation and the Sexual Division of Labour: A Case Study from Oaxaca, Mexico', in A. Kuhn and A. Wolpe (eds), *Feminism and Materialism: Women and Modes of Production* (London, Routledge and Kegan Paul, 1978).

26. C. D. Deere and M. Leon de Leal, 'Peasant Production, Proletarianization, and the Sexual Division of Labour in the Andes', *Signs*, 7, 2 (1981).

27. M. Smith, 'Domestic Service as a Channel of Upward Mobility for the Lower-Class Woman: The Lima Case', in A. Pescatello (ed.), *Female and Male in Latin America* (Pittsburgh: University of Pittsburgh Press, 1973) pp. 193, 205.

28. E. Jelin, 'Migration and Labor Force Participation of Latin American Women: The Domestic Servants in the Cities', in Wellesley Education Committee, *Women and National Development: The Complexities of Change* (Chicago: University of Chicago Press, 1977 (*Signs*, 3, 1 (1977)).

29. S. Lobo, *A House of My Own* (Tucson, University of Arizona Press, 1982) p. 37.

30. L. Arispe, 'Women in the Informal Sector in Mexico', in Wellesley Education Committee, *Women and National Development*.

31. J. Alonso, 'The Domestic Clothing Workers in the Mexican Metropolis and their Relationship to Dependent Capitalism', in J. Nash and M. P. Fernandez-Kelly (eds), *Women, Men and the International Division of Labour* (Albany: State University of New York Press, 1983).

32. See for example H. Saffioti, *Women in Class Society* (New York: Monthly Review Press, 1979).

33. J. Humphrey, 'Gender, Pay and Skill: Manual Workers in Brazilian Industry', in H. Afshar (ed.), *Women, Work, and Ideology in the Third World* (London: Tavistock, 1985).

34. M. P. Fernandez-Kelly, *For We Are Sold, I and My People: Women Industrial Workers on the Mexican Frontier* (Albany: State University of New York Press, 1983).

35. For some comparisons, see L. Lim, 'Capitalism, Imperialism, and Patriarchy: The Dilemma of Third-World Women Workers in Multinational Factories', in Nash and Fernandez-Kelly (eds), *Women, Men*.

36. E. Stevens, 'Marianismo: The Other Face of Machismo', in Pescatello (ed.), *Female and Male*.

37. E. Chaney, *Supermadre: Women in Politics in Latin America* (Austin: University of Texas Press, 1979).

38. See J. Aviel, 'Political Participation of Women in Latin America',

Western Political Quarterly, 34, 1 (1981), and J. Jaquette, 'Female Political Participation in Latin America', in Nash and Safa (eds), *Sex and Class*.

39. N. Saadawi, *The Hidden Face of Eve: Women in the Arab World* (London: Zed Press, 1980) pp. vi–vii.
40. Amal Rassam, 'Revolution within the Revolution? Women and the State in Iraq', in T. Niblock (ed.), *Iraq: The Contemporary State* (London: Croom Helm, 1982) p. 94.
41. See L. Bahry, 'The New Saudi Woman: Modernizing in an Islamic Framework', *Middle East Journal*, 36, 4 (1982).
42. E. Friedl, 'Women and the Division of Labour in an Iranian Village', *MERIP Reports*, 95 (March–April 1981).
43. Friedl, 'Women and the Division of Labour', p. 17.
44. H. Afshar, 'The Position of Women in an Iranian Village', in Afshar (ed.), *Women, Work and Ideology*, pp. 76–7.
45. P. Higgins, 'Women in the Islamic Republic of Iran: Legal, Social and Ideological Change', *Signs*, 10, 3 (1985).
46. Afshar, 'The Position of Women', p. 72.
47. M. Hegland, 'Political Roles of Iranian Village Women', *MERIP Reports*, 138 (January–February 1986).
48. H. Afshar, 'Women, State and Ideology in Iran', *Third World Quarterly*, 7, 2 (1985) p. 269.
49. Afshar, 'Women, state', pp. 269; 277.
50. E. Taylor, 'Egyptian Migration and Peasant Wives', *MERIP Reports*, 124 (June 1984) p. 10.
51. See F. Khafagy, 'Women and Labour Migration: One Village in Egypt', *MERIP Reports*, 124 (June 1984).
52. See A. Bandaranage, 'Women in Development: Liberalism, Marxism, and Marxism-Feminism', *Development and Change*, 15, 4 (1984).
53. Higgins, 'Women in the Islamic Republic', p. 493.
54. L. Beck, 'The Religious Lives of Muslim Women', in J. Smith (ed.), *Women in Contemporary Muslim Societies* (Lewisberg: Bucknell University Press, 1980).
55. See B. Callaway, 'Ambiguous Consequences of the Socialisation and Seclusion of Hausa Women', *Journal of Modern African Studies*, 22, 3 (1984); L. Ahmad, 'Western Ethnocentrism and Perceptions of the Harem', *Feminist Studies*, 8 (1982).
56. U. Wikan, *Behind the Veil in Arabia: Women in Oman* (Baltimore: Johns Hopkins University Press, 1982) p. 185, and discussion pp. 68–9.
57. See, for example, A. Tabari, 'The Women's Movement in Iran: A Hopeful Prognosis', *Feminist Studies*, 12, 2 (1986).
58. M. Molyneux, 'Family Reform in Socialist States: The Hidden Agenda', *Feminist Review*, 21 (1985) p. 50; see also 'Mobilization Without Emancipation? Women's Interests, State and Revolution in Nicaragua', *Critical Social Policy*, 4, 1 (1984).
59. M. Nazzari, 'The "Woman Question" in Cuba: An Analysis of

Material Constraints on Its Solution', *Signs*, 9, 2 (1983).
60. S. Urdang, 'The Last Transition? Women and Development in Mozambique', *Review of African Political Economy*, 27/28 (February 1984).

7. The International Context

1. A. A. Mazrui, *Africa's International Relations. The Diplomacy of Dependency and Change* (London: Heinemann, 1977) p. 158.
2. R. Hodder-Williams, *An Introduction to the Politics of Tropical Africa* (London: Allen & Unwin, 1984), p. 220.
3. Tangri, *Politics in Sub-Saharan Africa*, p. 137; Dr Tangri provides a good and succinct account of the international politics of southern Africa (*Politics in Sub-Saharan Africa*, pp. 135–46).
4. *The Guardian* (London), 3 April 1986.
5. See C. Hoskyns, 'Pan-Africanism and Integration', in A. Hazelwood (ed.), *African Integration and Disintegration: Case Studies in Economic and Political Union* (London: Oxford University Press, 1967); Tordoff, *Government and Politics in Africa*, pp. 239–60; D. Mazzeo (ed.), *African Regional Organisation* (Cambridge: Cambridge University Press, 1984).
6. Today, there are six states in the 'front line' of the struggle against South Africa: the original three – Botswana, Tanzania and Zambia – plus Mozambique (1974), Angola (1975), and Zimbabwe (1980).
7. See J. Mayall, 'African Unity and the OAU: The Place of a Political Myth in African Diplomacy', *The Handbook of World Affairs*, 27 (1973).
8. See R. I. Onwuka, *Development and Integration in West Africa: The Case of the Economic Community of West African States (ECOWAS)* (University of Ife Press, 1982), especially pp. 112ff.: 'The Organs and Decision-Making Process of ECOWAS'; S. K. B. Asante, 'Trade Problems and Prospects', in *West Africa* (London) 24 May 1982, and 'ECOWAS/CEAO: Conflict and Cooperation in West Africa, in R. I. Onwuka and A. Sesay (eds), *The Future of Regionalism in Africa* (London: Macmillan, 1985).
9. Tangri, *Politics in Sub-Saharan Africa*, p. 133.
10. The account which follows is based especially on P. Goodison, 'SADCC: Propects and Problems until the year 2000' (University of Liverpool, 1982) (mimeo.); R. Leys and A. Tostensen, 'Regional Co-operation in Southern Africa: the Southern African Development Coordination Conference', *Review of African Political Economy*, 23 (January–April 1982); and R. Sakapaji, *Regional Cooperation in Southern Africa: The Southern African Development Coordination Conference (SADCC) – Collective Self-Reliance or Collective Dependence?*, M.A. Econ. Dissertation in Development Studies, University of Manchester (December 1984). It has been amended in the light of Douglas G. Anglin's informative paper, 'SADCC after Nkomati',

African Affairs, 84, 335 (April 1985). For another account, see L. Abegunrin, 'The Southern African Development Coordination Conference: Politics of Dependence', in Onwuka and Sesay (eds), *The Future of Regionalism in Africa*.

11. E. A. Friedland, 'The Southern African Development Co-ordination Conference and the West: Co-operation or Conflict?, *Journal of Modern African Studies*, 23, 2 (1985) pp. 290–1.

12. Anglin, 'SADCC after Nkomati', p. 163. South Africa's 'coercive diplomacy' (to use Anglin's apt expression) led Swaziland also to sign an unequal treaty with South Africa in 1982. See also R. D. A. Henderson, 'The Southern African Customs Union: Politics of Dependence', in Onwuka and Sesay (eds), *The Future of Regionalism in Africa*.

13. Tangri, *Politics in Sub-Saharan Africa*, p. 129.

14. See W. J. Foltz, *From French West Africa to the Mali Federation* (New Haven: Yale University Press, 1965).

15. J. Pearce, *Under the Eagle: US Intervention in Central America and the Caribbean* (London: Latin American Bureau, 1981), p.11.

16. Ibid., p. 20.

17. S. Schlesinger and S. Kinzer, *Bitter Fruit: The Untold Story of the American Coup in Guatemala* (London: Sinclaire Brown, 1982) and R. Immerman, *The CIA in Guatemala: The Foreign Policy of Intervention* (Austin: University of Texas Press, 1982).

18. See C. Blasier, *The Hovering Giant: US Responses to Revolutionary Change in Latin America* (Pittsburgh: University of Pittsburgh Press, 1976).

19. J. Levinson and J. Onis, *The Alliance that Lost its Way* (Chicago: Quadrangle Books, 1970).

20. J. Petras and M. Morley, *The United States and Chile: Imperialism and the Overthrow of the Allende Government* (New York: Monthly Review Press, 1975).

21. W. Lafeber, 'The Reagan Administration and Revolutions in Central America', *Political Science Quarterly*, 99, 1, (1984).

22. See P. Sigmund, *Multinationals in Latin America: The Politics of Nationalisation* (Madison: University of Wisconsin Press, 1980).

23. See ibid. and G. Philip, *Oil and Politics in Latin America: Nationalist Movements and State Companies* (Cambridge: Cambridge University Press, 1982).

24. See T. Moran, *Multinational Corporations and the Politics of Dependence – Copper in Chile* (Princeton: Princeton University Press, 1974).

25. See the case studies in D. Becker, *The New Bourgeoisie and the Limits of Dependency: Mining, Class and Power in 'Revolutionary' Peru* (Princeton: Princeton University Press, 1983).

26. See R. Jenkins, *Dependent Industrialization in Latin America: the Automotive Industry in Argentina, Chile and Mexico* (New York: Praeger, 1977).

27. See G. Gereffi and P. Evans, 'Transnational Corporations, Dependent

Development, and State Policy in the Semiperiphery: A Comparison of Brazil and Mexico', *Latin American Research Review*, 16, 3, (1981).
28. See R. Fagen (ed.), *Capitalism and the State in US-Latin American Relations* (Stanford: Stanford University Press, 1979, and P. Evans, *Dependent Development: The Alliance of Multinationals, State and Local Capital in Brazil* (Princton: Princeton University Press, 1979).
29. See Sigmund, *Multinationals in Latin America*, p. 29.
30. See R. Jenkins, *Transnational Corporations and Industrial Transformation in Latin America* (London: Macmillan, 1984).
31. 'North–South Monitor', *Third World Quarterly*, 8, 3, (1986).
32. For Britain see W. R. Lewis, *The British Empire in the Middle East* (Oxford: Oxford University Press, 1984).
33. For United States policy in this period see J. C. Campbell. *Defence of the Middle East* (New York: Praeger, 1960); for the 1960s see W. Quandt, *Decade of Decisions: American Policy Toward the Arab–Israeli Conflict* (Berkeley: University of California, 1977); for the contemporary period see S. P. Tillman, *The United States in the Middle East* (Bloomington: Indiana University Press, 1982).
34. A. and K. Dawisha, *The Soviet Union in the Middle East* (London: Heinemann, 1982).
35. *U.S. Department of State Bulletin* 81/2056 (June 1981).
36. J. Stork and J. Paul, 'Arms Sales and the Militarization of the Middle East', *Middle East Research and Information Project* (February 1983).
37. See M. Kerr, *The Arab Cold War* (3rd edn) (London: Oxford University Press, 1971).
38. A. al-Sowayegh, *Arab Petropolitics* (London: Croom Helm, 1984).
39. See J. Stork, *The Middle East and the Energy Crisis* (New York: Norton, 1982).
40. See S. E. Ibrahim, *The New Arab Social Order: A Study of the Social Impact of Oil Wealth* (Colorado: Westview Press, 1982) p.73.

8. Famine, Petrodollars and Foreign Debt

1. M. Benjamin and J. Collins, 'Is Rationing Socialist?: Cuba's Food Distribution System', *Food Policy*, 10, 4 (1985).
2. S. Barraclough and P. Marchetti, 'Agrarian Transformation and Food Security in the Caribbean Basin', in G. Irvin and X. Gorostiaga (eds), *Towards an Alternative for Central America and the Caribbean* (London: Allen & Unwin, 1985).
3. *Accelerated Development in Sub-Saharan Africa: An Agenda for Action* (Washington, D.C.: The World Bank, 1981) p. 45. These trends in agricultural development are discussed in R. Vengroff and A. Farah, 'State Intervention and Agricultural Development in Africa: A Cross-National Study', *Journal of Modern African Studies*, 23, 1 (1985). For general discussions of African agriculture drawn upon here, see J. Barker (ed.), *The Politics of Agriculture in Tropical Africa* (Beverly

Hills: Sage, 1984), and R. Chambers, *Managing Rural Development, Ideas and Experience from East Africa* (Uppsala: The Scandinavian Institute of African Studies, 1974).

4. G. Hyden, *Beyond Ujamaa in Tanzania: Underdevelopment and an Uncaptured Peasantry* (London: Heinemann, 1980) p. 18 and *passim*.

5. A. Sen, *Poverty and Famines: An Essay on Entitlement and Deprivation* (Oxford: Clarendon Press, 1981) pp. 104–5.

6. R. Palmer, 'The Agricultural History of Rhodesia', in R. Palmer and N. Parsons (eds), *The Roots of Rural Poverty in Central and Southern Africa* (London: Heinemann, 1977) p. 237.

7. Palmer, 'The Agricultural History', p. 243.

8. G. Jan Van Apeldoorn, *Perspectives on Drought and Famine in Nigeria* (London: Allen & Unwin, 1981) chs 8–11.

9. L. Vail, 'The State and the Creation of Colonial Malawi's Agricultural Economy', in R. Rotberg (ed.), *Imperialism, Colonialism and Hunger: East and Central Africa* (Lexington: Mass., Heath, 1983).

10. Sen, *Poverty and Famines*, pp. 111–2.

11. Sen, *Poverty and Famines*, pp. 125, 126–7.

12. Abd al-Aziz Sowayegh, *Arab Petropolitics* (London: Croom Helm, 1984) p. 177.

13. P. Smallwood and S. Sinclair, *Oil, Debt and Development: OPEC in the Third World* (London: Allen & Unwin, 1981) p. 151.

14. Sowayegh, *Arab Petropolitics*, p. 177.

15. J. Nyerere, Address on the Occasion of Mainland Tanzania's Twentieth Anniversary of Independence, Dar es Salaam (December 1981).

16. F. Saddy, 'OPEC Capital Surplus Funds and Third World Indebtedness', *Third World Quarterly*, 4 (1982) p. 746.

17. R. Sobhan, 'Enhancing Trade between OPEC and the Developing Countries of Asia', *Third World Quarterly*, 4 (1982) p. 719.

18. Sobhan, 'Enhancing Trade', p. 735.

19. Sowayegh, *Arab Petropolitics*, p. 23.

20. Smallwood and Sinclair, *Oil, Debt*, p. 101.

21. F. Halliday, 'Labour Migration in the Arab World', *MERIP Reports*, 123, (May 1984) p. 9.

22. R. Dornbusch, 'Dealing with Debt in the 1980s', *Third World Quarterly*, 7, 3 (1985).

23. H. Lever and C. Huhne, *Debt and Danger: The World Financial Crisis* (Harmondsworth: Penguin, 1985) pp. 26–7.

24. Dornbusch, 'Dealing with Debt', p. 541.

25. See P. O'Brien, ' "The Debt Cannot Be Paid": Castro and the Latin American Debt', *Bulletin of Latin American Research*, 5, 1 (1986).

26. See W. Cline, *International Debt and the Stability of the World Economy* (Washington: Institute of International Economics, 1983), and Lever and Huhne, *Debt and Danger*, ch. 7, for estimates of the consequences of default.

27. Latin America Bureau, *Peru: Paths to Poverty* (London: Latin America Bureau, 1985) p. 90.

28. See R. Kaufman, 'Democratic and Authoritarian Responses to the Debt Issue: Argentina, Brazil and Mexico', *International Organization*, 39, 3 (1985).
29. R. Roett, 'Latin America's Response to the Debt Crisis', *Third World Quarterly*, 7, 2, (1985) p. 227.
30. See P. Smith, 'Reaping the Whirlwind: Brazil's Energy Crisis in Historical Perspective', *Inter-American Economic Affairs*, 37, 1 (1983).
31. See R. Castro de Andrade, 'Brazil: The Economics of Savage Capitalism', in M. Bienefeld and M. Godfrey (eds), *The Struggle for Development: National Strategies in an International Context* (Chichester: J. Wiley and Sons, 1982).
32. J-P. Bertrand, 'Brésil: modernisation agricole et restructuration alimentaire dans la crise internationale', *Revue Tiers-Monde*, 26, 104 (1985).
33. W. Saint, 'Farming for Energy: Social Options under Brazil's National Alcohol Programme', *World Development*, 10, 3 (1982).

Bibliography and Further Reading

1. General

Third World

E. A. Brett, *World Economy Since the War: The Politics of Uneven Development* (London: Macmillan, 1985).
C. Clapham, *Third World Politics. An Introduction* (London: Croom Helm, 1985).
V. Randall and R. Theobald, *Political Change and Underdevelopment. A Critical Introduction to Third World Politics* (London: Macmillan, 1985).

Africa

G. M. Carter and P. O'Meara (eds), *African Independence. The First Twenty Five Years* (Bloomington: Indiana, 1985).
R. Tangri, *Politics in Sub-Saharan Africa* (London: James Currey, 1985).
W. Tordoff, *Government and Politics in Africa* (London: Macmillan, 1984).
C. Young, *Ideology and Development in Africa* (New Haven: Yale University Press, 1982).

Latin America

C. Abel and C. Lewis (eds), *Latin America, Economic Imperialism and the State* (London: Athlone Press, 1984).
T. Skidmore and P. Smith, *Modern Latin America* (Oxford: Oxford University Press, 1984).
G. Wynia, *The Politics of Development in Latin America* (Cambridge: Cambridge University Press, 1984).

The Middle East

F. Ajami, *The Arab Predicament: Arab Political Thought and Practice*

Since 1967 (Cambridge: Cambridge University Press, 1981).
J. Bill and C. Leiden, *Politics in the Middle East* (Boston: Little Brown, 1974).
M. Halpern, *The Politics of Social Change in the Middle East and North Africa* (Princeton: Princeton University Press, 1963).
M. Hudson, *Arab Politics: The Search For Legitimacy* (New Haven: Yale University Press, 1978).

The Heritage of the Past

B. Albert, *South America and the World Economy from Independence to 1930* (London: Macmillan, 1983).
E. Archetti, P. Cammack and B. Roberts (eds), *Latin America* (London: Macmillan, 1987) part II.
E. A. Brett, *Colonialism and Underdevelopment in East Africa. The Politics of Economic Change, 1919–39* (London: Heinemann, 1973).
F. H. Cardoso and E. Faletto, *Dependency and Development in Latin America* (Berkeley: University of California Press, 1979).
R. B. Collier, *Regimes in Tropical Africa: Changing Forms of Supremacy. 1945–75* (Berkeley: University of California Press, 1982).
M. Crowder (ed.), *Colonial West Africa: Collected Essays* (London: Frank Cass, 1978).
A. Hourani, 'The Ottoman Background of the Modern Middle East', in K. H. Karpat (ed.), *The Ottoman State and its Place in History* (Leiden: Brill, 1974).
R. Owen, *The Middle East in the World Economy 1800–1914* (London: Methuen, 1981).

State and Society

C. Allen and G. Williams (eds), *The Sociology of Developing Societies: Sub-Saharan Africa* (London: Macmillan, 1982).
T. Asad and R. Owen (eds), *The Sociology of Developing Societies: The Middle East* (London: Macmillan, 1983).
D. Collier (ed.), *The New Authoritarianism in Latin America* (Princeton: Princeton University Press, 1979).
N. Hamilton, *The Limits of State Autonomy: Post-Revolutionary Mexico* (Princeton: Princeton University Press, 1982).
J. Iliffe, *The Emergence of African Capitalism* (London: Macmillan, 1983).
J. Malloy (ed.), *Authoritarianism and Corporatism in Latin America* (Pittsburgh: University of Pittsburgh Press, 1977).
R. Sandbrook and R. Cohen (eds), *The Development of an African Working Class: Studies in Class Formation and Action* (Toronto: University of Toronto Press, 1975).
J. Waterbury, *The Egypt of Nasser and Sadat* (Princeton: Princeton

University Press, 1983).

C. A. O. van Nieuwenhuijze, *The Sociology of the Middle East* (Leiden: Brill, 1971).

Political Parties and Participation

J. Dunn (ed.), *West African States: Failure and Promise. A Study in Comparative Politics* (Cambridge: Cambridge University Press, 1978).

C. Gertzel (ed), C. Baylies and M. Szeftel, *The Dynamics of the One-Party State in Zambia* (Manchester: Manchester University Press, 1984).

I. Harik, *The Political Mobilization of Peasants* (Bloomington: Indiana University Press, 1974).

R. A. Hinnebusch, *Egyptian Politics under Sadat. The Post-Populist Development of an Authoritarian-Modernizing State* (Cambridge: Cambridge University Press, 1985).

D. Levine, *Conflict and Political Change in Venezuela* (Princeton: Princeton University Press, 1973).

R. S. Morgenthau, *Political Parties in French-Speaking West Africa* (Oxford: Clarendon Press, 1964).

R. Olson, *The Ba'th and Syria 1947–82: The Evolution of Ideology, Party and State* (Princeton: Kingston Press, 1982).

J. Peeler, *Latin American Democracies: Colombia, Costa Rica, Venezuela* (Chapel Hill: University of North Carolina Press, 1985).

A. Valenzuela, *The Breakdown of Democratic Regimes: Chile* (Baltimore: Johns Hopkins University Press, 1978).

The Military

M. H. M. Alves, *State and Opposition in Military Brazil* (Austin: University of Texas Press, 1985).

H. Batatu, 'Some Observations on the Social Roots of Syria's Ruling Military Group', *Middle East Journal*, XXXV, 1 (Summer 1981).

T. S. Cox, *Civil–Military Relations in Sierra Leone: A Case Study of African Soldiers in Politics* (Cambridge, Mass.: Harvard University Press, 1976).

S. Decalo, *Coups and Army Rule in Africa: Studies in Military Style* (New Haven: Yale University Press, 1976).

H. Dekmejian, *Egypt under Nasir* (Albany, New York: State University of New York, 1971).

J. Dunkerley, *The Long War: Dictatorship and Revolution in El Salvador* (London: Junction Books, 1982).

M. Janowitz, *The Military in the Political Development of New Nations* (Chicago : Chicago University Press, 1964).

R. Luckham, *The Nigerian Military: A Sociological Analysis of Authority and Revolt, 1960–67* (Cambridge: Cambridge University Press, 1971).

P. O'Brien and P. Cammack (eds), *Generals in Retreat: The Crisis of*

Military Rule in Latin America (Manchester: Manchester University Press, 1985).
N. van Dam, *The Struggle for Power in Syria* (London: Croom Helm, 1979).

Revolution

E. Abrahamian, *Iran Between Two Revolutions* (Princeton: Princeton University Press, 1982).
G. Black, *The Triumph of the People: The Sandinista Revolution in Nicaragua* (London: Zed Press, 1981).
D. Hopwood, *Egypt: Politics and Society 1945–84* (London: Allen & Unwin, 1985).
K. S. Karol, *Guerrillas in Power: The Course of the Cuban Revolution* (London: Jonathan Cape, 1971).
N. Keddie (ed.), *Iran: The Roots of Revolution* (New Haven: Yale University Press, 1981).
J. Markakis and M. Waller (eds), *Military Marxist Regimes in Africa* (London: Frank Cass, 1986).
B. Munslow (ed.), *Africa: Problems in the Transition to Socialism* (London: Zed Press, 1986).
J. O'Connor, *The Origins of Socialism in Cuba* (Ithaca: Cornell University Press, 1970).
C. G. Rosberg and T. M. Callaghy (eds), *Socialism in Sub-Saharan Africa: A New Assessment* (Berkeley: Institute of International Studies, University of California, 1979).

Women in Third World Politics

H. Afshar (ed.), *Women, Work and Ideology in the Third World* (London: Tavistock, 1985).
L. Beck and N. Keddie (eds), *Women in the Muslim World* (Cambridge, Mass.: Harvard University Press, 1978).
M. Etienne and E. Leacock (eds), *Women and Colonization: Anthropological Perspectives* (New York: Praeger, 1980).
M. D. Fernandez-Kelly, *For We Are Sold, I and My People: Women Industrial Workers on the Mexican Frontier* (Albany: State University of New York Press, 1983).
N. Hafkin and E. Bay (eds), *Women in Africa: Studies in Social and Economic Change* (Stanford: Stanford University Press, 1976).
J. Nash and M. P. Fernandez-Kelly (eds), *Women, Men and the International Division of Labour* (Albany: State University of New York Press, 1983).
J. Nash and H. Safa (eds), *Sex and Class in Latin America* (South Hadley: Bergin, 1980).
J. Nash and H. Safa (eds), *Women and Change in Latin America* (South

Hadley: Bergin, 1986).

R. S. Oboler, *Women, Power and Economic Change: The Nandi of Kenya* (Stanford: Stanford University Press, 1975).

Review of African Political Economy, 27/28 (February 1984): a 'Women's Issue' on the theme Women, Oppression and Liberation.

N. Saadawi, *The Hidden Face of Eve: Women in the Arab World* (London: Zed Press, 1980).

A. Tabari, 'The Women's Movement in Iran: A Hopeful Prognosis', *Feminist Studies*, 12, 2 (1986).

The International Context

C. Blasier, *The Hovering Giant: US Responses to Revolutionary Change in Latin America* (Pittsburgh: University of Pittsburgh Press, 1980).

G.Chaliand, *The Struggle for Africa. Conflict of the Great Powers.* (London: Macmillan, 1983).

A. and K. Dawisha (eds), *The Soviet Union in the Middle East: Policies and Perspectives* (London: Heinemann, 1982).

R. Jenkins, *Transnational Corporations and Industrial Transformation in Latin America* (London: Macmillan, 1984).

M. Kerr, *The Arab Cold War* (3rd edn), (New York: Oxford University Press, 1971).

D. Mazzeo (ed.), *African Regional Organisations* (Cambridge: Cambridge University Press, 1984).

R. I. Onwuka and A. Sesay (eds), *The Future of Regionalism in Africa* (London: Macmillan, 1985).

J. Petras and M. Morley, *The United States and Chile: Imperialism and the Overthrow of the Allende Government* (New York: Monthly Review Press, 1975).

S. P. Tillman, *The United States in the Middle East* (Bloomington: Indiana University Press, 1982).

Famine, Petrodollars and Foreign Debt

Abd al-Aziz al-Sowayegh, *Arab Petropolitics* (London: Croom Helm, 1984).

J. Barker (ed.), *The Politics of Agriculture in Tropical Africa* (Beverly Hills: Sage, 1984).

H. Lever and C. Huhne, *Debt and Danger: The World Financial Crisis* (Harmondsworth: Penguin, 1985).

R. Sandbrook, *The Politics of Africa's Economic Stagnation* (Cambridge: Cambridge University Press, 1985).

A. Sen, *Poverty and Famines. An Essay on Entitlement and Deprivation* (Oxford: Clarendon Press, 1981).

P. Smallwood and S. Sinclair, *Oil, Debt and Development: OPEC in the Third World* (London: Allen & Unwin, 1981).

Special Issue, 'Perspectives on Global Debt', *Journal of International Studies*, 38, 1 (1984).

Index

302